D0563967

AND PROMISES TO KEEP

AND PROMISES TO KEEP

THE SOUTHERN CONFERENCE FOR HUMAN WELFARE, 1938–1948

THOMAS A. KRUEGER

VANDERBILT UNIVERSITY PRESS NASHVILLE

NASHVILLE, TENNESSEE
LIBRARY OF CONGRESS CATALOGUE
CARD NUMBER 67-13996
PRINTED IN THE UNITED STATES OF AMERICA
BY KINGSPORT PRESS, INC.
KINGSPORT, TENNESSEE

FOR MY MOTHER AND FATHER

PREFACE

THIS is a history of the Southern Conference for Human Welfare, a voluntary organization whose brief life was devoted chiefly to the propagation of the New Deal in the South. I have attempted to tell both the inner and the outer history of the organization; policy decisions, reform demands, finances, internal power struggles, and changes in function have been related wherever possible to important contemporary events and organizations: to the New Deal, the popular-front movement, Southern reform groups ranging from the Southern Regional Council to the Communist party, the Southern labor movement, the diplomatic prelude to World War II, domestic aspects of the war, the development of the cold war, the Negro rights movement, and the election of 1948.

This, I hope, constitutes a major revision in the treatment of the Southern Conference. Previous accounts hostile to the organization have been almost exclusively concerned with its connections with the Communist party. Previous friendly accounts—the work of former Conference leaders—have stressed the importance of the Conference's reform activities; they have avoided serious treatment of the Conference's relations with American Communists and they have glossed over several internal disputes which debilitated the organization. I reject the contentions and the approach of the Conference's critics; the Southern Conference for Human Welfare was not a Communist front, and its history is more than a study in Communist infiltration. I also try to avoid the evasions of the Conference's former leaders; the Southern Conference had important connections with native American Communists.

These and other conclusions in this study may derive from my liberal biases, and so may the evidence included in the text. Although much evidence has been omitted for the sake of brevity, I hope that no evidence counter to the major interpretation has been suppressed. Ideally, every fact about the organization not mentioned should be accounted for by some generalization in the text. The conclusions presented are the best I can do. I have tried to present the reader with sufficient evidence to decide whether my best is good enough.

Three additional warnings to the reader: Two words used in this study, "propaganda" and "tract," have acquired invidious connotation which, when I use them, I do not intend them to have. Every organization with a program or an encompassing philosophy—whether the Catholic Church, the Communist party, or the John Birch Society—resorts to propaganda. Where these organizations lack power, they propagate their views through didactic pamphlets and newspapers: tracts. Our impoverished political vocabulary does not provide us with better words to describe one of the Southern Conference's main activities; it attempted to propagate a point of view and a program and for this purpose printed tracts and a newspaper. A similar deficiency in vocabulary, together with a lack of evidence, has made necessary the occasional use of such terms as "liberal" and "progressive" as synonyms; where they occur together, they are equivalent to "reformer," which in turn covers most, if not all, the members of the Southern Conference for Human Welfare. They all agreed on the Conference's reform program; in this they are reformers. Without further evidence, nothing more accurate can be said; motives cannot be impugned; ultimate purposes cannot be divined. Where "liberal" occurs together with "Communist," "Socialist," "laborite," or "radical," it is intended to distinguish the right wing of the Southern Conference, an ill-defined organism including college professors, women from the League of Women Voters, journalists, and an occasional businessman. To avoid cluttering up the text with a large number of notes, I have gathered most of the references for each subsection of the text at the end of the subsection for which they were used. Only the sources for direct quotations are given immediately, and where the source of the quotation is obvious from the discussion in the text I have included the reference in the general note at the end of the subsection of the text in which the quotation appears.

I owe debts of gratitude to a large number of persons: to James A. Dombrowski of the Southern Conference Educational Fund for loan of valuable materials from his organization's files, for permissions to use the Southern Conference Records at Tuskegee Institute, and for granting an interview; to Mr. and Mrs. C. J. Durr of Montgomery, Alabama, for gracious hospitality and for numerous anecdotes and insights; to Clark Foreman of the Emergency Civil Liberties Committee, New York City, and to Atlanta University for permission to use and quote from materials in the University's Negro Collection; to Frank Graham of New York City for permission to use his files at the University of North Carolina and for granting an interview; to Guy Johnson of the University of North Carolina for permission to examine the Howard W. Odum papers; to the late Aubrey Williams for permission to use his papers at the Franklin D. Roosevelt Memorial Library, Hyde Park, New York; to Claude Williams of Helena, Alabama, for hospitality and for insights; to Mrs. Jessie P. Guzman, formerly head of the Department of Research and Records at Tuskegee Institute, and her staff, especially Mrs. McCoy, for making a large, comfortable working space available and for other kindnesses; to Mrs. G. W. Barksdale and Mrs. Theodore Gould of Atlanta University Library for similar consideration; to Miss Mattie Russell and Virginia Gray of the Manuscripts Division of Duke University Library; to Mr. James W. Patton and his staff at the University of North Carolina Southern Historical Collection, especially Miss Allen; to the staff of the Manuscripts Division of the Library of Congress; and to Elizabeth Drewry and the rest of the wonder-workers on the staff at the Franklin D. Roosevelt Memorial Library, Hyde Park. Professional aid has come from Dr. Warren Ashby of the University of North Carolina, Women's College, Greensboro, who showed me portions of the manuscript of his biography of Frank Graham and provided other information; to Kenneth Douty of the United States Department of Labor for permission to examine his unpublished study of the Southern Conference; to Donald Grubbs of the University of the Pacific for information about the Southern Tenant Farmers' Union and the Southern Conference; to George B. Tindall of the University of North Carolina for suggestions and for permission to examine a rough-draft section of his forthcoming volume in Louisiana State University's "History of the South" series dealing with the Southern Conference. I hope my disagreements with these historians in no way lessens my gratitude to them. The University of Minnesota provided two fellowships which made possible most of the research for this study, including a prolonged trip through the Southern and Eastern United States. I owe special thanks to W. Donald Beatty, Assistant Chairman of the History Department of the University of Minnesota, for innumerable kindnesses over the years; and more especial thanks to Clarke A. Chambers of the University of Minnesota who directed this study as a doctoral dissertation and who, together with Professor Dewey Grantham of Vanderbilt University, was responsible for its preliminary definition. I am grateful to Professor Grantham for suggestions and for encouragement. I wish also to thank the Macmillan Company for permission to use as my introductory quotation a passage from Herbert Croly's *The Promise of American Life* (New York: Macmillan, 1909), p. 3. Lastly, I am indebted beyond my ability to repay to my wife, Susan, who typed the manuscript and who, more importantly, endured the author's crotchets and pecadillos with tolerance and charity.

THOMAS A. KRUEGER

CONTENTS

From the beginning Americans have been anticipating and projecting a better future. From the beginning the Land of Democracy has been figured as the Land of Promise. Thus the American's loyalty to the national tradition rather affirms than denies the imaginative projection of a better future. An America which was not the Land of Promise, which was not informed by a prophetic outlook and a . . . constructive ideal, would not be the America bequeathed to us by our forefathers. In cherishing the Promise of a better national future the American is fulfilling rather than imperiling the substance of the national tradition.

HERBERT CROLY

AND PROMISES TO KEEP

1

ORIGINS

LATE in the evening of September 23rd, 1936, in Birmingham, Alabama, a thin unprepossessing man was assaulted by three men as he returned home from a meeting. He was blackjacked, punched, and forced onto the rear floor of an automobile. There one of his assailants sat over him, punching and kicking him until at last he feigned unconsciousness.

The kidnappers drove south from Birmingham to the vicinity of Clanton, Alabama, where they pulled onto a back road, stripped their captive, pushed him face-down on the ground, and whipped him with a thick leather strap. Once they turned him over: one kicked him in the stomach; another blackjacked him across the mouth. After their victim lost consciousness they left, taking his wallet, his watch, and his loose change with them.

When the man regained consciousness he dragged himself to help; at one town the doctor refused to treat such "a mess." Eventually he got to the hospital in Clanton, where his wounds were successfully treated. Although he lived until 1950, his death then, at the age of 51, can be partially attributed to the injuries he sustained that night in the darkness of rural Alabama.

The victim was Joseph Gelders, a scion of one of Birmingham's few Jewish families. Until the depression he had led an ordinary, placid life. Educated in the city's public school system, he briefly attended the University of Alabama and Massachusetts Institute of Technology. He joined the army in the summer of 1918—too late to see combat. Upon his release he returned to Birmingham, where during the next ten years he worked at several jobs: in a local department store, in the Ensley works of the Tennessee Coal and Iron Company, in the automobile business. In January 1929 he returned to the University of Alabama, where in 1930 he received a B.S. and, six months later, an M.A. in physics. From 1930 to mid-1935 he was an assistant professor of physics at the University.

The great depression troubled him deeply—as it deeply troubled nearly every American. He found time, in the midst of his academic duties, to search in the classics of politics and economics for an explanation and a cure for the nation's crisis. As his search for answers progressed his pedagogical interests declined; he became increasingly interested in civil liberties. In August 1935 he joined the National Committee for the Defense of Political Prisoners, an organization including on its published membership list such worthies as Lincoln Steffens, Ella Winter, Granville Hicks, Rockwell Kent, Sidney Hook, Bennett Cerf, Matthew Josephson, John Dos Passos, Upton Sinclair, and Crane Brinton. The Committee, he later testified, afforded him a chance to work in

> an organization . . . interested in the maintenance of civil rights, in . . . maintaining democratic government, in maintaining such conditions as will prevent political imprisonments and in helping . . . persons . . . ar-

rested because of their opinions or their economic situations or their economic struggles, [or] race, [or] religion. . . .[1]

Frequently labeled a Communist front, the organization, in its own words, stood for the defense of "militant labor and the victims of racial oppression."

In October 1935 Gelders went to New York as the Committee's secretary. In August 1936 he returned to Birmingham as its Southern representative.

Earlier that summer the police of Bessemer, an industrial suburb of Birmingham, had arrested the local secretary of the Communist party, one Jack Barton, under a law prohibiting the printing, distribution, possession, and display of printed matter which advocated or taught that "organized government should be overthrown by force, violence, or any unlawful means." Although the police had entered Barton's home with a warrant to search for liquor, they took him into custody for possessing several political publications, including the Communist party's theoretical journal, *The Communist, The Nation, The New Republic,* and the Birmingham AFofL organ. The day after his arrest, Barton was tried, convicted, and sentenced to 180 days at hard labor and fined $100. The trial judge refused to examine the materials to determine whether any of them advocated or taught the necessity of overthrowing "organized government . . . by force, violence, or any unlawful means." "It is all Communist stuff," he told Barton, "and you cannot have it in Bessemer."

Gelders took up the case for the National Committee for the Defense of Political Prisoners. In September, he and Mrs. Barton, along with three ministers, protested to the mayor of Bessemer about the brutal conditions of Barton's imprisonment. Several weeks

1. United States Congress, Senate, Subcommittee of the Committee on Education and Labor, *Violations of Free Speech and Rights of Labor,* 74 cong., 2 sess. (Washington: Government Printing Office, 1937), pt. 3, p. 773 (hereinafter cited as La Follette Committee, *Hearings*). All subsequent quotations in this section come from this part of the hearings pp. 773ff., pp. 960ff. On the Committee see Jerold S. Auerbach, "The La Follette Committee: Labor and Civil Liberties in the New Deal," *The Journal of American History,* LI (December 1964), 435–459.

later, doctors were permitted to examine Barton who was found to have tuberculosis. In the middle of October he was transferred to a sanatorium. Gelders, meantime, was kidnapped and flogged.

Despite his positive indentification of two of his attackers and independent confirmation of one of his identifications, Gelders's assailants were never brought to trial. Jefferson County Grand Juries twice failed to return true bills.

Despite the Grand Juries' hesitations, one of Gelders's identifications seems beyond reasonable doubt. An independent witness later saw the man dispose of papers from Gelders's wallet; on the afternoon of the kidnapping, according to a second witness, the man had asked what could be done about that "so-and-so Gelders"; sometime after, during a conversation about the beating, the man told a third witness that he would like to take a baseball bat to all the "reds"; he was then secretly employed by the Tennessee Coal and Iron Company, a subsidiary of United States Steel, as an investigator of Communist and labor problems.

Both the men Gelders identified refused to appear before the La Follette Committee to answer the charges against them. Both had worked for the Tennessee Coal and Iron Company as special guards during labor disputes. Both were intimate with the leaders of public and private anti-Communist organizations in north central Alabama. Affidavits and testimony of Negroes, unionists, and Communists on file in the La Follette Committee records mention the pair as principal agents in several intimidations, whippings, and beatings. Both had motive, opportunity, and the means to attack Joseph Gelders.

Gelders's beating was thus more than an isolated incident of senseless violence in an area seemingly addicted to senseless violence. It was a bloody footnote to the story of the attempt to organize the Tennessee Coal and Iron Company plants in Alabama. And it was an extreme example of the frequent public and private violation of basic constitutional rights that disgraced the Birmingham region throughout the depression.[2]

2. La Follette Committee, *Hearings*, pt. 15C, pp. 6318–6321; Interviews, Mrs. C. J. Durr, Montgomery, Alabama, January 11–12, 18–19, 1964.

II

Birmingham nestles in Jones Valley in the southern end of the Appalachian Mountains. During Reconstruction the region's rich deposits of coal, iron, and limestone, all essential to steel production, attracted capitalists, speculators, and promoters who came to buy land, to build railroads, and to exploit the region's natural resources. By 1870 the South and the North, and the Alabama and Chattanooga railroads had built into Jones Valley. Birmingham grew around the junction and axes these two lines provided. In the late 1870s the town boomed. By 1890 it had a population of 26,178; land sold for as much as a thousand dollars per foot; major organizations of capital had located in the area. By 1892 the Tennessee Coal and Iron Company, the largest Southern steel corporation, had built thirteen large blast furnaces in northern Alabama and attained a dominant position in the state's coal and iron mining industries. In 1907 United States Steel Corporation, a national leader in the open-shop campaign, bought control of the Tennessee Coal and Iron Company. By 1930 the region produced between 6 and 8 percent of the nation's total output of pig iron; the population had grown to 250,000, including 100,000 Negroes. The city had expanded to include several suburbs. Nearby were the separately incorporated industrial towns of Fairfield and Bessemer.

From its beginnings, Birmingham suffered from endemic violence; in a region notorious throughout the late nineteenth century for its crimes of violence the city held a prominent position. Policemen once referred to it as "bad Birmingham." To this day most bombings and dynamitings go unpunished. To this day some Southerners refer to it, half regretfully, half boastfully, as the murder capital of the world.

From the first, public and private violence was used to control the region's labor force. In 1894 the National Guard and Pinkerton spies broke up a coal miners' strike. In 1908 Governor Braxton Bragg Comer declared martial law to break a United Mine Workers' strike. During the red ore miners' strike of 1934 one company imported a thousand special guards; at least two Negro workers were murdered and twenty homes and buildings were bombed and burned, most of them belonging to Negroes. Although pay increases were granted, the union failed to gain recognition. During a miners' strike in 1935–1936, detonation of a company-planted booby-trap under a column of marching miners killed one striker and injured several others. Public officials openly co-operated with industry. For many years, the Tennessee Coal and Iron Company hired special guards through the county sheriff, who got a bonus for every man the company hired; in return, he deputized the guards during periods of labor difficulties.

The efforts to control labor were generally successful until the New Deal; in 1933, for example, Birmingham's miners and steel workers were practically without effective union organization. Then section 7a of the National Industrial Recovery Act stimulated union activity. After a year and a half of bitter disputes with the mine operators, the United Mine Workers claimed to have 23,000 members in 90 Alabama locals; only 1,000 miners, the union further claimed, remained to be organized. All but two coal companies had signed collective bargaining agreements. In the area's red ore mines, where more than 80 percent of the 5,000 miners were Negroes, unionism also took hold. Although the red ore miners lost a bitter strike in 1934, they were about 80 percent organized by the end of the year. The steel industry proved toughest to organize: in 1934, eight or ten blast furnaces operated in Jones Valley; only two of these were unionized, both of them independent of United States Steel. Not until 1937 did TCI sign a contract with the CIO Steel Workers' Organizing Committee.

The depression and the New Deal not only increased union efforts, they also brought the first serious efforts of the Communist party to organize in the South. Birmingham, the center of Southern heavy industry, was a prime target. In mid-1930 the party began a newspaper, *The Southern Worker.* It organized a sharecroppers' union in Alabama. In Birmingham it began to recruit members among the black and white unemployed. Later it filled or controlled important positions in the International Union of Mine, Mill and Smelter Workers. In 1932 the party attained a place on the state ballot. By the middle of the decade there were 250 members of the Communist party in the Birmingham area, many of them Negroes attracted by the party's promise of equality for all races; perhaps an additional 1,000 to 1,500 persons had connections with the party through the International Labor Defense, the League of Struggle for Negro Rights, and the Young Communist League. By 1938, according to official party publications, Jefferson County had more than 300 party members; at a party convention, 50 of the 82 delegates were Negroes.

Although a legal organization attempting to shed at least some of the vestiges of its underground past, the party's increased activities aroused increased opposition and increased violence against real and imagined party members. To halt radical public gatherings, the suburb of Fairfield prohibited interracial meetings. Bessemer and Birmingham enacted laws prohibiting the printing, possession, or distribution of literature advocating the overthrow of "organized government by force or unlawful means." The Birmingham police department set up a special section for the investigation of radical activities—popularly known as the "red squad." Homes of active unionists and suspected Communists, both Negro and white, were raided without warrant or with liquor search warrants, their inhabitants terrorized and intimidated. In 1934 police officials asked for state laws prohibiting "agitation of strike violence . . . meetings which would end in riot . . . [and] spreading of propaganda advocating racial intermarriage and inciting race hatred." [3]

Private groups formed to fight the red menace; local anti-Communist organizations included the Ku Klux Klan, the White Legion, the Silver Shirts, the Alabama Black Shirts, and several private detective agencies. Police and private investigators collaborated; one private detective was seen on several occasions giving orders to red-squad minions. They both may have secretly worked with the more unsavory organizations.

Besides flogging Gelders and railroading Jack Barton, police or local vigilantes:

—kidnapped Blaine Owens, a known Communist, beat him severe-

3. Quoted in Horace Cayton and George Mitchell, *Black Workers and the New Unions* (Chapel Hill: The University of North Carolina Press, 1939), p. 339.

ly about the face and head, ripped off portions of his scalp and stuffed them into his bleeding mouth;

—arrested Jane Speed, white, in May 1933 for attempting to hold a May Day meeting, twisted her arms while making the arrest, slugged her at least once during the booking, bloodily beat one of her male Negro companions;

—entered the home of Emily Mabel Owen under a liquor search warrant, seized and confiscated several pieces of Communist and Socialist party literature in her possession;

—arrested Robert Washington, a Negro sharecropper organizer, in Selma, Alabama, during a sharecroppers' strike in 1935, released him after dark, whereupon he was kidnapped and flogged for the better part of an hour with a thick leather strap;

—took into custody a young Negro who had come to look for Washington, also released him after dark, whereupon he too was kidnapped. He was never seen again;

—illegally entered and illegally searched the dwelling of Helen Longs, Negro and Communist, later arrested her while she distributed Communist leaflets, took her into custody, beat her with a leather strap until she nearly lost consciousness;

—broke up a picket line during a strike of W.P.A. sewing project women during the course of which they severely beat two Negroes;

—arrested two union officers incidentally connected with the W.P.A. sewing strike and held them incommunicado for two days;

—arrested, during the red ore strike of 1934, as a suspected Communist, one Paul Weller, released him, whereupon he was kidnapped and flogged.

—illegally entered the home of Ben Winston, a Negro, during the same strike, kidnapped him and two other Negroes, severely beat the three of them with a weighted rubber hose.

Gelders's acquaintance with these and other barbarities and his personal experience led him to broach the idea of a regional conference on civil liberties to publicize police and vigilante brutality, to elicit suggested solutions to the violations of the Constitution incident to the class war in Birmingham, and to establish a permanent organization devoted to the protection of Constitutional rights in the South. For more than a year, his idea received polite, interested attention; but nothing was done.

Meanwhile, national political developments prepared persons in Washington to be interested in Gelders's proposals and to be willing to help him.[4]

III

By late winter 1938, Franklin Roosevelt's reform program had been thwarted in nearly every detail. The Court Reform Bill had been defeated; many were still deeply angered over the President's attempt to alter the national Sanhedrin for political purposes. Sit-down strikes, federal spending, and the recession of 1937–1938 (which diminished Roosevelt's prestige with Congress) provoked conservatives in both parties to obstruct proposed New Deal legislation. Congress increasingly asserted its independence of the presidential will: the special congressional session of November-December 1937 failed to produce a single measure the president requested; the regular session of Congress, convened in January 1938, did little better: by March Roosevelt's pains had got him the second Agricultural Adjustment Act—nothing more. Something had to be done.

A ruthless but impracticable plan would have called for an attempt to chop off the conservative wing of the party. A less dangerous and more workable strategy required Presidential intervention in select Democratic primaries. Eventually Roosevelt adopted the latter course of action.

The President may have assumed that the Southern conservatives

4. Writers' Program, *Alabama: A Guide to the Deep South* (New York: R. R. Smith, 1941), pp. 69–73, 164–170; Cayton and Mitchell, *Black Workers*, pp. 314ff.; C. Vann Woodward, *Origins of the New South, 1877–1913* (Baton Rouge: The Louisiana State University Press, 1951), pp. 158–160, pp. 299–302; T. Spradling, "About a Branch in the South: How We Brought Street Lights to Pratt City," *Party Organizer*, XI (July 1938), 31–32; Rob Hall, "Establishing the Party in the South," *Party Organizer*, X (August 1937), 28–31; La Follette Committee, *Hearings*, pt. 3, pp. 773ff., pp. 960ff., pt. 15C, pp. 6318ff., pt. 2, pp. 726–729; interviews with Mrs. C. J. Durr previously cited; interviews, Claude Williams, Helena, Alabama, January 13–14, 1964; for a different perspective on Birmingham in the 1930s, see William Bradford Huie's autobiographical novel, *Mud on the Stars* (New York: L. B. Fischer, 1942).

would be the easiest to defeat. The South had benefited from the New Deal and had greater need of federal largess than any other section of the country. An adopted Southerner, the President had been deeply solicitous of Southern welfare; and he knew the region in intimate detail. Whatever the case, he began his campaign against the party's obstructionists in the deep South.

March 23, 1938, at Gainesville, Georgia, he addressed a celebration in honor of the city's reconstruction following its virtual destruction by a tornado two years before. After praising the townspeople for their public-spirited initiative, he pointed out that an RFC loan and P.W.A. and W.P.A. projects had also contributed to the city's recovery. He used Gainesville as a lesson for the nation: "Today, national progress and national prosperity are being held back chiefly because of selfishness on the part of a few. If Gainesville had been faced with . . . minority selfishness your city would not stand rebuilt as it is today." Minority selfishness, minority greed, had effected a dangerous maldistribution of the national wealth. Consequently, the

> buying power of the people . . . is . . . so low today that [they] . . . cannot purchase the products of industry. Therefore, industry itself is cut off from an outlet it otherwise would have. People cannot buy at stores unless they have cash or good credit. Stores cannot fill their shelves unless they have customers. [I challenge] Georgia and the lower South . . . [to] face facts. . . . The purchasing power of . . . this whole area is far too low. . . . On the present scale . . . of buying power, the South cannot and will not succeed in establishing successful new industries.

Increased purchasing power, he reminded his listeners, would make possible "better schools, better health, better hospitals, better highways. These things will not come to us in the South if we oppose progress—if we believe in our hearts that the feudal system is still the best system." Feudal reaction and its twin, fascism, had thrown down the gage to the champions of peaceful progress. Sadly, feudal reactionaries held public office in the United States;

> To those in and out of public office, who still believe in the feudal system . . . the people of the United States and in every section of the United

States are going to say "We are sorry, but we want people to represent us whose minds are cast in the 1938 mold. . . ." [5]

The reactionaries had been warned: defeat was imminent—if only effective candidates could be found to run against them.

Later in the spring, Roosevelt asked a native Georgian in the administration, Clark Foreman of the P.W.A.'s Power Division, whether he knew a liberal who could defeat Walter George in Georgia's forthcoming senatorial primary. Unfamiliar with the state's internal politics, Foreman could not think of an opponent for the Senator. Instead he passed on a suggestion he had picked up at a Washington dinner meeting of the Southern Policy Committee, a small group of liberal Southern congressmen and bureaucrats who met regularly to discuss public affairs. There he had heard Jerome Frank, also of P.W.A., recommend publication of a pamphlet on the South's major economic problems. Foreman told Roosevelt the pamphlet could be used during the summer primaries to dramatize the benefits the New Deal had brought to the South. The pamphlet, Roosevelt countered, should present simply, factually, the South's most pressing economic problems. Foreman agreed.

At Roosevelt's suggestion, Foreman asked Lowell Mellett, Director of the National Emergency Council (NEC), to have his agency produce the document. Mellett and Foreman enlisted several Southerners in the administration to do the preliminary work. Their instructions were explicit: to summarize existing knowledge of Southern economic conditions.

Mellett and Foreman next assembled an advisory committee of distinguished Southerners to criticize the preliminary work and, in Roosevelt's words, make it "representative of the South's own best thought." The committee included Frank Graham, President of the University of North Carolina, Barry Bingham, publisher of the Louisville *Courier-Journal,* Carl Bailey, Governor of Arkansas, Lucy Randolph Mason, a direct descendant of the author of the Virginia

5. Franklin D. Roosevelt, *The Public Papers and Addresses of Franklin D. Roosevelt,* ed. Samuel I. Rosenman, 13 v. (New York: Random House, Macmillan, and Harper, 1938–1950), VII, 164–168.

Declaration of Rights, H. L. Mitchell, an executive of the Southern Tenant Farmers' Union, John C. Persons, President of the First National Bank of Birmingham, Paul Poynter, publisher of the St. Petersburg *Times,* and a number of other prominent Southerners. The group convened on July 5. It considered the preliminary report line by line and made a few minor changes. On July 25 Mellett transmitted the National Emergency Council's *Report on the Economic Conditions of the South* to the President.

The *Report* expressed Roosevelt's conviction that the South was "the Nation's No. 1 economic problem—the Nation's problem, not merely the South's." It was therefore more than a factual presentation; its facts were arranged to lead the reader to conclusions that were iterated and reiterated throughout the *Report.* Although the South was the nation's poorest region, the *Report* argued, it had the potential to be richer than any other section of the country. Deficiencies in the region's institutions kept it from realizing its potential: they were inadequate to the task of exploiting Southern natural resources; they failed to provide Southerners with means to fulfill their ambitions; they were tributaries and lackeys of non-Southern corporations, unconcerned with the region's vital interests. The *Report's* fifteen subsections—Economic Resources, Soil, Water, Population, Private and Public Income, Education, Health, Housing, Labor, Women and Children, Ownership and Use of Land, Credit, Use of Natural Resources, Industry, Purchasing Power—amplified and played variations on this major theme. Thus the section on Economic Resources:

> The paradox of the South is that while it is blessed by Nature with immense wealth, its people as a whole are the poorest in the country. Lacking industries of its own, the South has been forced to trade the richness of its soil, its minerals and forests, and the labor of its people for goods manufactured elsewhere.

Thus the section on Private and Public Income:

> The wealth of natural resources in the South . . . benefit the South only when they can be turned into goods and services which its people need. So far the South has enjoyed relatively little of these benefits, simply be-

cause it has not had the money or credit to develop and purchase them.

Thus the section on Population:

The search for wider opportunities than are available in the overcrowded, economically undeveloped southern communities drains away people from every walk of life.

Thus the section on Credit:

There has never been enough capital and credit in the South to meet the needs of its farmers and its industry. Its people have been living so close to poverty that the South has found it almost impossible to scrape together enough capital to develop its natural resources for the benefit of its own citizens.

Beneficent nature in institutional chains—a refrain that haunted Southern liberals and progressives throughout the 1930s and 1940s and appeared frequently in their writings and public speeches.

And with justification. The *Report,* for example, pointed out that:

—erosion annually carried away 300 million dollars worth of fertile topsoil;

—in 1929 the average gross annual income of Southern farmers was $186, that of other American farmers $528;

—in 1937 common laborers in twenty Southern industries received 16 cents an hour less than their counterparts in other sections of the country;

—the South educated one third of the nation's school children with one sixth of the nation's school revenues;

—in 1936 the region spent only one half as much per pupil as the rest of the country;

—the South had 28 percent of the nation's population, but less than 11 percent of its bank deposits;

—Southern rates of syphilis, pellagra, industrial disease, and tuberculosis were higher than the rates of these diseases in other parts of the country;

—half the families in the region—four million in round numbers—needed to be rehoused;

—more than half the region's farmers were tenants.

Clearly something had to be done. Clearly solving the region's economic problems required private, local, state, and federal action. Less clearly, little could be done until the Democratic party had dealt with its conservative wing. By mid 1938, Roosevelt had at least decided to try to pluck out a few of its larger feathers.

August 9, the *Report* came to the President. Two days later, in an address at Barnesville, Georgia, he publicly declared his opposition to the re-election of Senator George, while the latter sat silently behind him on the speakers' platform. Roosevelt drew attention to the NEC *Report,* calling it a concise account of the South's economic problems, and recommending action to ameliorate the conditions it described. Promising to do what he could, he reminded his listeners that what he could do depended on Congress; without congressional sanction, he was powerless. If the people of the South desired his help they would have to elect liberal congressmen and senators favorable to his programs. Regretfully and hesitantly, he told his audience that his "old friend, the senior Senator," Walter George, could not be classified as a liberal, and he asked support in the primary election for Lawrence Camp, one of George's two opponents.[6]

Meanwhile, early in 1938, during a strike at Tupelo, Mississippi, Joseph Gelders had discussed his proposed conference on civil liberties with Lucy Randolph Mason. She arranged for Gelders to confer with her good friend Mrs. Franklin D. Roosevelt. Shortly thereafter he met the President's wife. Mrs. Roosevelt liked his idea, but she thought the conference should be broadened to include all the South's major problems. Gelders agreed.

Mrs. Roosevelt arranged for Gelders to meet her husband. The two met at Hyde Park sometime in June. Since no transcript of the conversation has survived—if indeed one was made—the substance of their interview can only be surmised. No doubt they discussed the proposed conference. Probably the President also wished the conference extended to include all the South's major problems; probably Roosevelt suggested tying the conference in with the

6. *Ibid.*, VII, 463ff.

forthcoming NEC *Report*. Undoubtedly the President asked Gelders to begin a national campaign against the poll tax; presumably he suggested that the proposed conference lead the campaign. This much is certain: two years later, while lobbying for a federal anti-poll tax bill, Gelders telegraphed Roosevelt to ask presidential support for the measure. "In June 1938," he wired, "you urged me to undertake a crusade to abolish the poll tax as a requirement for voting in the Southern states, in the interest of democratic government...." Six days later, Presidential Aide General Watson acknowledged receipt of the telegram. Roosevelt remained silent. This much more is certain: the President liked Gelders's idea for a conference in its amended form; he sent letters of greeting to the organization's first three plenary conventions. And until 1945 Mrs. Roosevelt took an active interest in the group.[7]

The President must have expected a successful campaign against the poll tax to help liberalize the Democratic party. The tax disenfranchised numerous poor voters of both races—extravagant estimates placed the figure as high as eleven million—whose votes, once freed, were expected to go for candidates who supported Roosevelt's programs. The voters might eliminate the Southern conservatives without implicating the President.

The means were ideal. While others worked against the poll tax, the President could continue cordial relations with Southern poll-tax congressmen and senators, many of whom held powerful positions on congressional committees. Whether the campaign failed or succeeded, Roosevelt avoided taking responsibility. If the campaign succeeded he would reap the reward: a united liberal Democratic party behind him.

When Gelders returned to the South he sought out H. C. Nixon, a renegade from the Vanderbilt agrarians, and other Alabamans active in the state branch of the Southern Policy Committee, including Louise O. Charlton, United States Commissioner in Birming-

7. Gelders to Roosevelt, July 10, 1940; General Watson to Gelders, July 16, 1940, Roosevelt Papers, Hyde Park, OF 1113.

ham, and Cooper Green, Birmingham Postmaster. Formed in August 1936, the Alabama Policy Committee numbered among its members prominent industrialists, publicists, labor leaders, civil servants, and professional people. It studied state political, social, and economic problems, published its findings, fostered discussion of them, and lobbied for specific reform laws. Late in 1937 the Committee considered the possibility of a regional conference on basic Southern problems; and in the summer of 1938 one of its members, Noel Beddow of the Steel Workers' Organizing Committee, advocated a coalition of Southern reform groups for an assault on the obstacles to regional progress. Gelders and the members of the Policy Committee thus had a common aim; together they began arrangements for the conference.

At the suggestion of Josephine Wilkins, head of the Citizens' Fact-Finding Committee of Georgia, a liberal organization devoted to realistic studies of state conditions, they interviewed Clark Foreman "in Atlanta with a view to hooking up the conference with the recent work of the President's Committee on Southern economic problems." [8] Others made similar suggestions: Mark Ethridge of the Louisville *Courier-Journal*, his publisher, Barry Bingham, and Lowell Mellett, NEC director.

The proposed conference would thus serve numerous purposes. Gelders would have a chance to plead for organized work in defense of Constitutional rights in the South. Southern liberal organizations could be invited to send delegates and a coalition, such as Noel Beddow had suggested, might be established. The conference would respond to the NEC *Report* with specific prescriptions to cure the ills the *Report* described; these would challenge Congress to act when it convened in December. The conference might begin a campaign against the poll tax. It would constitute

8. H. C. Nixon to Brooks Hays, July 27, 1938, National Policy Committee Papers, Manuscripts Division, Library of Congress (hereinafter cited as LC), box No. 3. This letter is basic to the interpretation offered in the text. Boxes No. 3 and No. 5 of the National Policy Committee records contain considerable information on the Alabama Policy Committee and some pertinent details on the preparations for the Conference.

an informal alliance between the progressive South and the National Administration.[9]

9. For an analysis of the conservative coalition in Congress see James T. Patterson, "A Conservative Coalition Forms in Congress, 1933–1939," *The Journal of American History*, LII (March 1966), 757–772. National Emergency Council, *Report on the Economic Conditions of the South* (Washington: Government Printing Office, 1938). For a different interpretation of the *Report* see Clarence H. Danhof's "Four Decades of Thought on the South's Economic Problems," in Melvin L. Greenhut and W. Tate Whitman, eds., *Essays in Southern Economic Development* (Chapel Hill: The University of North Carolina Press, c. 1964), pp. 7–68, especially pp. 30–35; Danhof considers the *Report* "a curious episode in the depression-stimulated concern with economic-political-social problems;" a storehouse of "ammunition for an upsurge of sectionalism which was to see some of the South's distinguished liberals allied with some of its most notorious demagogues"; a transformation of Howard W. Odum's Regionalism into a revived sectionalism: a misconceived interpretation of the South as an economic colony of the North: subservient, exploited. Thus "Odum's pursuit of a constructive regionalism was now converted into a renewed sectionalism of a peculiarly vitriolic character." For a more balanced, less acidulous account from the same point of view, see George B. Tindall, "The 'Colonial Economy' and the Growth Psychology: The South in the 1930's," *The South Atlantic Quarterly*, LXIV (Autumn 1965), 465–477. Materials deposited by Clark Foreman at the Atlanta University Library, in the Negro Collection, Atlanta, Georgia (hereinafter cited as Foreman Papers, AU) contain a file on the *Report*, including minutes of the Advisory Committee's deliberations; also Foreman to Jonathan Daniels [draft of a letter], June 8, 1948; Foreman to Gay Morenus, November 24, 1948. Mrs. C. J. Durr to author, September 3, 1963; Clark Foreman, "Decade of Hope," *Phylon*, XII (1951), 137–150. Lowell Mellett to John Persons, October 18, 1938; Mark Ethridge to Howard Odum, October 24, 1938, Odum Papers, Southern Historical Collection, University of North Carolina (hereinafter cited as UNC), box No. 21. For what it may be worth, as early as October 1937, the Administration had begun to look for liberal allies in the deep South (Brooks Hays to F. P. Miller, October 24, 1937, National Policy Committee Papers, LC, box No. 2); in February 1938, James Roosevelt announced the administration's support of Claude Pepper in the Florida primaries. Frank Freidel, *F. D. R. and the South* (Baton Rouge: Louisiana State University Press, 1965), pp. 97ff. offers evidence of Roosevelt's interest in repeal of the poll tax and of his refusal to commit himself to work against it. This account of the origins of the Southern Conference for Human Welfare differs from the official account in *Proceedings of the Southern Conference for Human Welfare, Birmingham, 1938.* (n.p.: n.p., n.d.), pp. 3–6., which credits the Alabama Policy Committee exclusively. Judge Charlton, who wrote the account, came to the Conference from the Policy Committee and was presumably ignorant of the parts played by Gelders and the Roosevelts. Members of the Policy Committee began to prepare for the Conference after Gelders returned from his interview with President Roosevelt and enlisted their aid; their role was therefore secondary, not primary.

2

THE BIRMINGHAM CONVENTION OF 1938

GELDERS and the members of the Alabama Policy Committee worked quickly. By the end of July, they had a temporary organization and by early September a permanent one. They named the organization the Southern Conference for Human Welfare—a clear indication of its general purpose—selected a place for its first meeting, lined up numerous eminent sponsors, and solicited financial aid for it.

They decided to hold the convention in Birmingham. The city could accomodate a sizable delegation and it was centrally located. Alabamans were primarily responsible for the convention preparations; they naturally preferred an Alabama city. Birmingham had an additional symbolic value; as the major center of Southern heavy industry, the city embodied Henry Grady's New South, both in its potential beneficence and in its abuses. The Southern Conference for Human Welfare intended to remedy the abuses of the Southern industrial order. What better place to start than in the center of that order? "Birmingham," Gelders later wrote, "is *potentially* . . . the most progressive and [actually] the most reactionary city in the South. This is the point in the South at which, above all others, the struggle between absentee ownership and Southern labor heads up."[1]

Invitations to the convention were sent to every organization or person who might have an interest in the Conference; Southern radio stations and newspapers publicized the forthcoming gathering. Accompanying the invitations was a statement of the organization's general purpose. The South, the statement proclaimed, had studied itself intensively; academic and civic fact-finding organizations had produced numerous studies. Now the "pertinent facts and studies must be put into the language of the people" whose "experience and aspirations . . . must be discovered and made available for students and leaders. The needs of our region must bind us, the Southern people, together for collective effort. Only in this way can genuine democracy prevail." While the people and their leaders enlightened one another, the activities of Southern liberal organizations could be harmonized. "In order to co-ordinate, strengthen, and modernize democratic activities it is important to know parallel lines of endeavor." The Southern Conference for Human Welfare would provide Southern liberals with a chance to get acquainted. All who sympathized with the statement, both Northerners and Southerners, would be welcome at Birmingham: the former as visiting, the latter as voting delegates. The Southern Conference would answer the NEC *Report* in Southern terms and in Southern tones.[2]

By early September the list of sponsors and convention partic-

1. To John B. Thompson, July 3, 1940, Southern Conference for Human Welfare Records (hereinafter SCHW Records) box No. 3, located at the Department of Research and Records, Tuskegee Institute, Tuskegee, Alabama (hereinafter TI). His italics.

2. Copies of the Statement are in Foreman Papers, AU.

ipants included Lister Hill, Hugo Black's replacement in the Senate; Luther Patrick, congressman from Birmingham; Brooks Hays, Democratic National Committeeman from Arkansas; Howard K. Beale, a liberal historian; George Fort Milton, journalist and biographer of Stephen A. Douglas and Andrew Johnson; Josephine Wilkins; Governor and Mrs. Bibb Graves of Alabama; Ralph McGill, then at the threshold of his distinguished career; John Temple Graves, II, Birmingham journalist; Clarence Poe, editor of the onetime Populist journal, the *Progressive Farmer;* and W. T. Couch, head of the University of North Carolina Press. Later additions to the list included William E. Dodd, Sr., historian and former ambassador to Germany; Virginius Dabney, editor of the Richmond *Times-Dispatch;* Edwin A. Elliott of the National Labor Relations Board's regional office in Texas; Mrs. Raymond Robbins, Honorary President of the National Women's Trade Union League; Mark Ethridge; H. L. Mitchell; and Frank Graham.

Indeed, the convention delegate and guest lists could have formed the nucleus for a who's who in Southern liberalism, and a list of the guests' and delegates' organizational affiliations could have formed the nucleus of a who's who in Southern liberal organizations. Politicians and New Dealers from Washington attended: Justice Hugo Black to receive the Southern Conference's first annual Thomas Jefferson Award given to "the Southerner who has done most to promote human and social welfare in line with the philosophy of Thomas Jefferson;" [3] Mrs. Roosevelt to make a major address; Claude Pepper to preside over the session at which Mrs. Roosevelt spoke; Aubrey Williams of the W.P.A. to speak on labor relations and unemployment; R. W. Hudgens of the Farm Security Administration to participate in a panel discussion on Southern health problems; John Bankhead to attend the Thomas Jefferson award ceremony and appear on the panel on farm tenancy. Politicians from less powerful organizations also decided to come: six avowed members of the Communist party and, so accusations have run, perhaps a score of covert members and conscious fellow-

3. *Birmingham Proceedings of the Southern Conference*, p. 24.

travelers from such organizations as the International Labor Defense, the American League for Peace and Democracy, the Workers' Alliance, and the American Youth Congress. A judicious H. C. Nixon balanced the avowed six Communist party members with six Catholic representatives designated, at Nixon's request, by the Bishop of Mobile. The Socialist party sent a contingent of twenty-seven, either openly or in organizations with large Socialist factions: the Southern Tenant Farmers' Union, the Southern Workers' Defense League, and the Southern branch of the Amalgamated Clothing Workers of America. Economic interest groups sent representatives. The CIO sent a sizable delegation, both black and white, from its regional councils and from its industrial unions; the AFofL and the Railroad Brotherhoods sent smaller contingents. The dispossessed farmers took an interest: members of the Tenant Farmers' Union and the National Farmers' Union agreed to tell of their experiences in the harsh Southern agricultural system. Donald Comer, Alabama textile magnate, came to lobby for a declaration against freight-rate differentials. Men of the cloth, Protestant, Jew, and Catholic, graced the gathering and, indeed, many of the delegates, being products of the Social Gospel tradition, came as plain-clothes clergymen. Prominent Negroes agreed to attend: Mary McLeod Bethune, founder of Bethune-Cookman College in Daytona Beach, Florida, and indefatigable fighter for Negro rights; F. D. Patterson, President of Tuskegee Institute; Rufus Clement, President of Atlanta University; Benjamin Mays, President of Morehouse College; and Forester Washington from the Atlanta University School of Social Work. Negroes less well known came from other organizations: from the National Negro Congress, from the Southern Negro Youth Congress, from integrated CIO unions, from other Southern Negro schools. Eminent educators and scholars attended: Frank Graham, Arthur Raper, George S. Mitchell, Charles S. Johnson, and Wilson Gee. The National Women's Trade Union League, the League of Women Voters, youth groups, penal reformers, and Highlander Folk School were other organizations that sent representatives. All of the delegates presumably shared the desire to answer the NEC *Report.* Many of them came to air their pet panaceas and to propagate the views of the special interests they represented.

Educators concentrated on resolutions in favor of federal aid to education, labor delegates on strong labor resolutions, the young on the problems of Southern youth, politicians on dramatizing themselves and their views, farmers on strong farm resolutions. The Southern Conference for Human Welfare was from its inception a congeries of progressive interest groups, any one of whose policies might conflict with the Southern Conference's program. The Conference's demise in 1948 was in part a result of conflicts between its program and the policies of some of its constituent groups.

In this connection, Howard W. Odum's relation to the Conference is instructive. An outstanding sociologist, Odum had led the movement for realistic studies of Southern conditions; he had attracted a number of first-rate students to the University of North Carolina where, under his direction, they had done valuable work on contemporary Southern problems. His own work was basic to the NEC *Report.* The Southern Conference interested Odum as a potential agent for Southern change and as a means for furthering his own reform programs. He was then maturing plans for a Southern regional reform organization "analagous to our best universities for making more articulate the researches in the universities and for utilizing the sentiment, action, and facts gained by all these groups." [4] He hoped to assimilate the Southern Policy Committee and the Commission on Interracial Co-operation into the new organization and to be invited to present his plan to the Birmingham convention. "My position is . . . [that] if the Alabama Conference is adequate we can present our plan to them, since by that time we shall know which way we are going." [5]

But Odum's conception warred with the conception of the Southern Conference. "The difference between the agency and the conference," he wrote to Wilson Gee, "is fundamental; namely, the

4. Odum to Mark Ethridge, November 14, 1938, Odum Papers, UNC, box No. 21.
5. Odum to Charles Johnson, September 21, 1938, *ibid.*

agency is a permanent, full-time functioning organization, well endowed and with its staff composed of men everywhere comparable to our university presidents and faculty members." [6] H. C. Nixon expressed the differences more forcefully:

> Odum's undertaking must inevitably be academic, the Welfare Conference is close to the labor movement with strong labor-farmer participation for action. . . . Odum's plan will cost more money and furnish material for the others to use but will not directly touch the people. . . . The Conference must make a mass appeal, if it makes the grade at all.[7]

Odum was invited to Birmingham, but not to present his plan. Fearful lest his presence at Birmingham be taken as an endorsement of the Southern Conference program and so compromise his own plans, Odum decided to stay home. He asked Mark Ethridge to look after his affairs at the convention.

With Odum absent the progressive groups present at Birmingham could work in harmony. Their common desire to bring the New Deal to the South in greater measure united them. The Southern Conference's most pressing problem lay elsewhere.

Conference officers budgeted $6,760 for the convention. According to the extant records—which may be unreliable—about $3,000 was raised. Roy Lawrence, CIO Southern regional director, gave $500 on behalf of the CIO; for the United Mine Workers, William Mitch donated $900. John Temple Graves gave $250; Sam Zemurray, an officer of the United Fruit Company, gave $100. The delegates' one-dollar registration fee accounts, on the basis of the minimum estimate of the number of delegates, for $1,250; on the basis of the maximum estimate it accounts for $1,500. The former figure leaves a deficit of $100 unaccounted for; the latter a surplus of $250. If the former figure is correct, the chances are that Mrs. Roosevelt and other wealthy friends of the organization made up the difference. Whichever is correct, the Southern Conference had raised less than

6. October 13, 1938, *ibid.*
7. H. C. Nixon to Francis P. Miller, October 19, 1938, National Policy Committee Papers, LC, box No. 3.

half its budgeted figure. Here originated a chronic financial problem which the Conference never got over.[8]

II

On November 20, 1938, the Southern Conference for Human Welfare convened in Birmingham's Municipal Auditorium. The city accorded the Conference a friendly reception: most of the city's liberally inclined were on hand for the opening session; the major white newspapers genuinely desired an honest answer to the NEC *Report;* the Women's Civic Club took the delegates on a tour of the city; Birmingham's main hotel, the Tutwiler, housed most of the white delegates and opened its special conference rooms to several panel discussions. Although Negroes and whites ate and slept separately, they mingled freely during the convention's opening session. On the second day, however, Birmingham police, acting under orders from City Commissioner Theophilus Eugene Connor (the same Bull Connor of recent notoriety), enforced the City's segregation statute, and for the remainder of the convention Negroes and whites sat on opposite sides of the Municipal Auditorium. Other-

8. Foreman Papers, AU, National Policy Committee Papers, LC, box No. 3 for the Conference preparations. Charles Johnson to Howard Odum, September 6, 1938; H. C. Nixon to Odum, October 5, 1938; Odum to Nixon, October 8, 1938; Odum to Wilson Gee, October 13, 1938; Odum to Mark Ethridge, October 8, 1938; same to same, November 14, 1938: Odum Papers, UNC, box No. 21. *Birmingham Proceedings of the Southern Conference, passim.* Socialist Party Papers, Duke, August-December 1938. Letter Box has a list, dated November 20, 1938, of the Socialists who attended the convention. Figures on the known Communist vary: some say six, some say five, others say four. At different times H. C. Nixon used four and six. Graham Papers, UNC, have some materials on finances: H. C. Nixon to Graham, November 20, 1939. Foreman Papers, AU, also have information on early finances. This account rejects the Dies Committee charge that in the spring of 1938 Communist Party Treasurer William Weiner sent $2,000 to the South which was used to finance the Southern Conference. Like so many things said before that unfortunate committee, the charge stands unsupported by any credible evidence. Weiner explicitly denied it. United States Congress, House of Representatives, Special Committee on Un-American Activities, *Investigation of Un-American Propaganda Activities in the United States,* 76 cong., 1 sess. (Washington: Government Printing Office, 1939), VII, 4765–67. Howard Kester comes to similar conclusions about Conference financial sources on the basis of even less credible evidence. Interview, Howard Kester, Black Mountain, North Carolina, February 26, 1964.

wise, relations between the Southern Conference and local authorities remained cordial.

The delegates, the official chronicle of the convention relates, "poured into Birmingham like a cleansing flood, animated one and all with one selfless purpose—to help the South through the democratic process of free speech and frank discussion." [9] Forced segregation could neither stay the flood nor stifle discussion. "All shades of thought, many ideas of how the job could be accomplished; many pet foibles, a few panaceas; much sound doctrine" had come together to express a Southern liberal consensus; not

Southern in the sense of magnolia blossoms and sweet dim memories of a by-gone age, but a solid, sensible South, aware that the War between the States is over and that the South is the garden spot of the country, but that we must till the soil, or the fairest garden soon over-runs with weeds.

The delegates, George C. Stoney, a young journalist, reported "were a southern crop . . .; talk was thick as molasses. Although I had lived 'up no'th' less than a year, they pinned a blue visitor's badge on my lapel that labeled me 'Yankee'." He was one of the few who had reservations about the convention.

I joined my old friends among the student delegates and tried to lay bets on what the speakers would say. They were veterans of southern conferences, too, and as cocksure as I that the old line liberals, sociologists and welfare workers, stray ministers and educators we had heard so many times before would repeat themselves.[10]

Repetitions no doubt occurred; the main speakers were prominent persons who had been propagating their opinions for decades. But new tones appeared. In their addresses, Frank Graham and Mrs. Roosevelt made oblique, critical references to Southern treatment of the Negro. Graham challenged the delegates to work for "helpless minorities and the underprivileged," to "demonstrate, in our stumbling and defective way that we wish to go the Jesus way,"

9. Unless otherwise noted, all quotations are from *Birmingham Proceedings of the Southern Conference.*

10. "Southerners Write Their Own Prescription," *Survey Graphic*, XXVIII (January 1939), 42–43.

and to "show that this Conference stands for the Sermon on the Mount, the American Bill of Rights and American democracy." Mrs. Roosevelt asked the delegates to work to demonstrate the vitality of American democracy to the world, and to take pride in "every one of our citizens, for regardless of nationality, or race, every one contributes to the welfare and culture of the nation." Both offered education as the cure for the region's problems. For Graham, the "Jesus way" was "the slow way of education and revelation of the inner life" and freedom and democracy, then in retreat throughout the world, meant a "geater equality of opportunity for all the children everywhere." For Mrs. Roosevelt "the real basis of democracy" was "universal education" which prepared "every individual" to "be able to bear his responsibility fully." Both favored federal aid to education.

In his acceptance of the Thomas Jefferson award, Hugo Black reiterated some of the NEC *Report*'s salient findings and then strung quotes from Jefferson implicitly critical of Southern life. The great Virginian, Black said, had championed public discussion, public education, the freedoms of the Bill of Rights, a widespread franchise, and gradual reform of human institutions to keep pace with technological, scientific, and industrial changes. These Jeffersonian beliefs not only implicitly criticized the South, they also afforded a rationale for the Southern Conference. "I understand," the Justice's peroration ran,

> this Conference has not turned to the past to lament events beyond control; that you have examined the facts of the present; that you look to the future. Those who accept the dynamic philosophy of Jefferson as sound must believe such deliberation and actions will not be in vain. Such free and open conferences should promote the welfare of the South and of the Nation.

The promotion of Southern and national welfare required detailed recommendations. These came from panel discussions on credit, farm tenancy, constitutional rights, education, labor relations, women wage-earners, freight-rate differentials, youth, health, and child labor. At these, resolutions were introduced, debated, and accepted or rejected. The accepted resolutions went to the Resolutions Committee, chaired by Clyde Mills of the Amalgamated Clothing Workers, where they were reworded and, on occasion, toned down.

The result was a wholesale demand for immediate reforms embodying the programs and panaceas of every conceivable interest group—including George C. Stoney and his sceptical friends. There was something in the resolutions for the sociologist, the stray minister, the welfare worker, the educator, the worker, the farmer, the Negro, the businessman, and the doubting youth.

The Conference's labor resolutions favored shorter hours for women, liberal state workmen's compensation laws, women's bureaus in state departments of labor, laws requiring prompt payment of employees and severance pay, state Wagner acts, state enforcement of the child labor provisions of the Fair Labor Standards Act, civil service laws guarantying tenure to qualified personnel, and continuation of the La Follette Committee. Other resolutions opposed amendments to the Wagner Act, denounced remnants of the domestic, or putting-out, system of labor, criticized regional wage differentials, spoke out against eviction of workers from company housing to prevent them from organizing their own unions, and opposed the use of W.P.A. labor in munitions plants. The Conference endorsed Roosevelt's efforts to re-unite the labor movement and declared its support for the W.P.A.'s cultural projects.

The numerous labor resolutions reflected the heavy labor representation at the convention. A comparable number of resolutions on the Negro problem reflected the large number of the South's minority present—estimates place the figure between 300 and 400. Here the intricacies of Southern race relations became clear. Here the perplexities of Southern interracial reform organizations became clear; generous impulses were nearly everywhere checked by qualifications or silence: perhaps they had to be. Thus the Conference denounced forced segregation of the races—but only in its own meetings; it condemned "the action of Birmingham City officials in enforcing existing segregation ordinances, as affecting sessions of this conference." Future Conference meetings should be held in cities where "the practices of the past few days would not be applied." Thus the Conference recommended greater Negro participation in Southern politics through "the abolition of poll-taxes as a prerequisite to voting" and through the "extension of the franchise to all our citizens of proper educational qualifications"; yet the poor Negroes whom the poll tax kept from the polls were not likely to have the "proper educational qualifications" for voting. The Conference demanded freedom for the remaining Scottsboro boys and state and federal anti-lynching statutes; and it opposed "the practice of wage differentials between racial groups." Yet it failed to denounce discriminatory hiring practices. It recommended basing "appropriations for public education ... upon school populations." It supported giving "qualified Negro physicians ... an opportunity to render professional service to Negro patients in tax supported institutions." It urged the federal government to build "a playground and recreational facility for the Negro youth of Birmingham." It recommended "adequate appropriations ... for Negro graduate work in Southern state-supported Negro institutions." The Southern Conference would integrate its meetings and try to get a few Negroes the vote; it would not yet attempt to integrate Southern schools, hospitals, or playgrounds. Had it gone any farther than it did, most if not all of the liberals and radicals in the Conference would probably have scurried away. That would have been the end of the organization.

Conference solicitude for farmers extended itself to endorsements of increased appropriations for implementing the Bankhead-Jones Farm Tenancy Bill, for additional funds for the Farm Security Administration to enable it to expand its group medical and co-operative programs, for legal aid to farmers, for federal rural housing, for written contracts to govern landlord-tenant relationships, for minimum housing standards on plantations, and for cheaper agricultural credit.

Resolutions on industrial problems included endorsement of the Southern governors' fight against freight-rate differentials, and proposals for taxes on the incomes of absentee owners, for lower interest rates on loans to industry, and for extension of federal credit to the South through regional federal banks or a federal insurance company to guarantee private banks' long-term loans.

On civil liberties, the Conference resolved in favor of uniform federal and state voter-registration procedures, an end to the poll tax, flexible election laws to permit printing of the names of independent candiates and minor parties on the ballot, WPA legal-aid bureaus to provide counsel for those otherwise unable to afford it, strict regulation of the private use of deputy sheriffs, laws guaranteeing the right to parade and meet in public places, and a La Follette Committee investigation of corporate subsidies which "threaten the freedom of the press."

The Conference also recommended other state and federal action: state graduated income taxes to replace the sales tax; federal aid to education, including money for vocational training programs and student co-operatives in high schools and colleges; extension of the Social Security Act's coverage; an increase in federal housing and slum-clearance programs; an antidelinquency and penal-reform program to include a "broad system of playground and recreation centers . . . parole and probation administration" systems free from political considerations, more diversified vocational training in prisons, and adequate playgrounds in housing projects; medical and dental clinics for the many Southern counties where they were lacking; birth-control clinics in state public health agencies; combination of the National Youth Administration and the Civilian Conservation Corps into a single federal youth agency.

Finally, the Conference endorsed the First Congress of the Mexican and Spanish-American Peoples of the United States, an action the House Committee on Un-American Activities later considered significant, although it stands isolated and irrelevant in Southern Conference history; and it endorsed the peace policy of President Roosevelt and Secretary Hull, an action which later involved it in serious internal dissention.

The Southern Conference had demanded much—so much that it could not end with the close of the Birmingham convention. Its fair words and bold pronouncements needed implementation. Although older liberals and some of the middle-class representatives may have expected to demand much and do nothing, most of the delegates expected more. Both Gelders and Nixon hoped for a permanent organization to carry out part of the program. The skepticism of George C. Stoney and his friends indicates a readiness among the young for action to supplement words. Presumably, the Negroes and organized labor were either in favor of a permanent organization or were willing to cooperate when the subjcet was broached. Whatever the case, on November 21 the chair appointed a committee on permanent organization under W. T. Couch. Two days later the committee returned with a plan of organization which was quickly adopted.

The organization's declared purposes were to promote the general welfare, improve the economic, social, and cultural standards of the Southern people, "advance Southern functional growth in accordance with American democratic institutions and ideals," initiate and support progressive legislation, and co-operate with other Southern progressive organizations. Annual membership meetings would draw up general programs of action. A Southern council of 118 members—seven from each of the thirteen Southern states, nine selected at large, and the organization's eighteen general officers—constituted the plenary authority; when not in session its functions devolved to the Executive Board. Special study committees were provided for, and the Executive Board was given the power to organize regional, state, and local councils, to appoint organizers, to raise money, and to act to carry out the Conference's policies. The Conference elected Frank Graham chairman. Clark Foreman became treasurer.

The Conference made news. The New York *Times* sent a correspondent. The Associated Press wire service sent out scraps of information—some of it misleading—to its member newspapers; these ran in Southern as well as Northern newspapers. National and regional liberal magazines ran notices of it. Nationally and internationally known intellectuals paid it heed.

The coverage was generally favorable, even in the South. Much of the unfavorable Southern coverage resulted from an Associated Press story which reported the resolution deploring enforced segregation in the City Auditorium as a unanimously voted "condemnation of the South's Jim Crow laws for the separation of whites and Negroes." The Richmond *Times Dispatch*, more in sadness than in anger, wrote: "This resolution we venture to guess has gone farther in arousing opposition on the part of the masses of Southern whites to the Conference's entire program than anything the gathering could have done." The Montgomery *Advertiser*, then under editorial guidance of Grover Hall, Sr., who had braved the wrath of the Klan in the 1920s, was equally saddened: "Surely there was enough work for this Conference to do to soften the rigors of life in the Deep South without challenging the folkways of our people- and raising extraneous issues. . . . " The Birmingham *News* hoped the furor over the segregation resolution would not distract attention from the positive contributions the Conference had to make.[11] The New Orleans *Tribune* refused to be saddened:

For that conference, we believe, most southerners have the common sense to be grateful. . . . What chiefly matters is that the South, after decades of denouncing its critics as damn-yankees, has decided that much in this part of the country must be improved, and that the job of changing it belongs to us, not to outsiders, although they, too, may be helpful. The first Southern Conference for Human Welfare means that the barriers against free discussion of new ideas in the South have come down. We want to keep them down.[12]

Outside the South, few if any interested liberals or radicals had serious reservations about the Conference. The New York *Times* correspondent, Winifred Mallon, thought the Conference unique in its "policies, personnel and program."[13] Charles and Mary Beard called the Conference a "sign of determined resistance to the ar-

11. These quotes were taken from clippings in the possession of Mrs. C. J. Durr of Montgomery, Alabama.

12. Quoted in Lucy Mason, "Southerners Look at the South," *The North Georgia Review*, III (Fall and Winter, 1938–1939), 17–18, 40.

13. The New York *Times*, November 23, 1938, p. 23.

bitrary spirit," noted its free discussion of efforts "to raise the standard of living," and praised the attempt at "a permanent pooling of interests and for moving in a solid phalanx upon the menaces to liberty and welfare everywhere in the South." [14] Gunnar Myrdal, then at work on his *An American Dilemma,* came away from the Conference with

> a feeling that the real importance of this meeting was that here for the first time in the history of the region, since the era of the American Revolution, the lonely Southern liberals met in great numbers . . . and that they, in this new and unique adventure, experienced a foretaste of the freedom and power which large-scale political organization and concerted action give.[15]

Myrdal, himself a Socialist, had his echoes in the American left. The Socialist *Call,* having warmly greeted the Conference and having predicted that it would be "one of the most significant movements ever launched," happily reported that "the conference adopted stacks of strong resolutions on the basic issues, many of which were drafted by Socialist leaders who took an active part in the meetings." [16]

Communists wrote of the conference with unaccustomed modesty. Ernest Moorer in the *Daily Worker* found impressive the "free and easy association of white and Negro delegates and the complete naturalness with which the conference democratically [proceeded]." [17] "The conference," the *New Masses* editorialized, "marks the opening of a new, hopeful epoch in the South. The forces of Southern progressivism have become articulate and the battle to reclaim the South for democracy has now acquired courageous leadership." [18] Only Rob Hall, party secretary in Alabama, departed from the tasteful, disinterested treatment the party journals accorded the Conference. Its attempt to forge a union of all progressives was, so Hall argued, a brilliant confirmation of the policy line Earl Browder had laid down at the Tenth Party Congress. At

14. *America in Midpassage* (New York: Macmillan, 1939), p. 571.
15. *An American Dilemma* (New York and London: Harper, 1944), p. 469.
16. IV, November 19, 1938, p. 1; December 17, 1938, p. 4.
17. November 22, 1938, p. 6.
18. XXIX, December 6, 1938, p. 21.

that, Hall's boast was almost incidental; elsewhere he wrote that the Communist party had played only a minor role in the Conference preparations and proceedings. He was more concerned with reporting, intoning hymns of praise, and offering minor criticisms. "Here was a gathering of intensely patriotic Southerners," he exulted, "wrapped up in Southern problems, and jealous of their obligations to solve these problems. But this did not mean the narrow, fanatical sectionalism of the past." The Conference was a sign that the solid South was melting, if not thawing and resolving itself into a progressive flood. "The Southern Conference indicated that the Southern people, harassed by deep-seated problems... are determined to secure for themselves and their families more of the fruits of the New Deal...." He criticized the Conference because the middle class and the AFofL were inadequately represented, and because no representative from the Farm Bureau Federation had been present. To such a pass had the requirements of popular-front tactics brought the once radical Communist movement.[19]

Members of the Southern Conference were equally enthusiastic. Stanton Smith thought the Conference had the "color of a representative section of the progressive" South, and that the Conference had "struck fire," though "whether the fire will burn... remains to be seen." [20] Lucy Mason and W. T. Couch agreed, in Miss Mason's words, that the Conference was "a people's movement, representing every strata of society from capitalist to sharecropper." Tarleton Collier, reporter for a Hearst journal in Atlanta, called the Conference the "first large gathering in the South ever to be concerned with the total picture rather than with detached elements of work that must be done." [21]

Members of Negro protest groups took note of the Conference. Charles Johnson analyzed it at length for the *Crisis*, the N.A.A.C.P.'s house organ. The Conference, he wrote, marked "the first bold

19. "The Southern Conference for Human Welfare," *The Communist*, XVIII (January, 1939), 57–65.

20. "South's Answer," *American Teacher*, XXIII (December 1938), 7–8.

21. Lucy Mason, "Southerners Look at the South," *The North Georgia Review*, III, 17–18, 40. The Collier quote comes from this article. W. T. Couch, "Southerners Inspect the South," *The New Republic*, XCVII (December 14, 1938), 168–169.

emergence of the liberal South as a self-conscious group. . . . " It had achieved "a comfortable tolerance in diversity" and projected "a philosophy which revealed the organic relationship of many of the problems of the area, the solution of any one of which is conditioned upon the solution of the others." He exhorted the Conference's Negro members to become conversant with the broad range of Southern problems instead of concentrating on the race question; Negroes "can never be presumed to speak wisely . . . unless they are known to be acquainted with the total structure of Southern life and the confusing interrelationships of all its problems." [22] The Conference, wrote Sterling A. Brown in the pages of *Opportunity*, "is a sign that the South is on the move. The hind wheel may be off and the axle dragging, but the old cart is moving along." [23]

However they interpreted the Birmingham convention, nearly all of the commentators agreed that the Southern Conference for Human Welfare was a unique event in the annals of Southern liberalism. This was an exaggeration; the Southern Conference both developed out of and departed from Southern reform precedents.

The Conference's insistence on interracial organization and integrated meetings could have derived from the practices of the United Mine Workers, many of the CIO unions, the Commission on Interracial Co-operation, some state social welfare organizations, and some church groups. Its attempt to cut across class lines had been anticipated by the Southern Policy Committee, whose Alabama branch, for example, had included labor leaders and businessmen. The Conference's wish to set the facts before the people frankly derived from the fact-finding work of Southern academic and civic organizations.

Here the Conference departed from these kindred organizations. Where they were either small groups of limited membership or large groups representing a single interest, the Southern Conference anticipated a mass membership and expected to have every Southern progressive organization represented on its executive board. All

22. "More Southerners Discover the South," *Crisis*, XLI (January 1939), 14–15.
23. "South on the Move," *Opportunity*, XVI (December 1938), 366–368.

persons willing to pay one dollar a year in membership fees were welcome, whether businessman, farmer, worker, teacher, or Negro. Persons willing to attend board meetings were sought from labor organizations, farm groups, colleges, and business. Where the fact-finding organizations worked quietly, concentrating on a few issues, the Southern Conference began with a direct, noisy attack on all Southern problems. Where the fact-finding groups had been chary of political action the Conference was prepared, if necessary, to stumble headlong into the thicket of Southern politics. And if all else failed or nothing else was available the Conference would attempt to bring down the whole battered mansion of Southern reaction with huffs and puffs of hot rhetoric.

Here, indeed, was perhaps its most distinguishing feature: where previous organizations had contented themselves with quiet repairs on sections of the old Southern mansion, the Southern Conference for Human Welfare insisted at the least on complete renovation and at the most on immediate demolition and replacement by an entirely different structure. The Conference, as Tarleton Collier had said, was concerned with "the total picture rather than with detached elements of the work that must be done."

The Conference's wholesale attack on Southern institutions and the misrepresentation of its antisegregation resolution drew conservative criticism. The Selma *Times Journal*, the Tuscaloosa *News*, the Decatur *Daily*—all Alabama newspapers—scored the Conference for its stand on the race question. Their condemnations were heartily seconded by *Alabama: The News Magazine of the Deep South*, an organ of Birmingham's industrial elite, the so-called Big Mules. The Conference, it jeered, was a joint enterprise of Southern radicals and left-wing members of the Roosevelt administration with a "program vicious in its intended results"; the group would abolish the poll tax, achieve "universal voting, and adopt some sort of law . . . to equalize the economic, social and political condition of colored people with . . . the white race . . . ." Both *Alabama* and the Birmingham City Commission demanded a Dies Committee investigation. The Alabama Council of Women's Democratic Clubs, an organization without official connection with the Democratic National Committee, demanded Judge Charlton's resignation from her post on the Alabama State Democratic Executive Committee, charged that the Conference was Communist-inspired, and prophesied that it would retard Southern progress and disrupt peaceful relations between the South's two races. Early in December the ladies organized a public meeting to protest the Southern Conference's appearance in Birmingham.[24]

Whether as a result of these attacks or of the misrepresentation of the Conference's stand on the race issue, most of the prominent politicians quit the Conference soon after the Birmingham meeting. Lister Hill, who had once been among the most enthusiastic, was never heard from again; Luther Patrick, Cooper Green, and John Bankhead, when the Conference adjourned, severed their tenuous connections with it. Bankhead wrote an apology: "The expressions made in favor of social race equality and in favor of the sectional Wagner lynching bill demonstrate that a majority of those participating do not understand fundamental Southern conditions." He later told Kenneth McKellar he had been misled about the nature of the Conference. Francis Pickens Miller refused to serve the Conference in an official capacity because a known member of the Virginia Communist party, Donald Burke, had been present at the convention; off the record, he acknowledged that he not only opposed association with Communists on principle but also that if his connection with Burke became known it would ruin his chances of winning elective public office. Even Claude Pepper refused official association with the Conference. Both he and Brooks Hays continued their interest—Pepper openly, Hays behind the scenes; but neither would permit himself official connection with the organization.

Although the attacks on the Southern Conference and the resignations of prominent liberal politicians may have weakened it, they also benefitted the organization. Frank Graham had told his friends at Birmingham that he did not have time to serve the Conference in an official capacity. When he heard of the attacks on the organization and the criticisms of Judge Charlton he felt honor-

24. Material in this paragraph is from *Alabama,* III (December 5, 1938), 3ff. The quote from John Bankhead in the next paragraph is from the same source.

bound to acquiesce in his election to the Conference chairmanship. One of the outstanding Southern liberals of his generation, he inspired abiding loyalty in nearly all who knew him. His decision to take the Conference chairmanship was sufficient to persuade a number of prominent persons to remain in the organization, among them Mark Ethridge and Barry Bingham, and to lend it badly needed respectability. He wrote Ethridge:

> There was much about the conference that was impressive. . . . We should have the historical understanding and the social insight to know that with freedom and democracy inevitably go mistakes of judgment, tactics, and even action. The only way to have a mistake-proof meeting is to make the biggest mistake of all in not having the meeting free and democratic.[25]

"Despite some misunderstanding," he told Clark Foreman, "much and bitter misrepresentation, some resignations, and even some mistakes we must carry on." [26]

25. December 20, 1938, Graham Papers, UNC.

26. December 20, 1938, Foreman Papers, AU. Otherwise this section depends on Mark Ethridge to Howard Odum, November 25, 1938, Odum Papers, UNC, which discusses the problem of permanent organization and contends that only Nixon and a few others desired one. Since little or no opposition to the permanent organization appeared, it is safe to assume that the bulk of the delegates were either in favor or insufficiently concerned to oppose it. On the Southern Conference's predecessors see Wilma Dykeman and James Stokely, *Seeds of Southern Change* (Chicago: University of Chicago Press, 1962); this deals with the Commission on Interracial Cooperation and its guiding genius for many years, Will Alexander; Edward Flud Burrows, "The Commission on Interracial Cooperation, 1919–1944," unpublished Ph.D. Thesis, University of Wisconsin, 1954; an abstract of this can be found in University of Wisconsin, *Summaries of Doctoral Dissertations*, XVI, 265–267. E. Charles Chatfield, "The Southern Sociological Congress: Organization for Uplift," *The Tennessee Historical Quarterly* (December 1960), pp. 328ff; and *idem*, "The Southern Sociological Congress: Rationale of Uplift," in *ibid.* (March 1961), pp. 51ff.; Frank T. Wilson, "The Role of the Young Men's Christian Association," in William Stuart Nelson, ed., *The Christian Way in Race Relations* (New York: Harper, 1948), pp. 158–59; Cayton and Mitchell, *Black Workers and the New Unions*, *passim.* Frank Graham to L. A. Crowell, Jr., December 22, 1938, Graham Papers, UNC, was especially helpful. C. Vann Woodward to author, July 19, 1963; Harry Golden to author, October 7, 1963; Interview, Howard Kester, Black Mountain, North Carolina, February 26, 1964. For attitudes of various persons before and after the Convention see Joseph Gelders to Mrs. C. J. Durr, July 30, 1938, Foreman Papers, AU, which contains the remark that Lister Hill was the most enthusiastic about the Southern Conference; Mark Ethridge to Graham, November 30, 1938; Sallie F. Hill to Clarence Poe, December 7, 1938; Luther Patrick to Graham, December 1, 1938; H. C. Nixon to Graham, January 17, 1939; Claude Pepper to Graham, February 6, 1939: Graham Papers, UNC. Francis Pickens Miller to Graham, December 21, 1938, Odum Papers, UNC.

3

THE EARLY YEARS, 1938–1940

CARRYING ON required power: financial resources, dedicated workers willing to labor long hours for low wages, a program of action with the widest possible appeal. A voluntary organization, the Southern Conference depended upon private benefactions and the devoted efforts of a committed few. The plan of action had to reflect the common reform interests of its constituent groups. The Conference's dependence on financial donations, the concerns of its first full-time executive secretaries, and the need for a scheme of action satisfactory to all its supporters determined to a large extent the organization's early history.

During the first year and a half of its existence, Conference fund-raisers had worse luck than they had had prior to the Birmingham convention. Solicitations from wealthy Southern liberals and from affluent New Yorkers yielded little. For the period beginning December 1938 and ending January 1, 1940, Conference income was a scant $1,963.48: Robert Marshall, a former conservationist with the United States Forest Service, gave $500, as did Mrs. Luke Wilson, who remained a Conference benefactor during most of its existence; the Amalgamated Clothing Workers contributed $250; Mrs. Roosevelt, Barry Bingham, William E. Dodd's daughter, Martha, James K. Feibleman, a professor of philosophy from New Orleans, Frank Graham, and a Mrs. Schott gave $100 a piece. From this fund, the Conference's executive secretaries drew meager wages and occasional expenses.

Poverty nearly destroyed the fond hopes and the expectant idealism of the Birmingham convention. Few could live on the wages the Conference could afford to pay. Until the middle of 1939, H. C. Nixon traveled about the South to encourage formation of state branches of the Southern Conference and to interest liberals in its program. Unable, or unwilling, to live on Conference wages, he left the Conference in the summer to take a teaching position at the University of Missouri. The Conference could not afford a replacement until the following October. Its only full-time employee during the intervening months was Joseph Gelders.

If few could live at Conference wages, even fewer were willing to devote much time to the organization's affairs. Both Mark Ethridge's Committee on Freight Rates and Clarence Poe's Farm Committee remained inactive because their chairmen were busy with other projects. For similar reasons, the Committee on Finance, under Barry Bingham, did little; Gelders, Clark Foreman, Frank Graham, and Lucy Mason were the Conference's most active fund raisers. Although Graham and H. C. Nixon hoped the Conference would concentrate on a campaign for federal aid to Southern education, they did nothing about it. Nixon quit the Conference before its program of action got under way, and Graham's duties as President of the University of North Carolina limited his work for the Southern Conference to letter writing. The Conference's state groups—

organizations begun in Georgia, Louisiana, Virginia, Alabama, and Kentucky—seem to have been occasional study and discussion groups. The Conference was unable to present its answers to the NEC *Report* to Congress and that body never responded to them.

In February 1939, the Conference's executive council authorized the establishment of a Committee on Civil Rights, under the chairmanship of Maury Maverick and the executive secretaryship of Joseph Gelders, and directed it to begin a campaign against the poll tax. Two months earlier, the younger members of the Conference had established the Council of Young Southerners. For the early years of its life, the Conference's reform efforts were limited to the activities of these two groups. Like its predecessors, the Southern Conference had to begin with a few minor repairs on the old Southern mansion.[1]

II

Abolition of the poll tax was the most convenient repair to begin with. Enacted between 1889 and 1902 in the eleven former Confederate states, it was an annual capitation of one or two dollars for the privilege of voting in primary and general elections. Falling heavily on the rural poor, it limited both the Negro and the poor white vote. Levied in the late winter or early spring, it came when the rural areas were short of money. Where the tax was a dollar a year and no fines were exacted for previous delinquencies, the meager annual cash incomes of Negro sharecroppers and white tenants made the vote a luxury they could ill afford. Where nonpayment in one year entailed an additional impost the next, the vote was an extravagance they seldom considered. Exaggerated

1. H. C. Nixon to Graham, December 9, 1939; Lucy Mason to Graham, December 6, 1938; Tarleton Collier to Graham, January 2, 1938 [1939]; Lucy Mason to Graham, December 31, 1938; H. C. Nixon to Graham, December 26, 1938; James K. Fiebleman to Nixon and Graham, January 12, 1939; H. C. Nixon to Graham, January 17, 1939; H. C. Nixon to Mary McLeod Bethune, January 18, 1939; H. C. Nixon to Graham, January 24, 1939; same to same, February 16, 1939; Joseph Gelders to Graham, March 23, 1939; W. R. Bowie to Graham, April 10, 1939; Clark Foreman to Graham, July 31, 1939– Graham Papers, UNC. Financial details are from Howard Lee to Gelders, January 8, 1940, SCHW Records, TI, box No. 4.

estimates placed the number disenfranchised by the late 1930s as high as eleven million. In the late 1940's, the cautious and scientific V. O. Key claimed the tax disenfranchised a maximum of five to ten per cent of the total Southern adult population—far fewer than eleven million and probably even fewer than five million. Yet, Key estimated that repeal of the tax would increase the size of the Southern electorate by a minimum of one-fourth and a maximum of one-third—a significant increase whatever the total number of voters added might have been. In both its intent and its effects, the tax clearly violated democratic principles: it kept large numbers of otherwise qualified citizens from the polls; it enabled numerous petty autocrats to maintain unchallenged control over their pocket boroughs.

If its effects were pernicious, its justifications were hollow. In spite of the effusions of its more rhapsodic apologists, the tax had not, by trying to keep political power in the hands of the wealthy few, markedly purified Southern politics—unless Theodore Bilbo and Martin Dies are pure political types. Buying and selling of poll tax receipts were common practices in the poll tax states; the votes thus acquired were automatically cast for the purchasers' candidate. Claims that the tax was a major source of Southern public school funds were made in ignorance or mendacity; no Southern state got more than 5 per cent of its school funds from poll tax receipts.

In 1920, North Carolina repealed its poll tax. In 1934, Louisiana, where the Long organization sought more votes, followed suit. In 1937, Senator Claude Pepper's forces repealed Florida's tax. By the late 1930s, sentiment for repeal of the tax had spread throughout the South. The small, struggling Socialist and Communist parties in the region favored repeal. Southern branches of the League of Women Voters and Southern women in the Women's Division of the Democratic National Committee desired the reforms; in defiance of the Nineteenth Amendment's intentions, their husbands often refused to give them the money to pay their poll taxes. Organized labor opposed the tax; so did leading Negro groups. Prominent Southern politicians favored repeal. In 1938, President Roosevelt expressed approval of efforts in Arkansas to repeal the tax and that same year asked Joseph Gelders to begin a campaign against it. A war against the tax would have the support of most of the Conference's constituent groups, and it would maintain the informal alliance between the Conference and the Roosevelt administration.

The poll tax lay like a rotten timber across the threshold of the old Southern mansion. Once it had been cleared, so opponents of the tax contended, the way to the interior of the mansion, where the major rebuilding job awaited, would be open. Once it had been cleared, the millions of new voters would return to public office candidates who would vote for further extensions of the Roosevelt reformation. Once it had been cleared, Conference radicals would openly attack other obstacles to full Negro participation in Southern elections.

Gelders planned to attack the poll tax in the Federal Courts, in Congress, and in the eight Southern states retaining it. He began in the federal courts.

In 1939, in Tennessee, Henry Pirtle sued the Board of Election Commissioners of his congressional district for refusing to permit him to vote in a special election until he had paid his poll tax. The Civil Rights Committee took immediate interest in the case; it engaged Crampton Harris, Hugo Black's former law partner, to represent Pirtle.

The decision to involve the Conference is puzzling. In 1937, the American Civil Liberties Union had brought a case against the tax from Georgia to the Supreme Court where its constitutionality was unanimously upheld. In *Breedlove* v. *Suttles*, the Court decided: the Georgia poll tax did not violate the equal-protection clause of the Fourteenth Amendment; the franchise derived from the states, not from the federal government; and the poll tax was a tax, not a qualification on the exercise of the franchise. Although Gelders thought Breedlove had questioned the imposition of the tax on the vote for both state and federal officers, he was partially mistaken; in the Georgia Courts, the tax on both state and federal exercise of the right to vote had been challenged, but the Supreme Court had dealt solely with the tax as it pertained to federal elections. Gelders's eagerness for the reform may have got the better of his judgment and made him overlook the marked similarities between the Breedlove and Pirtle cases. Or, he may have thought the Supreme Court would, as it had in other cases, reverse itself.

Whatever Gelders had in mind, Crampton Harris's brief assumed the federal courts were ready to overrule the Breedlove decision. The poll tax, his brief contended, was a tax and could not be a qualification for voting; here he agreed with the Court's opinion in the Breedlove case. As a tax, he continued, it was an impost on a federally conferred function of citizenship and unconstitutional on the same grounds that Maryland's tax on the notes of the Second Bank of the United States had been declared unconstitutional in *McCulloch* v. *Maryland.* Here was the heart of Harris's argument: the right to vote in federal elections was granted and guaranteed by the Constitution. Two years before, the Supreme Court had denied this proposition; it had also denied another of Harris's main contentions: that the tax violated the privileges and immunities clause of the Fourteenth Amendment.

Neither Harris nor the Conference should have hoped to win such a weak case in the lower federal courts; they were asking the lower courts to reverse the Supreme Court. In 1939, the United States District Court for the middle District of Tennessee rejected Pirtle's plea. In March, 1941, the Sixth Circuit Court of Appeals upheld the District Court. Either for want of funds or for want of further hope of relief from the courts, the Conference dropped the case.

While the case pended, Gelders proceeded on other fronts. He raised $2,500 from the William C. Whitney Fund for a study of the poll tax. In 1941 the study was completed by Eleanor Bontecou with the aid of an additional $2,500 from the Whitney Fund. Early in 1940, the Conference and the National Council on Public Affairs produced a short pamphlet on the poll tax, a compendium of its history, its effects, and the arguments against it. Members of the Conference living in Tennessee joined in a major effort to have the state's poll tax repealed by the Tennessee legislature. To finance its work, the Civil Rights Committee issued poll tax stamps, bearing the inscription, "Free America First—Abolish the Poll Tax," and anti-poll tax buttons. Altogether, by April, 1940, the Committee had collected $3,825.

Gelders tried to persuade a Southern congressman to introduce a bill abolishing the tax in federal elections. Failing that, he prevailed on Congressman Lee Geyer of California to introduce such a measure on the last day of Congress in September 1939. Gelders hoped, in this way, to bring the poll tax to public attention; between sessions of Congress, congressional and public opposition to the tax could be organized. Some twenty thousand printed copies of the Geyer Bill were circulated.

By early 1940, Gelders's campaign was faltering. Then in an address to the American Youth Congress, John L. Lewis praised the renovated Supreme Court for overruling its earlier anti-New Deal opinions and denounced the poll tax. Calling it a denial of the poor whites' and Negroes' inalienable right to consent to the manner in which they were governed, Lewis asked that the new Supreme Court be put to the test; it should be given a chance to rule again on the poll tax's constitutionality.

Although he failed to mention either the Southern Conference or the Pirtle case, Lewis clearly had the latter in mind and probably meant to give indirect aid to the former. Late in 1939 and early in 1940, Southern Conference leaders worried over labor's apparent disaffection. Labor leaders grumbled about the number of college professors or college-educated in the Conference hierarchy and they complained of labor's inadequate representation on the Conference executive council. At the insistence of Gelders and Lucy Mason, William Mitch of the UMWA was added to the Civil Rights Committee; Mitch got $500 from the Mine Workers to help finance the Pirtle case. Lewis undoubtedly knew of this benefaction, and the United Mine Workers eventually paid more than two-thirds of Crampton Harris's $5,000 fee. Throughout 1940 and 1941, Lewis and his daughter, Kathryn, took a keen interest in Conference affairs; in April

1940, Kathryn attended the second convention of the Southern Conference; they both had detailed conversations with Conference members over the Southern Conference's plans of action. In 1941, Lewis hoped to merge the Conference with the CIO's political action organization, Labor's Non-Partisan League. After the American Youth Congress speech, Gelders, ever concerned to keep the Conference faithful to labor's interests, wrote: "It now appears . . . possible to draw labor into the Southern Conference for Human Welfare sufficiently to guarantee its policies." [2]

Lewis's public support revived the anti-poll tax campaign. The list of organizations interested in the reform grew rapidly. By the beginning of March, representatives of the United Mine Workers, the Southern Conference, the National Lawyer's Guild, the Descendents of the American Revolution, the International Ladies Garment Workers Union, the National Federation for Constitutional Liberties, the American Civil Liberties Union, the League of Women Voters, the American Newspaper Guild, the International Benevolent and Fraternal Order of the Elks either were attending or had been invited to attend strategy conferences in Geyer's office. Out of these, at Geyer's insistence, came the National Committee for the Abolition of the Poll Tax, an organization which took the lead in the national campaign against the tax for the next nine years.

Nearly every year between 1940 and 1948, bills to abolish the poll tax in federal elections were introduced in one or both houses of Congress. Although the Southern Conference opposed ending the tax by changing the constitution, it can take limited credit for the passage of the Twenty-fourth Amendent; its campaign for repeal helped make the tax a matter of national concern. That rotten timber got moved from the threshold of the mansion of Southern reaction.[3]

2. Gelders to George Marshall, February 27, 1940, Foreman Papers, AU.

3. Foreman Papers, AU, have several separate boxes of materials on the campaign against the poll tax. Gelders reported on his activities to the second convention of the Southern Conference held at Chattanooga, Tennessee, April, 1940. Copies of his report are in the Foreman Papers as are copies of Crampton Harris's brief. Separate files marked "Gelders" and "Mrs. Virginia Durr" have pertinent materials. The Court cases are *Breedlove* v. *Suttles*, 302 *U.S.* 277 (1937) and *Pirtle* v. *Brown*, 118 *F2nd* 218. SCHW Records, TI, boxes No. 3, No. 4, and No. 5 also have relevant

III

The most enthusiastic contingent within the Southern Conference was its youth group. At Birmingham, the young had been among those most eager to establish a permanent organization. Some had shocked the older conferees by smoking in church, addressing the patriarchs of Southern liberalism by their first names, and by pushing hard for a radical declaration on segregation. Although the older members of the Conference had limited the resolution on segregation to a condemnation of the enforcement of the city's segregation ordinance, they were unable to bottle up the younger spirits completely. At the Youth Panel, an executive committee to draw up a plan and a program for a permanent youth organization was appointed; Helen Fuller, a young Alabama lawyer, chaired the committee; her assistants included Howard Lee, Edward Strong, Mary Jeanne McKay, and William McKee.

In Washington in mid-December, the committee organized the Council of Young Southerners, provided for an executive committee and representation of the thirteen Southern states, and decided upon a program. Its "greatest immediate contribution," the committee concluded, "would be to develop youth forums throughout the South ... to provide an opportunity for young people to meet together and discuss their own problems and the problems of the South generally."[4] Studies of Southern youth problems would supply these forums with discussion materials; on the basis of these and the Southern Conference program, specific plans of action might be developed. The organization's motto reflected the determination and

material. W. M. Brewer, "The Poll Tax and the Poll Taxer," *The Journal of Negro History*, XXXIX (July 1944), 260–300 is useful. Lewis's speech is in the New York *Times*, February 11, 1940, p. 45; Mrs. C. J. Durr to Gelders, undated [summer, 1940]; Gelders to George Marshall, October 30, 1940; Lucy Mason to Frank Graham, January 4, 1940; SCHW Records, TI, box No. 3. Gelders to Mrs. Durr, December 9, 1939; Gelders to Lincoln Kirsten, February 27, 1940, Foreman Papers, AU. Minutes Executive Board Meeting, June 21, 1940, the Southern Conference Educational Fund, Inc., New Orleans, Louisiana (Hereinafter SCEF) possession. V. O. Key, *Southern Politics in State and Nation* (New York: Alfred A. Knopf, 1949), p. 617. Kenneth Douty, "The Southern Conference for Human Welfare," unpublished study, Douty's possession, Washington D.C., p. 30.

4. Helen Fuller to Frank Graham, January 20, 1939, Graham Papers, UNC.

the optimism of both the Southern Conference for Human Welfare and the Council of Young Southerners; it was: "Stay South, Young Man."

In Washington in early February 1939, the Council formally established itself at a dinner attended by several prominent persons, including Justice Black, Will Alexander and Mrs. Roosevelt. The first lady thought "there should be some way to dramatize the significance of coming of age and the . . . responsibilities of citizenship in our democracy." [5] The Council accepted Mrs. Roosevelt's suggestion. The Council learned shortly afterward of a similar program in Wisconsin which inspired it to plan for a series of citizenship day ceremonies in the fall to point up

> the rights and duties of American youth . . . [and] ritualize the ballot so as to create wider interest in government among young people. . . [;] the Young Southerners believe that young people can . . . find some of the answers and contribute their share to programs in the South. By playing a more active role in government, young people will demonstrate their faith in Democracy, and answer . . . the challenge of regimented youths in totalitarian states.[6]

Forums and voting ceremonies were intended to awaken Southern youth and to educate them in their public responsibilities. The Council of Young Southerners would conduct remedial civics courses for young adults.

The Council established headquarters in Nashville. Mary Jeanne McKay of the National Student Federation assumed the office of president, and Howard Lee, one of Mrs. Roosevelt's protegees, assumed the post of executive secretary. They organized several nonpartisan young voters clubs in Nashville. They collaborated with the Davidson County (Nashville) Youth Citizenship Day Program; Miss McKay helped prepare a pageant for the program depicting "the responsibilities of young people for government in a democracy." The Council worked with the Georgia Education Association on the state's first annual Youth Citizenship Day, held on Columbus

5. News of the Young Southerners, Vol. I, no. 1, August 29, 1939,
6. *Ibid.*

Day, during which more than 15,000 new Georgia citizens of both races "solemnly dedicated themselves to their responsibilities" at 1,200 places throughout the state. The Council collaborated on similar programs in North Carolina, Texas, and Florida. It took its nonpartisan role so seriously that it refused to send a representative to testify before a committee conducting hearings on federal aid to education.

After 1939, the Council's history becomes difficult to trace. Its officers promised to have five hundred young persons present at the second convention of the Southern Conference; but they probably failed. In April 1940, at that convention, the Council changed its name to the League of Young Southerners and may have changed its purposes; there it elected Robert Russell of North Carolina chairman, Junius Scales vice chairman, Malcolm Cotton Dobbs executive secretary, and James Jackson, H. E. McConnell, Mike Ross, and Wiley Critz administrative secretaries. There it probably became an unofficial propagandist for the Southern labor movement. Late in 1940, a Southern Conference officer described the League as an organization designed to foster a better understanding of the labor movement among Southern youth. It planned to establish recreation workshops for Southern youth where work on posters and picket signs would stimulate interest in organized labor. Members talked of sending teams of puppeteers into the rural areas to dramatize the problems of urban workers to Southern farm children.

Both of these projects failed for lack of funds. The League of Young Southerners probably failed for similar reasons. The parent Southern Conference suffered acute financial distress during 1940 and 1941; the League undoubtedly had similar fiscal difficulties. The threat of war drew many away from League activities. Whatever the case, by 1941, the League was moribund. In March, some of its officers took part in demonstrations sponsored by the American Peace Mobilization. It later joined the Southern Negro Youth Congress and the Southern Conference in a letter of protest to the Governor of Alabama over a Fairfield policeman's alleged murder of a Negro sheet mill worker; a member of the Alabama league proposed a campaign among Southern youth to educate them about the gravity of war and the necessity of giving unstinting support to America's defense efforts. These were its last gasps.[7]

IV

According to the Southern Conference's plan of organization, the group was supposed to hold annual membership meetings to decide on a program of action. Lack of funds prevented a meeting in 1939. But by the latter part of the year Conference leaders anticipated increased revenues and so planned a convention for the winter of 1940. The gathering would publicize the Conference's campaign against the poll tax and authorize its continuation. Tentative arrangements were made to have reports on voting in each of the Southern states, describing existing regulations and suggesting possible reforms. If the reports were substantial, they might be published following the convention.

Conference leaders wished to avoid the mistakes made at Birmingham, where panels held simultaneously in different parts of the city and the Conference's diffuse purposes had rendered central control difficult, if not impossible. The second convention would consist of general sessions with all delegates in attendance and it would have a unifying theme: "Democracy in the South."

The theme and the organization of the convention were put into effect according to plan. But the program, owing to criticisms from Conference members, was broadened.

Late in August, George C. Stoney toured the South to look into prospects for a Southern liberal magazine. The Southern Conference paid part of his expenses and he, in turn, discussed with interested progressives the plans for the second convention.

Middle-class liberals were divided about the Conference and its

7. In addition to the previous citations, this section draws on News of Young Southerners, vol. I, no. 2, October 21, 1939; H. C. Nixon to Frank Graham, May 11, 1939; Graham to Howard Lee, June 6, 1939; William McKee to Graham, June 6, 1939; Howard Lee to Graham, June 9, 1939; same to same, undated [summer 1939]: Graham Papers, UNC. SCHW Records, TI, box No. 3 contains a draft of an application for money from the Robert Marshall Fund where the information about the League's labor program was found. SCHW Records, TI, box No. 5, lists officers of the League chosen at the second convention. The *Daily Worker*, March 29, 1941, p. 5, May 21, 1941, p. 5 and May 6, 1941, p. 4.

purposes. In Virginia and North Carolina, they were eager for an extension of the anti-poll tax campaign. Farther south, several told Stoney that most Southerners equated abolition of the poll tax with race equality. Some feared the Conference demands were too extreme; others that the Conference would degenerate into a middle-class discussion club. Yet others thought the proposed agenda was too narrow.

On the whole, Stoney had better luck with organized labor and with Negro leaders, both groups being wholeheartedly behind the drive to abolish the poll tax; they promised to attend and to send delegates. And Stoney had good luck with both labor and middle-class liberals in Chattanooga. Julian Harris of the Chattanooga *Times,* the New York *Times's* Southern outlet, and George Fort Milton of the Chattanooga *News* hoped the convention would meet in their city, and they both promised it editorial welcome. Chattanooga boasted of being the strongest union town in Tennessee. The head of the state AFofL, T. R. Cuthbert, promised to send delegates to the convention. City officials agreed not to interfere with the Conference's integrated meetings. Chattanooga was thus chosen as the site for the Conference's second general meeting.

Stoney had, however, encountered sufficient reservations about the proposed convention from middle-class liberals to warrant alterations in the content of its program. Early in October, the Southern Conference Executive Council met at Chapel Hill. There it resolved to broaden the convention's program; Frank Graham was appointed head of the program committee.

The committee decided to add to the dramatization of the campaign against the poll tax sessions dealing with the meaning of religion for democracy (one of Graham's favorite subjects), youth in the South, Southern rural life, Southern industrial conditions, and the problems of Southern children. Whether for want of interest or want of persons qualified to do the work, the plans for reports on state voting regulations were abandoned. The additional sessions were presumably intended to satisfy the interests of the Conference's Social Gospelers, its youth contingent, its industrialists, and its labor and farm delegations.

Conference committees on speakers, finance, and arrangements took care of the remainder of the major preparations for the convention. The hard work was left to Howard Lee, who became Conference executive secretary in October. He worked to attract delegates, to publicize the convention, to assure that speakers came, to placate local antagonists, and to raise money. The convention call went to every imaginable Southern liberal or radical organization; it addressed itself to "Southerners of all parties, races, and creeds who, with good will and devotion to the highest traditions of the South, ... desire to join the Southern Conference ... in its program to upbuild the South and to advance Human Freedom and Humane Democracy in *all* our Southern states." Lee conferred regularly with Julian Harris and George Fort Milton, whose editorials and influence helped counteract some of the attacks on the Conference. Shortly before the convention, he traveled to drum up additional interest. As many prominent Tennesseans as possible were included in the list of Conference officials. In addition to the delegates' fee of one dollar, the Conference got $1,000 from the Christian Social Justice Fund and $100 from Herbert Lehman. The organization was ready to meet again, more determined, if poorer, than before.[8]

V

On April 14, 1940, the second convention of the Southern Conference for Human Welfare met in Chattanooga, Tennessee. Although Aubrey Williams, Maury Maverick, Will Alexander, and Mrs. Roosevelt attended the gathering, the second convention lacked the prominent political names that had given luster to the first convention. Although Donald Comer remained a Conference supporter

8. Clark Foreman to Frank Graham, July 10, 1939; Lucy Mason to Graham, October 13, 1939; Graham to Rufus Clement, October 16, 1939; Jennings Perry to Graham, October 12, 1939; Barry Bingham to Graham, December 14, 1939; Stanton Smith to Graham, October 7, 1939; George C. Stoney to Graham, October 12, 1939: Graham Papers, UNC. George C. Stoney to Clark Foreman, September 6, 1939; same to same, September 13, 1939, and September 19, 1939: Foreman Papers, AU. Lucy Mason to Graham, November 28, 1939, SCHW Records, TI, box No. 3. Minutes Executive Council Meeting, October 6, 1939, SCEF possession. The author possesses a copy of the call to the Chattanooga convention; others may be found in the Foreman Papers, AU.

and industrialists appeared on the program, fewer representatives of the South's upper classes and industrial elite were present. In spite of the Conference's numerous middle-class sponsors and its middle-class leadership, the convention delegates were mainly Negroes and unionists. Of the number of delegates—estimates vary from 750 to 1064—at least 250 were Negro. (Editorialists for *Alabama* claimed that more than half the Conference delegates were Negro.) The bulk of the remaining delegates were regional leaders of organized labor: they came from the CIO industrial and regional organizations, from the AFofL local, national, and international unions, from the Railroad Brotherhoods, from the Southern Tenant Farmers' Union. Although both the Tenant Farmers and the National Farmers' Union sent representatives, Southern farmers were inadequately represented at the Chattanooga convention and, for that matter, at every other Conference convention. Although some members of the Southern Conference hoped to win mass farmer-labor support and for that reason worked actively against the poll tax, they failed to get effective support from the South's rural masses. Until after the war, the Southern Conference remained an unofficial propagandist for the New Deal; its leadership came in the main from the urban, industrial South.

The Chattanooga convention was part ritual, part development: a combination of ceremony and growth. Delegates were exhorted to rediscover themselves; speakers reminded them of truths and details they should never have forgotten. They were recalled to their purposes as Southern Conference members, to the fundamentals of their progressive convictions, and to the specific programs for which they had become champions. The convention offered them a chance to redefine their program to cope with changes that had taken place within the Southern Conference and in the world about them since their previous meeting. Old programs could be rephrased, new emphases added. In short, the convention was both a secular revival meeting and a conference on future tactics.

On the first night, Frank Graham, John B. Thompson, and Mordecai Johnson, President of Howard University, descanted on the religious basis of democracy. Graham reminded his listeners that the Judaeo-Christian tradition had transmitted to them the belief in "one God and . . . all men as brothers and sons of God"; from this belief had come the "conception of freedom and democracy in the modern world." [9] Thompson, a Presbyterian minister, adverted to the South's maddening contrasts: her religious zeal and her governmental corruption; her physical charm and her lynching record; her classical architecture and her illiteracy rate. A democracy based on religion, he contended, could end both the contrasts and the madness; it could absolve the South of her sins and give her the power to go and sin no more. "The faith of democracy makes more sense than the logic of aristocracy. We are for the people. If democracy is made self-conscious, if democracy is adequately defined in social terms, it will prove to be the most Christian form of government." In this spirit, the delegates could "plan the new life of a new day." Mordecai Johnson paid even higher tribute to the religion of the majority of the delegates: the Fascist, Communist, and anti-Colonialist revolts against western civilization could be beaten, he argued, if Christianity became aggressively reformist. The Christian religion had more radical potential than capitalism, fascism, or communism; where these took a partial, incomplete view of man's nature, Christianity dealt with man's total psychophysical constitution. Christian tenets implied emancipation from toil and the spiritualization of economic activity.

> The work which we undertake to do here in the South by increasing the fertility of the soil, by the diversification of crops, by the bringing of . . . [farm] machinery into the South, by bringing scientific intelligence in the South is not merely economics, it is religion, setting the individual souls free from slavery.

The next day the Conference moved from the pulpit into the fields, the factories, and the schools. In the session on rural life, the delegates heard one speaker contend, after pointing up the connection between economic and political democracy, that in view

9. Unless otherwise noted, all quotations are from a typescript of the convention proceedings in the Foreman Papers, AU.

of the nation's economic system democracy was a good idea which had never been tried. The wife of a tenant farmer provided details for the generalizations about the harshness of Southern rural life; she spoke warmly of the help she and her husband had received from the Farm Security Administration. Several speakers, including F. D. Patterson of Tuskegee Institute, dwelt on the special problems of the rural Negro poor. A farm labor organizer, stealing a march on Bruce Barton, called Moses the first great labor organizer. Rob Hall of the Communist party offered a broad resolution on the farm problem to translate the Southern rural poor from economic misery to material plenty.

In the session on Southern industry, the main speaker, Dr. F. E. Melder, presented a lengthy review of intersectional trade barriers, including freight-rate differentials. Former Senator James Pope, then with the Tennessee Valley Authority, summarized the benefits the Authority had conferred upon the region. A Cleveland industrialist, appearing at Donald Comer's behest, spoke for healthy industrial relations through what he called sound collectivisms—labor-management co-operation, collective bargaining, and high wages.

Elsewhere, old themes and old facts reappeared. In the session on children, one speaker contended that the high proportion of children to the total Southern population was at once the region's greatest problem and its greatest opportunity. Because so many of them came from the rural South and were thus raised close to nature, Southern children of both races had better moral and spiritual surroundings than any children in the country. Both races produced children of good stock. If they received better education, they would get better paying jobs; their increased purchasing power would increase the volume of Southern business. Mrs. Roosevelt, repeating her Birmingham plea, voiced the Conference's general conviction that Southern children were a national concern; they should be educated to understand their duties as citizens in a democratic country. Horace Mann Bond, noting the common problems of Negro and white children, pointed out that parsimonious Black

Belt-dominated state legislatures stinted the education of the children of the mountain whites as well as the education of the region's Negro children. Others lamented low teacher salaries, advocated teacher unionization, and described the miserable conditions under which Negro children were raised. All agreed with Mrs. Roosevelt: Southern children were a national problem whose condition could be bettered through federal aid to education.

In both the session on children and the session on citizenship the Conference moved away from ceremony toward action. The latter session heard Gelders report on the campaign against the poll tax, pleas for co-operation with the local branches of the NAACP, and a pungent oration from Maury Maverick. In the tradition of the early Tom Watson, the Texan argued that Negroes and whites must stand together not only to fight the poll tax but also, and more importantly, to fight for economic justice. "Democracy," he told them, "is the right of every man to talk, write and think as he pleases, live in peace, and eat regular." Although impressed with Maverick's speech and concerned that all should eat well, the delegates voted to have the civil rights committee continue the campaign against the poll tax.

Having sanctioned its own actions, the Conference went on to request action of others. It passed numerous resolutions; some repeated the demands of the Birmingham convention; others were new. Special concern was shown for the interests of labor, Negroes, and the Southern farmer.

The Conference labor resolutions asked the nation to recognize that unemployment constituted the country's primary economic concern and proposed a presidential conference of industry, labor, and representatives of the people to deal with the problem. The Conference recommended the purchase of union-made products and asked for the extension of the Fair Labor Standards Act to agricultural and domestic workers.

The resolutions on the race issue did not go significantly beyond the Birmingham resolutions. The Conference condemned "all organizations and individuals in the South who seek to maintain or attain power and privileges through dissemination of racial and religious prejudice" and declared that the

> special limitations of life imposed upon the Negro people through race discrimination, limited job opportunities, inadequate and unequal school and recreational facilities . . . [require] the Southern people to work toward the general equalization of opportunity in all spheres, and toward the development of the friendliest of relations between our two racial groups. [We ask] Southern states to rectify the injustices now being done the Negro in regard to state and local expenditures for educational purposes.[10]

The Conference wished, in a phrase, to refurbish Jim Crow's cage until it resembled the white dove's aviary. Here was true separation with equality.

In line with the Conference's desire to attract a larger rural following, a number of detailed resolutions on the Southern farm problem were adopted. The Conference championed 100 percent parity payments or guarantee of the cost of production—whichever proved higher; it added its voice to those favoring extension of crop insurance to cotton, rice, tobacco, and other Southern crops. It asked the federal government to aid co-operatives, to provide housing for poor farmers, to expand the Rural Electrification Administration's program, to include tenants, croppers, and farm laborers in the social security program, and to increase the Farm Security Administration's group medicine program. The Conference asked that small farmers participate unrestrictedly in all AAA elections, that federal farm agencies permit democratic voting for the choice of farmers who served on them, and that tenants' and sharecroppers' rights to organize and bargain collectively be secured. The states as well as the federal government could act to secure these rights. In addition, the states could provide employment agencies to aid farm laborers and build work camps for the region's migrant farm workers. Though solicitous of the welfare of all Southern farmers, these resolutions were especially concerned about "small-sized farm owners, tenants and sharecroppers, white and Negro"—all of whom

10. "Resolutions . . . Southern Conference for Human Welfare . . . Chattanooga, Tennessee," photostat copy, author's possession, pp. 4–5. Dr. Dombrowski kindly provided the author with this copy.

would have to be drawn into the Conference before it could become a mass organization.

The Thomas Jefferson Award went to Will Alexander, former director of the Commission on Interracial Co-operation and then head of the Farm Security Administration, for his work in behalf of the Southern rural dispossessed. Alexander's acceptance speech was monitory, sober, and realistic. Uninterested in the self-love implicit in the ceremonial aspects of the convention, he used the occasion to issue didactic warnings. The South's rural poverty, he cautioned, could not be eliminated in less than two generations; ending it demanded careful planning, devotion, and hard work. In a veiled criticism of the Conference's penchant to demand federal aid, Alexander scored most outsiders who concerned themselves with Southern problems for superficiality, insincerity, and sentimentality; since outsiders were untrustworthy, the South's problems would have to be solved by Southerners. He congratulated the Southern Conference for pointing up some Southern problems and for demonstrating that diverse Southern groups wished to co-operate to rebuild Southern civilization. Avuncular warnings tempered the congratulations; "I call you again to the fact that this is no Sunday School picnic, nor is it for those people who are simply looking for the tweaking of their emotions. It is a long-time job that calls for wisdom and patience and determination of the highest possible order."

The delegates left the convention feeling that the meeting had been more unified and more harmonious than the Birmingham gathering. They were undoubtedly correct; the meeting had been harmonious, except for a brief, bitter conflict over the convention's resolutions on foreign policy.[11]

11. For other details on the convention: the Chattanooga *Times*, April 14, 15, 16, 17, 1940; Rob F. Hall, "New Forces for Peace and Democracy in the South," *The Communist*, XIX (August 1940), 700–702; *New Masses*, XXXV (April 30, 1940), 22; *Daily Worker*, April 17, 1940, p. 4; *Socialist Call*, VI (May 11, 1940), 1; "Southerners Confer," *Survey Midmonthly*, LXXVI (May 1940), 170–171; Lillian Smith, "Southern Conference? Editorial," *The North Georgia Review*, V (Spring 1940), 23–26. Alexander's biography is the previously cited volume by Dykeman and Stokeley, *Seeds of Southern Change.*

4

PURGING "RED" HUMORS

A month before the Chattanooga convention, the Soviet Union forced Finland to cede her the Isthmus of Karelia, a naval base at Hangoe in the Gulf of Finland, and the city of Viborg. Five days before the meeting, German armed forces occupied Denmark and invaded Norway. Saturday, April 13, Great Britain destroyed all German naval vessels in the harbor at Narvik in northern Norway. The two great continental powers, Germany and Russia, had used the security afforded by the Molotov-von Ribbentrop pact to extend their aggressive expansion beyond the partition of Poland. The *Sitzkrieg* was clearly at an end. The fires of war were moving slowly, inexorably westward; only one fireback remained: the Maginot Line.

The international crisis threatened the Southern Conference's internal unity; although agreed on a program of domestic reform, the Conference's constituent factions disagreed on foreign policy. The pacifist element opposed any involvement in the European war. Socialists, then in an extreme isolationist phase, followers of John L. Lewis, and many liberals though the European war did not warrant diversion of funds from domestic reform programs to rearmament. Some of the liberals favored aid to the Allies and envisioned eventual American entry into the conflict. Many Conference members considered the Russian invasion of Finland as reprehensible as the Nazi absorption of Czechoslovakia; more found the Russo-German destruction of Poland unconscionable—except, of course, Communists and fellow travelers who were bound to defend both acts of Russian aggrandizement.

Prior to the Chattanooga convention, Conference leaders decided to confine the meeting to domestic affairs; persons as different as Frank Graham, later a member of William Allen White's Committee to Defend America by Aiding the Allies, and Rob Hall, Communist party leader in Alabama, thought it wiser to leave foreign policy off the convention's official agenda. They reckoned without W. T. Couch.

Couch, who had been chairman of the committee on permanent organization at Birmingham, was concerned with consistency, principle, and propaganda. The Southern Conference, he argued, had at the Birmingham convention denounced Nazi persecution of religious minorities and had supported Roosevelt's efforts to preserve national security, curb aggression, "and assist the democratic peoples of the world to preserve peace, liberty and freedom." If Nazi aggression in Czechoslovakia and Nazi persecution of the Jews were culpable, so, Couch went on, was the Russian invasion of Finland. "If I were to attend and if the Conference refused to take the same position with reference to the Communists that it took two years ago with reference to the Nazis, I would not want to have any further association . . . with the Conference and would have to walk out." [1] He

1. W. T. Couch to Frank Graham, April 12, 1940, Graham Papers, UNC.

proposed to introduce a resolution censuring Russian aggression in Finland. Couch further wished the Southern Conference to come out openly for American aid to the democracies, thereby taking a position in advance of the Roosevelt Administration.

April 14, at the convention's first business session, Couch introduced a resolution condemning Soviet aggression against Finland and favoring all-out aid to the western democracies. A brief scuffle followed. One angry conferee knocked Couch away from the microphone when he tried to defend his proposal. Frank Graham, presiding over the session, broke his glasses pounding on the rostrum for order. Finally, Graham's insistent thumping and calmer tempers restored peace. In the face of a small but vociferous protest that the Couch resolution lay beyond the convention's declared theme and was thus out of order, Graham directed the resolution to the rules committee with outspoken instructions that the committee rule the motion within the convention's purview. This done, the resolution went to the resolutions committee.

From here, the resolution's path is difficult to follow. All that can be said with certainty is that it came out altered in form and substance. The resolutions committee worked in the midst of divergent pressures. The combined caucus of the CIO and United Mine Workers seems to have had no objection to condemning Russian aggression in Finland. Presumably, it echoed John L. Lewis's opposition to aid to the Allies because such aid diverted funds from domestic reform; Kathryn Lewis was on hand to remind the unionists of her father's views. Liberals supporting the Couch resolution could have been dissuaded; the war had not become sufficiently grave to warrant all-out aid: the Maginot Line remained to break the Nazi conflagration. Although the Socialist caucus gleefully supported condemnation of the Soviet Union, the Socialists were then opposed to American aid to the Allies or American entry into the war, claiming the country had no concern in a war involving Hitler and the reactionary British and French governments. Only Communists and fellow travelers opposed both parts of the resolution. Compromise was possible, and so was a large vote for the condemnation of Russia. If the demand for aid to the Allies were dropped and all forms of aggression, Commuinst, fascist, and imperialist were condemned, an overwhelming vote for the resolution could be put together. All except Communists and fellow travelers would be satisfied: pacifists, anglophobes, Socialists, unionists, even most of the middle-class liberals.

The resolutions committee worked into early Monday morning. At one point several members suggested to William Mitch, committee chairman, that the resolution would be stronger if it were drafted without qualifying adjectives. Mitch, uncertain, phoned Frank Graham who told him that omission of qualifying adjectives would reduce the resolution to a general condemnation, since, as the resolution was worded, "Communist" appeared in it as an adjective. Alerted, Mitch returned to the committee. He stayed the rest of the night: so did the adjectives.

When the resolution came to a vote, members of the UMW were spotted around the auditorium to watch known Communists and suspected fellow travelers who might introduce crippling amendments. This was probably unnecessary. Such a large bloc of votes had been rounded up for the resolution that any amendments would have been voted down. In any case, the revised version of the Couch resolution passed overwhelmingly; it may even have passed without a dissenting vote.

The Conference foreign policy resolution deplored the rise of dictators, the suppression of civil liberties, persecution of minorities, aggression against the small and weak nations, and the violations of the neutral rights and democratic liberties of peoples by all fascist, Nazi, Communist, and imperialist powers, who, to achieve their ends, resorted to force and aggression. The convention opposed appropriations for armaments at the expense of appropriations for domestic reform programs. In the spirit of the neutrality laws, it opposed extension of credits to the Allies or any of the belligerents and opposed any actions which might compromise the country's neutrality and "serve as steps toward involvement in the present war." Finally it recommended taxation of war profits and the use of the proceeds for the solution of the country's domestic problems, especially for the elimination of "distress among our hungry and unemployed." This was radical isolationism. John L. Lewis, no doubt, was pleased.

The Communists were mildly displeased. Rob Hall wrote of "weaknesses in the Chattanooga conference, due partly to the failure of honest progressives to orient themselves to the new situation caused by the outbreak of the imperialist war and the abandonment of the New Deal by Roosevelt. . . ." The *Daily Worker* correspondent, although satisfied with the modification of Couch's original resolution, wrote: "The Conference, however, was not clear in its peace stand. In addition to the strong anti-war resolution, it adopted another resolution condemning 'aggression' by 'Nazis, Communists or imperialists.' "

The Southern Conference enemies were delighted by the Communists' interest in the Chattanooga program and in other aspects of the Conference's operations.[2]

II

From its inception, the Southern Conference was accused of Communist affiliations. Its enemies stigmatized it as a Communist plot or a Communist front. According to some of its friends, it either came under Communist domination or was subject to the baleful influences of a large contingent of covert Communists and conscious

2. Clark Foreman to Frank Graham, March 20, 1940; Barry Bingham to Clark Foreman, March 22, 1940; Graham Papers, UNC. Rob Hall to James Dombrowski, April 15, 1940; M. C. Dobbs to Joseph Gelders, March 13, 1940: SCHW Records, TI, box No. 5. W. T. Couch to Mrs. Clifford J. Durr, March 21, 1940, Foreman Papers, AU. After the convention Couch quit the conference to protest the modification of his resolution. The story of the manuevering at the convention comes from the following sources: Marc Friedlander to Carl Durham, February 12, 1949; William Mitch to Yelverton Cowherd, April 20, 1955; Frank Graham to William Mitch, April 21, 1955; William Mitch to Frank Graham, April 25, 1955; Frank Graham to Eugene Pfaff, June 3, 1955; William Mitch to Yelverton Cowherd, December 19, 1955; Cowherd to Frank Graham, undated [after December 14, 1955, probably before February 1, 1956]: all of these are in photostat in the possession of Dr. Warren Ashby of the University of North Carolina, Women's College, Greensboro, North Carolina; the author is indebted to Dr. Ashby for the use of these letters and for numerous other kindnesses. Interviews with Paul R. Christopher, Knoxville, Tennessee, February 25, 1964, with Mrs. C. J. Durr, Montgomery, Alabama, January 11–12, 18–19, 1964, with Frank McCallister, Chicago, Illinois, December 16, 1963, with Frank Graham, New York City, April 10, 1964 were also helpful. For Hall's comments see Rob F. Hall, "New Forces for Peace and Democracy in the South," *The Communist*, XIX (August, 1940), 702; *Daily Worker*, April 17, 1940, p. 4.

fellow travelers. The diagnoses of the friends and enemies of the Southern Conference had this in common: they agreed the patient suffered from a Communist virus. They differed over prescriptions for curing the ailing organization. Conference enemies frankly hoped the patient would die and frankly recommended mercy killing; most of their reports were wishful thinking rather than scientific description. The Conference's friends either prescribed localizing the virus or purging it. Subsequent critics thought the organization died when the virus grew and consumed it. Unfortunately, these diagnosticians were at worst quacks, at best simply consulting physicians whose inadequate acquaintance with the patient's case produced oversimplifications and serious mistakes in emphasis. All their diagnoses overlooked other viruses and neglected the patient's environment. All their diagnoses were thus either wrong or seriously inaccurate.

The earliest accusations of Communist control appeared during and immediately after the Birmingham Convention in Alabama conservative newspapers and organizations, and in the Big Mules' unofficial mouthpiece, *Alabama.* These spread to other conservative journals; prior to the Chattanooga convention, the Chattanooga *Free Press* repeated them. The accusations here were vague and diffuse, as much vilification as detailed condemnation: the list of plotters generally included New Deal bureaucrats, John L. Lewis and his minions in the CIO, as well as specific alleged Communists within the Southern Conference. Reduced to comprehensible terms, these accusations simply claimed the Conference was kin to numerous other organizations in the popular-front movement—organizations containing but not dominated by Communists. And they claimed the Conference was of alien, non-Southern origin.

Some of the conservative attackers demanded a Dies Committee investigation of the Southern Conference. (After the war, ex-Congressman Joseph Starnes of Alabama testified that the committee had had observers at the Birmingham meeting.) In 1939, the committee held extensive hearings on Communist propaganda activities. William Weiner, party treasurer, and Earl Browder, party secretary, both testified. Weiner's interrogators asked whether he had sent

$2,000 South during the spring of 1938 for the express purpose of organizing the Birmingham convention of the Southern Conference for Human Welfare. Weiner's explicit denial failed to convince either his interrogators or subsequent members of the Dies Committee. Browder's interrogator, J. Parnell Thomas, asked for a definition of a Communist transmission belt. After Browder's definition, Thomas then read a list of organizations, including the Southern Conference for Human Welfare, the American League for Peace and Democracy, and the American Civil Liberties Union. To the question whether each of these could be considered a Communist transmission belt, Browder answered, "Yes." This was sufficient to convince the Conference's enemies and to horrify the Conference's liberal members. From this point on, the Dies Committee and its offspring, the House Committee on Un-American Activities, remained convinced—if they had not been beforehand—that in one form or another the Southern Conference for Human Welfare was a Communist front: either organized and run by Communists, or organized by liberals, dupes and Communists and later captured by Communists. Its purposes, plans, and programs were thus polluted beyond purification.

Some Socialists and liberals suspected Communist domination, or, at least, excessive Communist influence. Howard Kester and H. L. Mitchell of the Southern Tenant Farmers' Union credited Joseph Gelders with the Conference's conception, successful organization, and subsequent execution. According to Kester, Gelders used his name to secure a large sum of money for the Birmingham convention and Gelders and covert Communists were in nearly complete control from then on. Mitchell and Kester were annoyed because representatives of the Tenant Farmers' Union were not included on the program at the Conference's conventions in 1940 and 1942; they took this and the election in 1940 of Gerald Harris to the Conference executive board over a Tenant Farmers' Union candidate as indications that the Stalinists effectively controlled the Conference. At best, these conclusions were ill-conceived and ill-founded; at worst, they were simple-minded.

Two other Socialists, Frank McCallister of the Southern Workers Defense League and Kenneth Douty, and Roger Baldwin of the American Civil Liberties Union made more substantial charges. All three specified persons within the Conference close to the Communist party; all three knew that a large number of liberals and laborites were aware of the existence of alleged Communists within the Conference. And they knew the charge of Communist domination could not be substantiated by a simple enumeration of the suspected Communists within the organization. Yet they overestimated the effects the alleged Communists had on the Southern Conference. Their errors stemmed in part from their failure to recognize that the insipidity of the Communists' popular-front policy rendered them nearly innocuous and in part from their ignorance of details of the case.[3]

III

Three years before the Southern Conference's inception, at the Seventh Congress of the Communist International, Georg Dimitrov articulated international communism's main tactical adaptations to

3. The charges against the Conference can be found in numerous places. For the view of some Southern conservatives, see *Alabama,* III (December 5, 1938), 3ff. United States Congress, House of Representatives, Special Committee for the Investigation of Un-American Propaganda Activities, *Hearings—Un-American Propaganda Activities,* 76 cong., 1 sess. (Washington: Government Printing Office, 1939), VII, pp. 4397, 4482–4483, 4765–4767; *Congressional Record,* 81 cong., 1 sess., 1949, pp. 2998–3000; House Committee on Un-American Activities, *A Guide to Subversive Organizations and Publications,* 82 cong., 1 sess. (Washington: Government Printing Office, 1951), pp. 45, 104. For the Socialist view: interviews with Kester and McCallister previously cited; "Confidential Report on the Southern Conference for Human Welfare," Southern Tenant Farmers' Union Papers, UNC, box No. 27; H. L. Mitchell, "Reminiscences," Oral History Project, Columbia; Kenneth Douty, "The Southern Conference for Human Welfare," *passim.* On Roger Baldwin: Roger Baldwin to author, March 15, 1964; Interview, Roger Baldwin, New York City, April 9, 1964. For two academic views: William Nolan, *Communism versus the Negro* (Chicago: Henry Regnery, 1951), which, based on an HUAC report of 1947, accepts the extreme view that the Communists were pulling all the wires from the outset (for criticism of that report see chapter 8 below); Wilson Record, *The Negro and the Communist Party* (Chapel Hill: North Carolina Press, 1951), pp. 165ff., and *Race and Radicalism* (Ithaca: Cornell Press, 1964), pp. 100–103, both of which claim that the Communists eventually took over the Conference. Dr. Record responded unhelpfully to an inquiry by mail.

the Nazification of Germany. He directed the revolutionery leaders of the workers of the world to seek agreements by whatever means necessary with all workers' organizations, whether Marxist, Catholic, or opportunist, with Socialists, pacifists, democrats, and middle-class reform organizations, with co-operatives, national liberation movements, and religious organizations, and with cultural, educational, and sporting clubs. This broad, popular front would oppose domestic expressions of fascism and nazism and oppose the expansion of Germany.

In 1936 and again in 1938, the American Communist party repudiated violence as a means for achieving the Communist utopia. During the former year, American communism became twentieth-century Americanism, indicating perhaps that the right does not have a monopoly on super patriotism; indeed, party meetings opened with the singing of the Star Spangled Banner. After Franklin Roosevelt's famous quarantine speech in October 1937, the party publicly championed unconditional support for the New Deal. At the Tenth Party Convention, in May 1938, Earl Browder proclaimed that President Roosevelt's leadership was vital to the struggle against monopoly capital; the Communist party, he went on, would ally with all groups who opposed monopoly capital and favored collective security, effectively excluding thereby only the conservative Republicans, a few Southern and Northern Democrats, and some Socialist sects, say the Trotskyites and the Thomasites, who could not forgive earlier injuries and insults: nearly every other political interest within the country was a potential ally, from the League of Women Voters to the CIO. Browder's advocacy of socialism for the United States hardly outweighed his faith in reforms under capitalism. "The improvement of living conditions under capitalism," the Communist leader confusedly remarked, "may delay the revolutionary change to socialism but it will provide a more peaceful, less difficult and less painful transition to socialism when the time comes." [4]

4. Quoted in G. P. Rawick, "From Faith to Dogma: The Development of the Communist Party Line, 1928–1939," *The South Atlantic Quarterly*, LIII (April 1954), 201.

Communists became accommodating, friendly. In 1939, before the Dies Committee, Browder claimed that since 1937 the party had ceased forming Communist factions in non-Communist organizations; party members in such organizations were under orders to work for the interests of the organization—to increase its membership, to advance its program—and within these limitations to work to advance the Communist line. Communists were to be good organization men first, good Communists second. The use of terms degenerated. For Stalin and for Lenin, Communist transmission belts were party-controlled organizations in Communist countries which transmitted party policy to sections of the society as yet unready for direct contact with the Communist party itself. During the early 1930s, one American Communist had defined a transmission belt as any mass organization either set up or controlled by a party faction, in which the party transmitted its message to the masses and in return received accurate information about the wants and aspirations of the people. In 1939, Browder defined a Communist transmission belt as any organization which wittingly or unwittingly transmitted the party line or which followed policies similar to the policies of the Communist party; any organization, from the American League for Peace and Democracy to the Congress of the United States, might be a Communist transmission belt. Communists substantially controlled the former; the party's leader had appeared before a special committee of the latter and there had transmitted the Communist line to all the auditors, including the unwitting Martin Dies. The Southern Conference, in its capacity as a Communist transmission belt, had unexpected and unwanted company.

Whatever else may be said about them, the politics of the popular front were not the politics of radical Marxism. Gone was the revolutionary militancy which promised the workers of the world release from the bondage of toil if they would become self-conscious and organize themselves under Communist leadership. American socialism would grow gradually, peacefully out of reformist capitalism; socialism would be the natural development of capitalism's beneficent implications, not a destructive antithesis. (American conservatives fearful of creeping socialism could take masochistic comfort: Communist party dogma confirmed their worst expectations.) Communism had become opportunistic, seeking the main chance; in return for an American foreign policy conducive to the protection of the Soviet Union, the American Communist Party would become an unwanted member of the New Deal coalition. Even when American and Russian foreign policy seriously diverged, as between 1939 and 1941, American party members continued to propagandize for New Deal domestic reforms. Party members' militancy changed; it was no longer the militancy of the dedicated sectarian, willing to sacrifice all without scruple for the coming millenium. Party members worked hard; they always had; they worked, no doubt, harder than others. But they were now hard workers in groups with reformist aims similar to the Communist party's. They became militant, dedicated, organization men, loyal members of whatever team they happened to be working for. Party members became minions of the CIO, of numerous voluntary organizations, and of the Southern Conference for Human Welfare. It is an interesting, but at the moment insoluble, question whether as organization men they served the real or imagined interests of the Communist movement or whether they served the real or imagined interests of the organizations for which they toiled. Did they serve both masters? Which master did they serve better? John L. Lewis's question—"Who gets caught? The hunter or the hunted?"—has never been satisfactorily answered.

Whatever the answer, this much seems clear: between 1935 and 1945, at least, the American Communist party did not constitute a clear and present danger to the American Republic. It had explicitly disavowed violent revolution; its reform demands were indistinguishable from the reform demands of a host of other organizations actively working for the New Deal. At every turn, it collaborated with groups formerly denounced as enemies of the working class. Browder's gradualism and popular-front opportunism—and perhaps the two are the same—emasculated revolutionary Marxism. The defense of the Soviet Union against fascism entailed the defense and propagation of the New Deal. The latter function was clearly legitimate. The former might have been made legitimate.

The activities of the American Communist party were a danger to the United States only in so far as they were part of the Russian espionage system. Within the various organizations to which they belonged, Communists were as loyal as other members with outside loyalties—say, for example, Catholics within the CIO, or Socialists and laborites within the Southern Conference. Their superior organization and discipline, together with their practice of concealed memberships, occasionally gave them an advantage over their opponents when divisive matters arose. In the period under consideration, the major divisive issues were American foreign policy and Russian aggression in Finland. Within the Southern Conference, the Communists lost the attempt to destroy the Couch resolution condemning the Soviet Union; had most of the other constituent groups within the organization not been radical isolationists, the Communists would not even have been placated by the declarations opposing diversion of funds from welfare programs to armaments and American involvement in the conflict.

In any case, the diagnosticians' conclusion that communism was the only alien virus in the Southern Conference bordered on malpractice. Every constituent element within the Southern Conference had outside loyalties potentially in conflict with the Conference's declared purposes. During the years before the war, the Communist virus lay nearly dormant; other viruses were intensely active. The Communist party, if its publications can be believed, took a friendly interest in the Southern Conference: nothing more. The liberals and the CIO factions actively worked to use the Conference for other purposes.[5]

5. In addition to the Rawick article cited in note 4 above, this section is based on: Irving Howe and Lewis Coser, *The American Communist Party* (New York: Praeger, 1962), pp. 319ff., and Daniel Bell, "The Background and Development of Marxian Socialism in the United States," in Donald Drew Egbert and Stow Persons, eds., *Socialism and American Life*, (2 vols.; Princeton: Princeton University Press, 1952), I, 213–407. These are severely critical works by anti-Communist Social Democrats; none would agree with the present attempt to minimize the maleficence of the Communist party. For a copy of the 1945 Communist party constitution, which

IV

When the popular front moved South it moved with special caution. As early as 1934, tentative overtures for a common front against Southern fascism passed between the small Southern branches of the Socialist and Communist parties; these involved proposals for joint action in defense of the right to organize, strike, and bargain collectively, in defense of the rights of victimized Negroes, in opposition to the Klan, and other secret organizations using violence against Negroes and workers, and for a minimum program, including the abolition of the poll tax. Subsequent critics of the Southern Conference were party to these negotiations; in 1935 both Howard Kester and H. L. Mitchell endorsed a call to an all-South conference to deal with lynching and the rights of Negroes and unionists. Other collaborative efforts occurred.

The Communist party came out of its conspiratorial cellar. Party gatherings convened in fraternal halls and in union meeting places. Members brought their wives and children. The party tried to help people redress their immediate grievances; in Alabama, in 1937, local Communists distributed petitions for the repeal of the 2 percent sales tax to local merchants who declared their gratitude to the party for its good work; a year later, the proudest boast of the Communists of Pratt City, Alabama, was that they had helped to bring street lights to the town. The party urged its members to become active in churches and in social clubs. By September 1937,

---

still spoke of the nonviolent establishment of Socialism in America, see House Committee on Un-American Activities, *Organized Communism in the United States* (Washington: Government Printing Office, 1958), pp. 122ff. J. V. Stalin, *Leninism*, tr. by Eden and Cedar Paul (London: George Allen and Unwin Ltd., 1928), I, 29ff.; Clarence Hathaway, "Transmission Belts," *The Communist*, X (May 1931), 412–414, 422; House Special Committee on Un-American Activities, *Hearings—Un-American Propaganda Activities*, VII, 4443–4445, 4453–4454, 4482–4483; *Daily Worker*, September 10, 1939, p. 5; interview, Earl Browder, Yonkers, New York, April 13, 1964—all contain material on the use of the term transmission belt. Browder is unreliable on some things, but not on all. Evidence will be offered below to substantiate the claim that Communists were often as good—if not better—organization men as they were party members. On the other hand, Browder's claim to have abolished secret party memberships during this period is in one instance contradicted. The almost meaningless use of the term transmission belt is in keeping with the insipidity of the popular front.

party leaders felt sufficiently secure to hold a public regional party conference at Chattanooga, to which more than one hundred Negro and white delegates came from Alabama, Virginia, Florida, Louisiana, Tennessee, Kentucky, and North Carolina.

Here and elsewhere, the party emphasized the need to extend its work among Negroes and the agricultural population; Browder, in attendance at the Conference, pointed up the significance of the CIO in the fight against Jim Crow and stressed the need to work for extension of democratic rights, a task that would attract a wide variety of reform organizations. Later in 1937, Donald Burke, whose presence at the Birmingham convention would frighten Francis P. Miller away from the Southern Conference, urged the party to work toward winning the right to vote for all the Southern people; and Rob Hall proclaimed that Southern Communists were "happy to be Communists. We would like to share this happiness with our non-Party friends, by bringing them together with us into the Communist Party so that they, too, may participate in the building and guiding of this great movement for a better, freer and happier world." [6] By 1938, party analysts had decided that the movement for a freer, happier world in the South required a united democratic front of workers, Negroes, farmers, and middle-class liberals around a program which involved, as Hall wrote in another place, bringing the New Deal to the South with a view to the eventual formation of a farmer-labor party. Thus committed to moderate tactics, to the program of the Democratic party, and to the long-term goal of a farmer-labor party that has haunted American radicalism since the Civil War, the Communists were receptive to the appearance of the National Emergency Council's *Report on the Economic Conditions of the South* and the announcement of the formation of the Southern Conference for Human Welfare. The former, Browder greeted as an historic indictment of Wall Street's domination of Southern economic life. "All progressives and true democrats," he said, "will, if they are at all awake to the realities of the day, rally around this report and help to develop its implied

6. *The New South,* I (November 1937), 15.

program of progress for the South." [7] Since the South was unready for the true remedy for its ills, namely socialism, Communists and "sincere Socialists" should work to form a minimum program of action on the basis of the report, around which progressives and liberals could unite. To that end, the Southern people should join in their own voluntary organizations—unions and farm co-operatives, for example—to work to regain political control within their states.

Browder wrote in August; he seems to have been ignorant of the plans for the Southern Conference. Two months later, Paul Crouch, editor of the Party's Southern organ, the *New South,* and later an informant for the House Committee on Un-American Activities, took notice of the proposed Southern Conference. Like his leader, Crouch thought the National Emergency Council's report should be followed with effective action. The Conference, he noted without editorial comment, would attract hundreds of the South's most progressive leaders: educators, ministers, labor leaders, industrialists, editors, congressmen, and senators. He approved proposed plans for a permanent organization. At the end, he invited inquiries to be sent to the Conference's leaders. It is difficult to see how this detached, dispassionate reportage could later be used to prove the Southern Conference was a Communist plot: but it was. Earlier, Crouch discussed the NEC *Report;* here he hoped the Southern Conference would adopt a program with specific recommendations in it, would unite leaders from all areas of the South, and would mark the beginning of a new epoch in Southern history. He wrote:

> Southern progressives are proud of the South, of the splendid role played by our ancestors in the Revolutionary War and the establishment of our Nation. They are proud of the scenic beauty and the great natural resources found in the South. It is because they love the South that they wish to abolish illiteracy, poverty and starvation and disease from our land. There are differences of opinion on details, but there is no reason why a common program cannot be worked out for improving the conditions of the Southern people and making our South a better place in which to live with conditions inferior to no other part of our Nation.[8]

7. Earl Browder, "The NEC Report," *New Masses,* August 23, 1938, pp. 3–4.
8. *The New South,* I (October 1938), 10.

Patriotism, sweet reason, and pious good wishes were thus the attitudes determining the Communist party's declared policy toward the Southern Conference.

The party wished to help in whatever way it could; it did not wish to capture or dominate the organization. After the Birmingham convention, Rob Hall claimed that Browder's comments on the NEC *Report* had anticipated the Southern Conference and that the Southern Conference brilliantly confirmed Browder's democratic front policies. Both of these were harmless comments: at most the former indicates Browder had guessed what many others knew: Southern liberals and progressives planned to reply to the NEC Report: it does not indicate any causal link between the Communist party and the Southern Conference. Nor does the latter remark; it was a conclusion based on the observation that the Southern Conference represented an attempt by the people of the South "to secure for themselves and their families more of the fruits of the New Deal...." This, after all was one of the main purposes of the Democratic front. At the end of his report Hall wrote:

> Our Party contributed in a modest but constructive manner to the success of the Conference. This participation of communist delegates... reflects the fact that Southern progressives are becoming aware of the progressive and constructive role played by our Party in the preservation ... of democracy and the raising of living standards.

The party's task, he admonished, was to aid the Southern progressive movement.

> On this basis, our Party can and must proceed to recruit from the progressive ranks many hundreds of new members. By our growth and greater participation our Party will gain for itself greater recognition as an integral part of the developing democratic front in the South.

This was modest enough. Perhaps it was too modest.[9]

9. For early united front proposals, see the party's first Southern publication, *The Southern Worker*, October 1934, p. 2; November 1934, p. 3; December 1934, p. 4; January 1935, pp. 1–2; February 1935, p. 2; March–April 1935, *passim;* May 1935, p. 1; June 1935, pp. 1, 4. In fairness to Kester, he frankly acknowledges that he worked in united front organizations and that he occasionally brought Communists into such groups. He agrees with the declared ends of Communism, a classless

V

Before the middle of 1942, the three most important alleged Communists or fellow travelers within the Southern Conference hierarchy were Joseph Gelders, executive secretary of the Civil Rights Committee, Howard Lee, executive secretary first of the Council of Young Southerners and then of the Southern Conference, and John B. Thompson, Frank Graham's successor in the Conference chairmanship.

The allegations against Gelders date back at least to the time of his beating; his assailants seem to have considered him either a member of the Communist party or a willing fellow traveler. During the preparations for the Southern Conference's first convention, other members of the preliminary organization were aware of Gelders's leftwing connections. Mrs. Roosevelt, so it was rumored, had been suspicious. H. C. Nixon and other members of the Alabama Policy Committee knew of Gelders's work in defense of the Scottsboro Negroes and other victims of racial injustice and of his connections with the National Committee for the Defense of Political Prisoners, an alleged communist front.

Gelders's alleged Communist affiliations were supposed to have vitiated his tireless work for progressive causes. His Birmingham office was in the same building as the office of the Alabama Communist party, and he worked with Rob Hall on specific cases. But

---

society composed of free and equal individuals, but deplores Communist means. He may suspect the Southern Conference because he was never in a position to control the organization. Rob Hall "Establishing the Party in the South," *Party Organizer*, X (August 1937), 28–31; T. Spradling, "About a Branch in the South: How We Brought Street Lights to Pratt City," *Party Organizer*, XI (July 1938), 31–32; John J. Ballam, "The First All-Southern Communist Party Conference," *Party Organizer*, X (November 1937), 13–16; *Daily Worker*, September 27, 1937, p. 5; *The New South*, I (November 1937), 3ff.; (March 1938), 2, 10–11; (May 1938), 10–11; Rob Hall, "The Lessons of Southern Populism," *The Communist*, XVII (July 1938), 652ff.; Earl Browder, "Speech at the Tenth Convention of the Communist Party," *The Communist*, XVII (July 1938), 59ff.; *The New South*, I (October 1938), 8–10, 15; Rob Hall in *The Communist* (January 1939), pp. 57ff. In the absence of unpublished, private party documents, nothing can be said about the party's undeclared attitude toward the Conference. For whatever it may be worth, Earl Browder told the author that he never considered the Southern Conference important enough to merit mention in his reports to the party's conventions.

Gelders told Nixon that he was a Marxist democrat; and Nixon and the rest of the members of the preliminary organization took him for an honest radical. They also took care to see that Gelders's authority and sphere of operations were limited.

Gelders repeated his denials to others who suspected him. At Birmingham, he told Aubrey Williams that he was not a member of the Communist party. After the convention, he made a similar denial to Clark Foreman. In 1940, he made a written denial of the charge to Frank Graham. Two independent, but biased, sources corroborate him. Earl Browder expressly denied that Gelders ever joined the party; he was, the former Communist leader contended, a valued ally but he was too independent to submit to Communist party discipline. In the late summer of 1940, Gelders and several other members of the Southern Conference's Birmingham contingent undertook a campaign for the repeal of a Birmingham ordinance permitting the arrest of suspected persons without warrant and their detention without charge for an indefinite period of time. In its report of the campaign, the *Daily Worker* referred to Gelders and his coworkers as Birmingham liberals.

On the contrary, the *Party Organizer's* report of the all-South convention of the Communist party, held in September, 1937, notes that the "Scottsboro case was made a prominent issue in the conference, as well as the struggle for the extension of civil rights epitomized in the report of Comrade Gelders of Birmingham." [10] Between September 1940 and June 22, 1941, Gelders actively worked for the American Peace Mobilization, an enterprise formed to propagandize against aid to the Allies and American rearmament; it ended several days after the German invasion of Russia. Gelders himself, although a Jew and a Marxist radical, defended the Russo-German agreement. Between the German invasion of Russia and the American entry into the conflict, Gelders wrote to a friend that Roosevelt had

> got himself so surrounded by agents of the monopolies that it's hard for him to move ahead against Hitler with any confidence. Hope he can pitch out of the hole. A declaration of war would make a tremendous differ-

10. Ballam in *Party Organizer*, X (November 1937), 14.

ence.... The main thing is to find ways and means to push the anti-Hitler movement and the anti-poll tax campaign. Everything else will take care of itself. Thank God for the Red Army.[11]

Thus Gelders at one point in his life may have belonged to the Communist party; he may have found the discipline unendurable and withdrawn. Whatever the case, he remained a conscious fellow traveler during his affiliation with the Southern Conference. This seems beyond dispute. It is endlessly arguable whether the Communist party encouraged his plans for the Southwide civil rights conference that eventually broadened into the Southern Conference for Human Welfare. According to one source (whose anonymity must be protected), the party took no more interest in the idea than did other Southern organizations, and the Roosevelts provided the necessary impetus. The House Committee on Un-American Activities claims to the contrary. The point is trivial. In addition to being close to the Communist party, Gelders was also a nearly honest radical and a tireless worker for progressive causes, especially causes involving civil rights. No evidence exists that he ever plotted, advocated or conspired to teach the necessity of the violent overthrow of the United States government. His motives for the establishment of the civil rights convention were thus presumptively as pure as the motives of, say, the League of Women Voters, the CIO, the Socialist party, and the Descendents of the American Revolution in their opposition to the poll tax.

Howard Lee, an Arkansas sharecropper's son, is an obscure figure. He attended Commonwealth College where he came under the influence of Claude Williams, a radical Presbyterian minister whose interpretation of the scriptures justified labor unions, strikes, collective bargaining and mass political action. From Commonwealth, Lee went to Vanderbilt, where he received a Bachelor of Divinity. He was interested in labor organization and youth work; he may have worked for a time as farm labor organizer; he was active in the affairs of the American Youth Congress.

Before Lee became Southern Conference executive secretary in

11. Gelders to Mrs. C. J. Durr, undated, Foreman Papers, AU.

October 1939, his political connections were investigated. The Socialist party members of the Conference insisted that he was either a member of the Communist party or a willing fellow traveler; one insisted that Lee had been a member of the Young Communist League. To Frank Graham, Lee denied that he was a member of the Communist party: "I am a democrat and have tried to adhere to the dictates of my own conscience in whatever activities I may have engaged for the benefit of the South and for the Country." [12] While executive secretary of the Council of Young Southerners, Lee attempted to involve the organization in Democratic party politics, thereby alienating some of the Council's members who thought Lee's efforts violated the group's nonpartisan ideals. His political affiliations did not, however, cause any difficulty; one member wrote accusatory letters, that was all. Owing to his ability, Conference liberal leaders decided to hire him despite the risk; his appointment had the approval of Lucy Mason, Mrs. Roosevelt, Frank Graham, Clark Foreman, George C. Stoney, Brooks Hays, Barry Bingham, and Josephine Wilkins. If Lee had not been hired the Conference would have gone without an executive secretary for an indefinite period.

After Lee left the Southern Conference, he organized for the International Union of Mine, Mill, and Smelter Workers, a job of greater interest to him than the executive secretaryship of the Southern Conference. Testimony given before the Subversive Activities Control Board indicates that after the war, at least, Lee organized for the IUMMSW and organized and collected dues for the Communist party. Granting the accuracy of the testimony, which went unimpeached by the union's attorneys, it is impossible to say when Lee joined the Communist party. He, too, was an American Peace Mobilization activist. Whether the German invasion of Russia transformed him into an ardent interventionist cannot be determined. After mid-1941, he ceased to have any significant connection with the Southern Conference.

Lee took part in the campaign against Birmingham's arbitrary

12. Lee to Frank Graham, November 4, 1939, Graham Papers, UNC.

arrest and confinement ordinance; he, too, by implication, was one of the *Daily Worker's* Birmingham liberals. No evidence exists that he advocated the violent overthrow of the United States government, or of any other American government. Nor is there any evidence that his motives were more corrupt than the motives of scores of other zealous young Americans on whom the depression had a profoundly disturbing effect. His main interest was labor organization and the interests of the Communist party may have been subordinated to the interests of his union. He may have been a member of the Communist party at the time he held the Southern Conference executive secretaryship, but he opposed the Couch resolution because he feared it would split the Conference, not because it attacked the Soviet Union. Later, he tried to use the Southern Conference for the promotion of an American Peace Mobilization meeting. Otherwise, his actions were above board. There is no evidence that he and Gelders conspired to subvert the Southern Conference; indeed, Lee's letters forever complained that Gelders kept everyone ignorant of his affairs.

If the charges against Lee and Gelders are accurate, it would be difficult to improve on the following characterization of their type of communism:

> the Communist Party in some countries, notably France, Italy, and, to a lesser extent, the United States, draws into its ranks many who in no sense seek the revolutionary overthrow of our institutions as does the hard core of the Communist Party, but who look to the Communist Party as a method of reform which will cure evils. [These find] in the Communist Party an outlet for a sense of grievance. But they are not in reality either agents of a foreign principal nor do they entertain treasonable plans.[13]

John B. Thompson was born in Tennessee in 1907. Educated in several Southern states and at Beloit College in Wisconsin, he received the B.D. from Union Theological Seminary in 1932. His

13. John Foster Dulles to Richard M. Nixon, February 3, 1948 in United States Congress, House Committee on Un-American Activities, *Hearings on Proposed Legislation to Curb or Control the Communist Party of the United States,* 80 cong., 2 sess. (Washington: Government Printing Office, 1948), pp. 492–493.

thesis, "The Social Consequences of Religious Orthodoxy in the South," was written under Reinhold Niebuhr. In 1937, he became part-time professor of philosophy and religion at the University of Oklahoma and pastor of the First Presbyterian Church in Norman. In 1940, when Frank Graham announced he could no longer devote time to the Southern Conference chairmanship, Thompson was a candidate to replace him. The labor unions, dubious about his political affiliations, blocked his election. Two months later, again unable to find anyone else for the post, the Conference executive board elected Thompson to succeed Graham. In September 1940, Thompson assumed the presidency of the American Peace Mobilization.

After the war, Thompson testified before an Illinois legislative investigating committee; he denied that the American Peace Mobilization was a Communist front and he denied that he had ever been a member of the Communist party. Although some of Thompson's testimony was evasive, his denial of Communist party membership was believable. At the Chattanooga convention, he told Frank Graham he was a Christian Socialist. Before the Illinois investigating committee, he remarked that he had a profound philosophical criticism of communism. Sadly, the members of the committee failed to ask for more detail. Possibly Thompson's criticism remained what it had been in 1936. Then, in an article for Reinhold Niebuhr's journal, *Radical Religion,* Thompson criticized communism's materialistic and deterministic system because it could not lead to man's fulfillment: only the truths of Christianity could. But, for the truths of Christianity to effect human fulfillment they would have to engage themselves in the fight for social and political reforms.

Nevertheless, Thompson's criticism of the Communist system did not preclude acceptance of the chairmanship of the American Peace Mobilization, which, indirect evidence indicates, he knew was closely associated with the Communist party. His justification for his action is unanswerable; it also establishes the point that he probably knew how closely the American Peace Mobilization and the Communist party were connected. He arrived at his isolationism, he wrote Frank Graham, on his own, not at the dictates of any party; since he had come by his views honestly, he did not care who agreed with him nor with whom he collaborated to give effect to his views.

Except in foreign affairs, his views were similar to the views of the rest of the members of the Southern Conference. Late in 1940, the work that Thompson and other members of the Southern Conference had done for the American Peace Mobilization became a matter of concern to the Conference's anti-Communist bloc. This was part of a general concern with Communist infiltration that had absorbed much of the time and energy of the Conference's non-Communist leaders from the beginning of the organization.[14]

VI

By mid 1939, charges that the Southern Conference was infiltrated by Communists had alerted its liberal leaders. They tried to get accurate details; most of the small amount of time Frank Graham alloted to Southern Conference affairs was devoted to a search

14. Interviews with Clark Foreman, New York City, April 7, 1964, Aubrey Williams, Washington, D.C., March 24, 1964; Kester, Browder, Durr interviews previously cited. *The Southern Patriot,* VIII (September 1950), 4; Roger Baldwin interview previously cited; *Daily Worker,* September 15, 1938, p. 6; April 6, 1938, p. 3; September 8, 1940, p. 3; Gelders to Frank Graham, January 17, 1940, Graham Papers, UNC. On Lee: Cedric Belfrage, *A Faith to Free the People* (New York: Dryden Press, 1944), p. 32; Jack Tolbert to Josephine Wilkins, October 19, 1939, Graham Papers, UNC; Lee to George C. Stoney, February 28, 1940, SCHW Records, TI, box No. 3; Lee to Barry Bingham, March 23, 1940, SCHW Records, TI, box No. 3; Subversive Activities Control Board, *Hearings . . . on the International Union of Mine, Mill, and Smelter Workers of America,* mimeographed copy, possession of the SCAB, Washington, D.C., pp. 2991ff., p. 3015, 3017, and 3021. Lee to Claude A. Barnette, January 16, 1941, SCHW Records, TI, box No. 3; *Daily Worker,* August 25, 1940, section 2, p. 2; liberals named included Gelders, Malcolm C. Dobbs, and Gerald Harris. On Thompson: a brief biographical file is in SCHW Records, TI, box No. 3; State of Illinois, Seditious Activities Investigation Commission, *Report of Proceedings: Investigations of the University of Chicago and Roosevelt College* (Springfield: n.p., 1949), pp. 92ff. John Beauchamp Thompson, "Prolegomena to a Proletarian Theology," *Radical Religion,* I Autumn 1936), 11–18, John B. Thompson to Frank Graham, March 29, 1941, Graham Papers, UNC. Other members of the Southern Conference who belonged to the American Peace Mobilization were Gerald Harris, John P. Davis, Louis Burnham, and Malcolm C. Dobbs.

for reliable information about the alleged Communists within the organization. An unusually fair man, Graham informed the accused of the charges against them and requested their replies. Both Graham and Clark Foreman agreed that Communists should be prohibited from serving in executive and administrative positions in the Southern Conference. Foreman recommended a complete ban on Communist participation, whether as officers or as Conference members:

it might be wise . . . to suggest to the various state committees that in determining their membership they exclude . . . any agent of a foreign government or any member of an organization which is committed to a totalitarian form of government. After all, this is a conference on democracy; and anyone who believes in despotism should not participate.[15]

Graham, on the other hand, favored admitting avowed Communists to membership:

We should give them the fair open chance of a democratic way by holding our own ground as believers in liberty and democracy. We owe this to the millions of Negroes, underprivileged, and disinherited people all over the South who, through injustice, could become the innocent victims of Communism.[16]

Their mutual concern to keep the Southern Conference free from Communist control prompted them to uphold Howard Lee's appointment to the Conference executive secretaryship; had another person been willing to take the position, they might have blocked Lee's appointment. Graham's sedulous inquiries netted denials from the alleged Communists who held official positions in the Conference, and the members of the Alabama Policy Committee who had prepared for the Birmingham convention wrote him to deny the charges of Communist control.

At the Chattanooga convention, the liberals and anti-Communists tangled openly with the Communists and their allies over the Couch resolution. Here they won a partial victory. Elsewhere, the Communists won the day; at least two members of the governing board

15. Clark Foreman to Frank Graham, October 19, 1939, Graham Papers, UNC.
16. Frank Graham to H. C. Nixon, December 2, 1939, *ibid.*

of the League of Young Southerners were either then or later members of the Communist party, namely, Junius Scales and James Jackson; the League's executive secretary was at least a willing fellow traveler. Shortly thereafter, the League became inactive. It was thus a side-show. The main divisive issue remaining involved the choice of Frank Graham's successor; except for Kathryn Lewis, all the labor delegates and many of the liberals opposed John Thompson's selection; they were strong enough to prevent his election.

For the next few months, Graham and Foreman fruitlessly sought a reputable liberal for the Conference chairmanship. Graham urged Barry Bingham to take the post. But Bingham's duties as publisher of the Louisville *Courier-Journal* left him with little spare time and he doubted the Conference had a viable future. He refused the job. Graham and Foreman next tried to persuade Will Alexander, then about to retire from the Farm Security Administration, to take the Conference executive secretaryship. The proposal interested Alexander. So did one from the Rosenwald Fund to become one of its vice presidents. Unable to match the Fund's salary offer, the Conference had only one position acceptable to a man of Alexander's stature: the chairmanship, an unsalaried position. Foreman and Graham offered Alexander the Conference chairmanship and offered Howard W. Odum the Conference's executive secretaryship. Odum, suspicious of the Conference, thought his academic talents ill suited to an administrative position; in mid-June he declined the offer. So did Alexander. Six days later, the Southern Conference executive board met in Chattanooga. Frank Graham had to be replaced; John B. Thompson was the only available candidate. By a vote of three to two, he became Conference chairman.

During Thompson's chairmanship, the Conference remained nearly inactive, beset with financial malnutrition and obsessed with the several humors throbbing within it. The Birmingham contingent fought against the city's arbitrary arrest ordinance and eventually won their battle. Several members of the Conference participated in the formation of an Oklahoma Federation of Constitutional Liberties and the Tennessee Commonwealth Federation, a coalition of organizations working for favorable labor legislation and for the abolition of the state's poll tax. In 1941, Gerald Harris, a member of the Conference executive board, tried to organize a state chapter of the National Farmers' Union in Alabama—a project that brought few tangible results. Plans to oppose Eugene Talmadge's violations of the Bill of Rights in Georgia and to oust Boss Crump failed for lack of funds and consequent lack of personnel. Perhaps Thompson, Gelders, Malcolm Dobbs, and Howard Lee were more interested in their work for the American Peace Mobilization.

Meantime, Conference anti-Communists continued to be active. Late in 1940, William Mitch and other members of the UMW in the Conference raised questions about Gelders's and Malcolm Dobbs's political affiliations; in addition, Gelders was accused of misusing Conference funds. John T. Jones of Labor's Non-Partisan League and Kathryn Lewis authorized Mitch to investigate the charges against Gelders and Dobbs. Although Mitch's investigation produced no known results, it indicates the growing antagonism between the Conference's laborites and liberals, on the one hand, and the Conference Peace Mobilization activists on the other. Early in 1941, Mark Ethridge and Barry Bingham wrote to Thompson demanding an explanation of his association with the American Peace Mobilization, an organization whose program so clearly coincided with the Communist party's. Thompson, then recovering from a serious automobile accident, failed to reply. Ethridge and Bingham resigned from the Conference. This presaged a major quarrel between the Conference's isolationists and its interventionists.

In March 1941, Thompson and Howard Lee cosigned a letter on Southern conference stationery announcing a forthcoming rally of the American Peace Mobilization. Although they carefully pointed out that they wrote in their private capacities, their use of official stationery seemed to constitute an official Conference endorsement of the rally. Graham immediately accused them of using the Southern Conference's name in support of "an apparently Communist-inspired meeting" and of attempting to break up the organization. Lee replied that support of anti-interventionist programs rested on the Chattanooga resolutions, which had opposed American entry into foreign wars. American rearmament, he continued, diverted funds from reform programs; the New Deal had been abandoned in favor of all-out support of the western Allies.

Whoever had the better of the argument, the split within the Conference could no longer be veiled. Graham, Mitch, Judge Charlton Mrs. C. J. Durr, Clark Foreman, and other members of the board were ardent in support of aid to the Allies; some of them hoped to have the Conference declare its support of President Roosevelt's efforts in behalf of the western democracies. The Lewises wished the Conference to continue to support increases in domestic reform expenditures and to oppose aid to the Allies. Even though Thompson and Lee wished the Conference to confine itself to domestic problems, their letter forced the issue.

All of the members of the Conference Board agreed that the dispute would have to be settled in a board meeting, or in a meeting of the authority superior to the board, the Southern Council. Thompson finally arranged for a meeting of the Southern Council, which convened on May 2, 1941, in Nashville. There Thompson moved that the Southern Conference limit its activities to domestic issues. Graham offered a substitute motion: the Conference should reaffirm its opposition to Nazi, fascist, and Communist dictatorships and voice its concern for the fate of democracy everywhere in the world. Clark Foreman offered a substitute for Graham's substitute: although the Conference was concerned with all threats to democracy, it should "use our small budget and staff until the next Conference solely to extend civil and political rights in the South and to increase the economic opportunities of all Southerners." [17] After considerable debate, Foreman's motion passed. Sometime later, Thompson apologized for announcing the American People's Meeting on Southern Conference stationery; Howard Lee concurred.

Lee's concurrence failed to save him. During the meeting he

17. Minutes, Meeting of the Southern Council, May 2, 1941, SCEF possession.

volunteered to go on leave without pay for two months; ostensibly, the Conference's financial position left him no choice; between December 1940 and December 1941, the group raised about $3,000. Unquestionably his activities for the American Peace Mobilization infuriated Conference liberals, some of whom threatened to resign from the Conference if Lee remained. Unquestionably, too, Lee's work had deteriorated; early in 1941, his inept handling of Conference finances together with his work for the American Peace Mobilization moved Clark Foreman to threaten to quit the Southern Conference. The leave of absence was simply a way for Lee to depart the organization with his honor intact. On August 2, 1941, at a meeting of the Conference executive board, Lee's leave of absence became a permanent resignation.

At that same meeting, Gelders's Civil Rights Committee, on his own motion, was dissolved, and his official connection with the Southern Conference was ended. Had he remained with the organization, other, more prominent members would probably have resigned.

Of the three most important suspected Communists and fellow travelers, only John B. Thompson was left; his chairmanship ended in 1942. From the meeting of the Southern Council until his departure from the South after the war, Thompson was one of the Conference's most loyal, least factious members.

The Conference needed administrative personnel to replace Lee, and perhaps Gelders. Owing to a lack of funds, it accepted the loan of Alton Lawrence from Labor's Non-Partisan League. Early in July, John T. Jones, head of the League, agreed to lend Lawrence's services to the Southern Conference and to provide funds for a secretary.

Howard Lee had suggested the loan to John L. Lewis the previous March. In a letter promising co-operation between the Southern Conference and Labor's Non-Partisan League, Lee wrote: "Because both organizations have the same general objective and because both complement each other . . . it would therefore be possible that . . . co-operation [could] lead to amalgamation of the two organizations at the next meeting of the Southern Conference. . . ." [18] John B. Thompson agreed. But Conference officials envisioned co-operation between equals. John L. Lewis and John T. Jones had other plans. "John T. Jones told me several weeks ago," Alton Lawrence remarked shortly before coming to the Southern Conference, "that LNPL and John L. Lewis would back the Southern Conference to the extent that it became a part of the general political perspective of LNPL and John L. Lewis." [19] Where Conference leaders anticipated collaboration and then amalgamation, Lewis and Jones expected collaboration and Labor's Non-Partisan League's eventual assimilation of the Southern Conference. Lawrence was lent to the Conference for that purpose alone.

Lawrence was then a member of the Communist party. He kept this as quiet as he could. He had joined the party because he thought it had the most realistic solutions to the problems confronting the American worker. He often placed his loyalty to the labor movement above his loyalty to the Communist party. He came to the Southern Conference as a minion of John L. Lewis, not of Earl Bowder or Joseph Stalin. He stayed with the Southern Conference as long as it suited John L. Lewis to have him there. After the German invasion of Russia, few serious differences on questions of foreign policy remained to split the Conference; the interventionists determined Conference policies. By October, a third convention of the Conference had been planned to consider the South's role in national defense. This presumably disenchanted John L. Lewis. John T. Jones recalled Alton Lawrence. A good organization man, he returned to the trade-union work that was his first interest.

Once again, Conference leaders had to find an executive secretary. After some time, they hired James Dombrowski away from the Highlander Folk School. Another graduate of Union Theological Seminary, Dombrowski came highly recommended. Sherwood Eddy and Lucy Mason assured Conference leaders that Dombrowski was

18. Howard Lee to John L. Lewis, March 11, 1941, SCHW Records, TI, box No. 3.
19. Alton Lawrence to J. P. Davis, June 19, 1941, SCHW Records, TI, box No. 3.

not a Communist. On behalf of the Robert Marshall Civil Liberties Trust Fund, Roger Baldwin approved his selection; the trustees of the Marshall Fund, acting on Baldwin's assurance that the Conference was free from Communist control, donated money to the Conference for its third convention. Although Dombrowski was subsequently accused of being either a Communist or a fellow traveler, he claimed to be a Christian Socialist and a Democrat. His reform interests have on occasion brought him into alliance with Communists, but this is insufficient to sustain the charges against him; so is the other evidence used against him. Dombrowski remains to this day a Christian Socialist and a Democrat.

By the time of the Conference's third convention, some of its alleged Communist humors had been purged; those remaining lay dormant. Dombrowski made half successful efforts to avoid further ill-founded charges. He kept Jack McMichael off the program because his work for the American Youth Congress and other alleged Communist fronts might embarrass Mrs. Roosevelt who was scheduled to appear at the convention. He asked Rob Hall to stay away lest he too prove an embarrassment; when Hall refused, Dombrowski made no further objections. He could not prevent—had he wished to—Paul Robeson's appearance at the convention. Although Robeson was not a Communist, he was embittered over American treatment of the Negro and he had praised the Soviet Union. During his performance at the convention, Robeson asked the delegates to work for Earl Browder's release from prison, where he was serving a sentence for violation of passport regulations. Robeson's appearance and his plea for Browder's release occasioned further suspicions of the Southern Conference. Together with the presence of John B. Thompson and John P. Davis on the executive board they sparked a minor disruptive incident during the convention and eventually caused Roger Baldwin's disillusionment.

Since late 1939, the leader of the Southern Conference's Socialist faction, Frank McCallister of the Southern Workers' Defense League, had battled vociferously to have the Southern Conference leadership purged completely of its Communist and Communist-tainted viruses. He wrote long letters of warning to Frank Graham. At the Chattanooga convention, he tried to have the Conference adopt a resolution, modeled after one adopted by the American Civil Liberties Union a few months before, barring from office any person belonging to an organization supporting a totalitarian dictatorship or whose public declarations defended a totalitarian dictatorship. Possibly because the substance of his resolution harmonized with the policies of Foreman and Graham and possibly because many of the other Conference leaders actively disliked him, his resolution failed to get out of committee. He continued his interest in the Southern Conference's political health: he willingly named persons whom he believed were Communists and fellow travelers; he sought a politically reliable executive secretary. But he was not involved in the internal convulsions that resulted in the resignations of Joseph Gelders and Howard Lee. He came to the third Conference still hot on the trail of the Communist virus; he came ignorant of the anti-Communist labors of other Conference members.

His prime suspects were John P. Davis and John B. Thompson, the former a member of the Conference executive board, the latter still Conference chairman. McCallister's case against Davis rested on the latter's admitted membership in the National Negro Congress. Although witnesses before the Dies Committee had accused Davis of being a member of the Communist party, McCallister simply charged that Davis belonged to a Communist front; he based his case on the statement of his fellow socialist, A. Philip Randolph, delivered when he resigned from the National Negro Congress in 1940. Yet Randolph's statement had been a masterpiece of ambiguity; he had in effect charged that the National Negro Congress might become a Communist front, that it was becoming a Communist front, that it had in fact become a Communist front. McCallister fastened on the last charge to the exclusion of the former two. When he publicly moved against Davis he merely said what everyone already knew: Davis belonged to an organization charged with being a Communist front. So did Frank McCallister and every other member of the Southern Conference for Human Welfare.

McCallister's case was not only weak in point of documentation, it was flimsy in point of fact. Davis and Thompson had been among the least contentious, the most helpful members of the Conference. Davis had opposed the Couch resolution, fearing it would disrupt the organization. Although a member of the American Peace Mobilization, he advised against the use of Southern Conference stationery to advertise its meetings. After the charges against him became serious, he offered to resign from the Southern Conference if his presence would further embarrass the organization. In short, neither man had ever tried to subvert the organization nor been part of any Communist plot to capture it. And Thompson quit the chairmanship at the third convention. Several months later, Clark Foreman, one of the Conference's anti-Communists, assumed the position.

Nevertheless, McCallister's suspicions were not stilled; and, strangely, Roger Baldwin's were aroused. Baldwin himself had been a popular front participant until the Molotov-von Ribbentrop pact convinced him that communism had become opportunistic beyond redemption. The burden of his criticism—although twenty-two years later he denied this contention—seems to have been that the Southern Conference had failed to fulfill its declared purpose to unite all Southern reform organizations. The presence of Robeson, Davis, Thompson, the local arrangements secretary, and other members of alleged Communist fronts at the convention and on the Conference executive board indicated "that the leaders of the Conference do not appreciate the risks they run in collaborating closely with fellow travelers. . . ." [20]

After the third convention, a long, acrimonious dispute occurred between Baldwin and McCallister on one side and Clark Foreman, James Dombrowski, Lucy Mason, and Mrs. Roosevelt on the other. The one side repeated its accusations and elaborated its suspicions; the other countered that the alleged fellow travelers were too few to control the Conference and that the accused were loyal, co-

20. Baldwin to Clark Foreman, May 19, 1942, SCHW Records, TI, box No. 5.

operative members of the organization. Whatever the merits of the arguments, Baldwin and McCallister had made two cardinal errors: they acted in ignorance of the labors of the anti-Communists before the Nashville convention: their timing was off. By 1942, the Conference had not only got rid of most of the suspected Communists in administrative positions, it had also adopted at Nashville a set of by-laws which, by banning from membership persons advocating the violent overthrow of the United States Government or belonging to organizations advocating the violent overthrow of the United States Government, could have been modeled on the Smith Act.

Baldwin and McCallister's accusations affronted the non-Communists who knew better than they the extent of the influence of real and imagined Communists within the organization and who had worked for over two years to prevent them from exerting any baleful influence over the Conference. By 1942, Conference anti-Communists could justly claim to have either purged or neutralized the red humors within the organization. And they could claim that American entry into the war had temporarily transformed the nation's Communists into superpatriots, the most loyal members of a country mobilizing for total war. McCallister and Baldwin should have withheld their attacks and remained vigilant until subsequent differences between the United States and the Soviet Union over foreign policy made Communists in the Conference once more an actual instead of a potential danger. They should have realized that fiscal anemia and the war's distraction of national attention from domestic reforms, not red humors, were the main dangers to the Conference's health.[21]

21. Frank Graham to Louise O. Charlton, November 19, 1939; Lucy Mason to Frank Graham, November 10, 1939; Clark Foreman to Graham, October 31, 1939; H. C. Nixon to Graham, December 7, 1939; Howard Kester to Graham, December 11, 1939; Graham to Joseph Gelders, January 15, 1940; Gelders to Graham, January 17, 1940; Clark Foreman to Graham, November 8, 1939; Roger Baldwin to Graham, January 9, 1940; Lucy Mason to Graham, May 8, 1940; Barry Bingham to Graham, May 27, 1940; Graham to H. W. Odum, June 15, 1940; Odum to Graham, June 15, 1940; Foreman to Graham, June 18, 1940; George C. Stoney to Graham, April 29, 1940: Graham Papers, UNC. Minutes Executive Board Meeting, June 21, 1940, SCEF possession. Malcolm C. Dobbs to Gelders and Lee, January 29, 1941; Mrs. Franklin Roosevelt to Howard Lee, undated; Lucy Mason to Lee, March 28,

1941; Graham to Lee, March 16, 1941 and March 27, 1941; Lee to Graham, March 29, 1941 and April 5, 1941; Graham to Lee, April 5, 1941; Thompson to Graham, March 29, 1941; Thompson to Lee, March 29, 1941; Mark Ethridge to Thompson, January 17, 1941; Lee to Mason Smith, April 10, 1941; Lee to Kathryn Lewis, April 10, 1941; SCHW Records, TI, boxes Nos. 2 and 3. Some of the same materials are in Graham Papers, UNC. Minutes Executive Board Meeting, August 2, 1941, SCEF possession. Foreman to Howard Lee, October 4, 1940; Foreman to Thompson, January 22, 1941; Foreman to Lee, January 25, 1941; Foreman to Lee, April 12, 1941: SCHW Records, TI, box No. 4. Gardner Jackson to Joseph Gelders, October 11, 1940; John B. Thompson to Alton Lawrence, June 10, 1941; Lawrence to Thompson, June 19, 1941; same to same, July 12, 1941: SCHW Records, TI, box No. 3. On Lawrence, see United States Congress, Senate Internal Security Subcommittee, *Hearings . . . Communist Domination of Union Officials in Vital Defense Industry —International Union of Mine, Mill, and Smelter Workers*, 82 cong., 2 sess. (Washington: Government Printing Office, 1952), pp. 134–135; The assertion of Lawrence's membership in the Communist party is contained in *United States of America* v. *Raymond Denis et al.*, U. S. District Court for the District of Colorado, No. 15124, typescript in possession of the Justice Department's Internal Security Division, pp. 1312ff. The author is indebted to officials of this division for permission to examine this transcript. Junius Scales never tried to conceal his membership in the party: see Laurent B. Frantz, "Junius Scales," *The Nation*, December 30, 1961, pp. 528–530. Neither did James Jackson; Ralph Lord Roy, *Communism and the Churches* (New York: Harcourt Brace and World, 1960), p. 108 and David Shannon, *The Decline of American Communism* (New York: Harcourt, Brace and World, c.1959), pp. 270, 304, 312, 345. Sherwood Eddy to Highlander Folk School, January 21, 1941, Mason Papers, Duke. Interview, James A. Dombrowski, New Orleans, January 3, 1964. Frank McCallister to Frank Graham, March 18, 1940; M. C. Dobbs and Howard Lee to Graham, March 21, 1940; Foreman to Graham, March 27, 1940: SCHW Records, TI, box No. 4. Baldwin to Clark Foreman, May 19, 1942; Foreman to Baldwin, May 19, 1942; Baldwin to Foreman, May 25, 1942; Foreman to Baldwin, May 26, 1942; Lucy Mason to James Dombrowski, May 25, 1942; Dombrowski to Mason, May 27, 1942; Dombrowski to Baldwin, May 27, 1942; McCallister to Foreman, May 4, 1942; Foreman to McCallister, May 12, 1942; Baldwin to Mason, July 14, 1942; McCallister to Foreman, July 25, 1942; Baldwin to Foreman, September 2, 1942; Gardner Jackson to Foreman, June 2, 1942; Mrs. Roosevelt to Baldwin, June 23, 1942; Baldwin to Mrs. Roosevelt, June 26, 1942; Lucy Mason to Baldwin, July 4, 1942; Baldwin to Foreman, July 14, 1942; Foreman to Mrs. Roosevelt, July 26, 1942; SCHW Records, TI, box No. 5. On Baldwin see Dwight MacDonald's sketches in *The New Yorker*, XXIX, July 11, 1953, pp. 31ff. and July 18, 1953, pp. 29ff. especially pp. 42ff.

5

AND THE WAR CAME

AUGUST 2, 1941, the Southern Conference Executive Board began preparations for the organization's third full convention. It unanimously agreed to devote the meeting to the South's role in national defense. One month later, the Finance Committee—consisting of Mrs. Clifford J. Durr, John P. Davis, Clark Foreman, and William Mitch—decided to hold the convention in Nashville in November, to have Paul Robeson appear on the program, and to invite Mrs. Roosevelt. It suggested linking mobilization for war with domestic reform; the former could provide means and justification for further extensions of the New Deal. And it recommended awarding the Thomas Jefferson medal to a white and a Negro. Most of these plans were put into effect.

Subsequently the Conference date had to be moved into 1942. The CIO convention was scheduled for the end of November; Conference leaders hoped the split between Philip Murray and John L. Lewis might there be mended and the Conference once more enjoy the support of a united industrial union movement. The Conference's empty treasury had to be filled. The return of Alton Lawrence to Labor's Non-Partisan League necessitated once more a time-consuming search for an executive secretary. Conference leaders first offered the job to Helen Fuller, who declined. Late in 1941, they were finally able to hire James Dombrowski.

Dombrowski's problems were the problems of his predecessors: he had to arouse interest in the convention, to get respectable endorsements, to maintain old alliances and to create new ones—and, of course, to raise money. He tried to get representatives from every Southern reform group. "Would it not be swell," he wrote to a friend, "if we could pull off a conference with all elements fully represented? The outlook at the moment is fine." [1] Copies of the Conference Call went to more than 2,500 church groups, 1,500 educators, 259 social workers, 2,000 youth group leaders, 7,000 to miscellaneous persons, 6,545 to CIO locals, and 1,542 to AFofL affiliates. In all, Dombrowski sent out more than 27,000 calls. He also wrote personal letters to every rabbi in the South to every CIO state and regional director, and 2,000 to officials of the railroad brotherhoods. He sent a personal letter to Paul Williams of the Catholic Committee of the South, a mild reform organization which aimed at Negro-white understanding and a sounder family life. He got endorsements from John L. Lewis, William Green, and James Carey; and Carey, David E. Lilienthal, Francis Biddle, Rupert Vance, and Jonathan Daniels either appeared on the program or transmitted statements for use during the convention. Through Mrs. Roosevelt, Dombrowski suggested to the President a government pamphlet on the South's part in winning the war; like the NEC *Report*, it would give the convention a general theme to center on and provide the Southern Conference with an un-

1. Dombrowski to Mrs. C. J. Durr, March 10, 1942, TI, box No. 5.

official but important connection with the Roosevelt Administration. The National Resources Planning Board had prepared an interim report on a plan for Southern regional development. But Dombrowski failed to use it; the report may not have fulfilled his expectations; since Mrs. Roosevelt received her copy sometime after March 25, it may have appeared too late. Mrs. Roosevelt attended and her husband sent a letter of greeting. He also sent FBI agents to look for racial incidents at the integrated gathering.

Dombrowski and other Conference leaders somehow scraped together enough money for the convention. The Marshall Fund grant was either $1,000 or $2,500; the conferees contributed an additional $1,297.11; and Paul Robeson's concert netted $527.28. Otherwise, the records are fragmentary; during the first five months of 1942, Conference income totaled $7,929.39, most of which presumably financed the Nashville meeting. Foundations donated $5,500 and private contributors $605. Although the Conference was richer than it had been during either of its previous conventions, it was poorer this time in delegates.[2]

II

On April 19, 1942, the third convention of the Southern Conference for Human Welfare assembled in Nashville, Tennessee. More than 500 official delegates attended. About one third of that number were Negroes, who once again had to be housed separately and to take their meals apart from the white delegates. Some 160 delegates came from organized labor, 112 of these from the CIO. Only 3 representatives from farm organizations showed up. Edu-

2. Minutes Executive Board Meeting, August 2, 1941; Minutes Finance Committee Meetings September 18, 1941; Minutes Executive Board Meeting, October 31, 1941; SCEF possession. John P. Davis to James Dombrowski, undated [March (?), 1942]; Dombrowski to Frank Graham, April 6, 1942; Dombrowski to Paul Williams, March 16, 1942; James Carey to Dombrowski, April 9, 1942: SCHW Records, TI, box No. 5. Dombrowski to Mrs. Roosevelt, March 6, 1942, OF 4675, Misc. box No. 45; Memo for the National Resources Planning Board, March 11, 1942, PPF 5664; F. A. Delano to Mrs. Roosevelt, March 25, 1942, OF 4675, Misc. box No. 45; J. Edgar Hoover to Marvin McIntyre, May 7, 1942, OF 4952: Roosevelt Papers, Hyde Park. Financial Report, Southern Conference for Human Welfare, January 1 to June 1, 1942, SCEF possession.

cational institutions had 41 delegates on hand; federal agencies 25; and unclassified organizations another 25. Youth groups sent 91. The rest of the delegates were without organizational affiliation. As at the Chattanooga convention Negroes and CIO representatives—even accounting for some overlapping between the two categories—accounted for the bulk of the Conference's strength. The delegates without organizational affiliation probably came from the South's middle classes, with a few from its new industrial aristocracy: professional persons, housewives, textile magnates such as Donald Comer. A geographic breakdown of the delegation showed 288 from Tennessee, 70 from Alabama, 18 from Georgia, 27 from Kentucky, 21 from Louisiana, and a like number from North Carolina. The remainder came from the other Southern states. The figures reflect wartime restrictions on travel; but, with the exception of the abnormally large number from Tennessee, they also accurately represent the geographic distribution of the Southern Conference's strength. Its most active contingents were in Tennessee, Georgia, North Carolina, Alabama, and Louisiana. The Southern Conference was largely an organization of persons from the border South and from the central portion of the deep South.

The convention speakers exhorted the delegates to give themselves over completely to mobilization for total war and to work for the extension of the New Deal. Roosevelt's letter entoned the theme:

> Victory over the Axis aggressors demands that neither man nor wealth be wasted, and that the privilege of participation in our great national undertaking be granted to every citizen. It also demands that our own democracy be maintained as a vital strengthening force. It is my hope that your Conference will present tangible suggestions for the full utilization of our resources within the principles of our democratic faith.[3]

John B. Thompson's reply played minor variations; he pledged "all the vigor of our democratic faith in the achievement of unity

3. Unless otherwise noted all quotations in this section come from Southern Conference for Human Welfare, *Proceedings of the Nashville Convention of the Southern Conference for Human Welfare* (Nashville: n.p., 1942).

within the South and within the nation for this great fight against dictatorships abroad and defeatism at home." His keynote address echoed the President's letter. Aware of the necessity of victory and national unity, Thompson hoped the country would not simply

> fight first and postpone all thinking about goals and values until afterward! We know that thinking about our democratic goals and values is not irrelevant. It is necessary! For the things we believe in will determine the kind of struggle we make: its quality, its persistence, its success.

Mary McLeod Bethune, the Negro recipient of the Thomas Jefferson award, repeated the theme of total mobilization and, in a major variation, took up the Negro's role in the war.

> As the Negro people march into battle they know that there are many hindrances to full participation in the country's battle for freedom; but march they must, and march they will, because they do understand that every hope they have for full democracy hinges upon the outcome of this war. They understand that the fate of America is the fate of the Negro people; we go up or down together. [Negroes will fight] for the perfection of the democracy of our own beloved America, and the extension of that perfected democracy to the ends of the world.

During that fight, they expected to win fuller participation in the promises of American life.

Frank Graham, the white recipient of the Jefferson medal, added a variation of his own: full mobilization of the South's Protestants, Catholics, and Jews, who in unwitting co-operation had given the world its conceptions of brotherhood, freedom, and democracy. The three religions "must stand together now" in spiritual defense of these conceptions "against ideas and forces which would tear them down." Like Thompson, Graham asked both for total mobilization and for further democratic reforms.

> The old victories for human liberty can be preserved only in the revised versions of the new struggles for democracy. Freedom can be protected by the advance of equality of opportunity. Liberty can be raised to higher levels by the widening of social security. The old Bill of Rights can be saved only by provision for the new bill of rights.

Then, in what may have been a veiled reference to the restrictions being imposed upon Japanese and Japanese-Americans on the Pacific coast (the only one officials of the Conference ever made) Graham conjured a vision of a multi-national America,

settled by peoples of many regions, races, religions, colors, creeds, and cultures [that should] by example, lead the way . . . in really helping "to make the world safe for democracy." The haven of heretics in the days of its weakness should not, in the days of its power, become the stronghold of bigots. The world has given America the vigor and variety of its differences. America should protect and enrich its differences, make for a better understanding of other differences and for an appreciation of the sacredness of human personality, as basic to human freedom.

Then, in keeping with his Wilsonian idealism, Graham championed a postwar association of nations. And he issued a declaration for the South which became the Southern Conference's battle cry for the remainder of the war.

We wish to declare that we have the economic resources, the industrial plants, the sciences and technology, the human skills, the creative intelligence, and the democratic responsibility, based on the faith of our fathers and the aspirations of our children, both to make total war an effective military and industrial offensive against the Axis powers, and to make total war a defense of, and a step toward total abundance for all the people, who are what the defense is all about, from whom all our defenses come, and without whose spiritual faith and democratic morale all our defenses collapse.

America, he concluded, must transform herself into "the cornerstone of the United Nations of the World as another step in our time toward the Kingdom of God."

Thus the theme and its major variations. The panel discussions on industrial production, agricultural production, youth and training, and citizenship and civil liberties, repeated the theme and added a few minor variations.

The Industrial Production panel included such worthies as Frank Graham, chairman, James Carey, Clark Foreman, Andrew Jackson Higgins, a New Orleans ship builder, Robert C. Weaver, and Ira DeA. Reid. It demanded preservation and extension of the New Deal's domestic reforms and total mobilization of Southern human and natural resources. In keeping with the latter demand, it asked for an end to wasteful production and it advocated conversion of all Southern industries to war production and a 7-day, 24-hour production schedule. It also deplored the "refusal to employ people because of their color, sex or creed" and so censured the city fathers of Mobile for importing rural whites for war work which Mobile's Negroes could have performed. The necessities of war had brought the Southern Conference out into the open against discrimination in employment.

The Agricultural Production panel—under the chairmanship of Arthur Raper and including Charles S. Johnson, H. C. Nixon, and M. L. Wilson—sought ways to mobilize Southern food production for the war effort; each segment of the population had to have enough food to work to full capacity. The panel recommended a balanced agriculture in place of the South's customary reliance on a few cash crops. It declared for co-operative purchase of fertilizer, seed, and machinery, and for co-operative ownership of crop processing and storage facilities. It asked the government to grant farmers first priority on agricultural implements and fertilizers. The panel re-expressed the Conference's concern for the mass of underprivileged Southern farmers: it came out for unemployment insurance for the thousands of tenants whom farm automation had driven off the land into the cities, landlord-tenant laws to protect tenants and laborers, adequate shelter, home gardens, and a living wage for them, and agencies to inform farm workers of opportunities for employment.

The panel on Youth and Training was under the chairmanship of Homer Rainey, then President of the University of Texas. It included Noel Beddow of the steel workers, Mary McLeod Bethune, Myles Horton of Highlander Folk School, and Mrs. Jessie Treichler of Antioch College. In a written statement, Jonathan Daniels, Assistant Director of the Office of Civilian Mobilization, advocated that "our young people, without discrimination as to class, creed or color, be given their part in our war effort, that they have the assistance and training they need to prepare themselves for that part." The panel's suggestions dealing with Negro youth added detail to Daniel's general recommendation. It advocated fullest possible enrollment of both races in Southern schools and "greater efforts at equal opportunities for all youth, regardless of race or circumstance." "To disbar a volunteer or draftee from service in any branch of the armed forces of our country because of race, creed, or color," it added in a direct criticism of federal military segregation practices, "is a waste of manpower and a denial of the democracy which we fight to defend." Both Negro and white youth should have civilian as well as military training. The panel recommended a war mobilization day during July 1942 to stimulate youth to support the war effort and a federal agency to "aid local communities by utilizing speakers, forums, discussion, and study groups in discovering the causes which have produced this war, how we may participate in this effort, and an examination of those sacrifices we must make if victory is to be assured and a just and lasting peace to be established." Finally, the panel opposed decreases in the appropriations for the National Youth Administration, the Farm Security Administration, the Civilian Conservation Corps, and the Tennessee Valley Authority, because these trained American young people and provided food essential to the war effort.

The last panel discussion, Citizenship and Civil Liberties, was under the direction of Jennings Perry, an editor of the Nashville *Tennessean*. Panelists included Louise O. Charlton, Rufus Clement, and Mrs. C. J. Durr. The panel reiterated the obvious: the war had to be won. Although it denounced violations of civil liberties as a hindrance to the war effort, it remained silent about the increasing violations of the civil liberties of Japanese-Americans on the Pacific coast. Under the pressure of war, it argued, some of the freedoms of the Bill of Rights might have to be denied to certain persons; freedom of speech and of the press should not be extended, it asserted in words that could have come from conservative diatribes against Roosevelt, to those who used them "to weaken our national government or to create disunion among our people by setting up race against race, class against class, religion against religion." It asked for restrictions on domestic fascists, on Father Coughlin, on the Klan, and on the Dies Committee; it recommended banning *Social*

Justice from the mails. It asked for state laws conferring the vote on all who served in the armed forces and for a federal anti-poll tax bill. It asked for both federal and state action to protect labor's rights to organize and bargain collectively and to safeguard the security of persons. Finally, it asked for an end to racial and religious bigotry.

Victory, the Nashville convention had thus declared, required

> full use of the South's material and . . . human resources—Negro and white alike. Many of the goals the Southern Conference set for the fulfillment of democracy three years ago are now the requisites of victory. Without this victory no further progress will be possible and no work for human welfare will go on. All our goals are unified by the sweeping threats of this war.

But the Nashville convention was unable to determine an effective course of action. With the exception of its criticism of discrimination in employment and in the armed forces, its goals were as far—if not farther—from its grasp than they had been in 1938. The Conference still lacked the means to achieve them. And it was still beset with financial and personnel problems.

At the Nashville convention, for example, the Conference had to find another chairman. John B. Thompson's work for the American Peace Mobilization had impaired his effectiveness; his duties as part-time minister, part-time pedagogue consumed most of his energy and he wished to resign. The convention elected Homer P. Rainey to succeed him. Although interested in the position, Rainey temporized. At one point he accepted the job—or at least Dombrowski thought he had—only to reject it several days later. The Southern Conference, he contended, represented a segment of Southern liberalism and he wished to work for all Southern reform groups. (Two years later, a University of Texas student claimed that a powerful member of the Texas Board of Regents had forced Rainey to refuse the post.) In June, following Rainey's definitive rejection, the Conference executive board selected Clark Foreman for the chairmanship.

By the middle of 1942, the Southern Conference had two accomplishments to its credit: it had managed to stay alive; and it had hired the two men, Clark Foreman and James Dombrowski, who were largely responsible for its policies for the rest of its life and partly responsible for its ultimate fate.[4]

III

Scion of a distinguished Georgia family—his maternal grandfather had been editor of the Atlanta *Constitution*—Clark Howell Foreman was born in Atlanta, Georgia, on February 19, 1902. Educated in Atlanta public schools, he subsequently attended the University of Georgia from which he was graduated in 1921 at the age of 19. He spent one year at Harvard and a second at the London School of Economics where he came under the influence of L. T. Hobhouse, the theorist of English liberalism, and he read G. H. Oldham's *Christianity and the Race Problem* from which he learned of the work of the Commission on Interracial Co-operation in his native city of Atlanta. Returning home, he worked for the Commission and, as did many other young Southern liberals of the era, came under the spell of Will Alexander, the Commission's guiding genius. He finished his education at Columbia, receiving the M.A. and the Ph.D. from that institution. His thesis dealt with "The Environmental Factor in Negro Elementary Education."

Sometime during the 1920s or the early 1930s, Foreman became convinced of the need to integrate Negroes fully into American society. During his undergraduate days at Georgia, he had witnessed a lynching and there began to question Southern racial customs. His work for the Commission on Interracial Co-operation and his studies at Columbia presumably led him from questions to answers. In 1933, he went to Washington to work as Harold Ickes's Advisor on the Economic Status of Negroes, a post created to help prevent discrimination in the administration of federal relief programs.

In 1938, Foreman suggested to Franklin Roosevelt the publication

4. Report of the Representation at the Third Meeting Nashville, Tennessee, SCEF possession. Homer Rainey to Dombrowski, April 23, 1942; Dombrowski to Members of the Board, May 5, 1942; Benjamin Ramey to Marge Frantz, November 21, 1944: SCHW Records, TI, box No. 5. Lillian Smith, "Crossing Over Jordan into Democracy," *South Today*, VII (Spring, 1942), 46–50.

of a pamphlet on Southern economic problems; the resulting document became an indirect cause of the Southern Conference for Human Welfare. From the organization's inception, Foreman was active in it: as treasurer, as a member of the finance committee, and then as chairman, a post he held until the Conference's demise in 1948.

A short, dark-haired man, with a firm gaze and a prominent lower jaw, Foreman was confident, aggressive, and, so his critics claimed, a little ruthless. Quick to decide and quick to suppress doubts about completed decisions, Foreman was a deeply traditional—if not stereotypical—American progressive. The Southern question, for him, was at bottom an economic question; the South's poverty and the South's colonial economy were at the root of her major problems. The Southern question had an economic answer: Northern-style industrialism humanized by New Deal social reforms. Only the sovereign people could write the answer; they had to elect candidates whose progressive enactments would increase purchasing power, thereby automatically stimulating Southern industrial development.

Foreman's interest in political action later brought him to take the lead in the postwar transformation of the Southern Conference from an educational into a political organization and after that to devote his energies to the Progressive party in 1948. Conservatives in Congress and several ex-Communists have accused him of being a member of the Communist party, but, on the basis of his consistent opposition to the employment of Communists by the Southern Conference, the charge is groundless. (On July 15, 1950, Foreman cast one of two votes against a Progressive party executive committee resolution demanding U.N. cessation of hostilities in Korea.)

James Anderson Dombrowski was born in Tampa, Florida, January 17, 1897, the son of a jeweler. His childhood was placid and he grew up with attitudes common to a young man who expects to inherit his father's business. Like so many other Americans of that sensitive and confident generation, Dombrowski had his complacency at least partly disturbed by the first World War. He volunteered for the ambulance service and served more than a year in the charnel house of the Western front. His experiences there convinced him of the inadequacy of his attitudes toward the vexing political, economic, and religious questions confronting the world. Yet they did not destroy his quiet conviviality or a taste for the good life which he had acquired from his father. After the war, he enrolled at Emory University, a Methodist college in Atlanta, in search of answers, but while seeking them found time to edit the student newspaper, join a fraternity, and lead the college glee club. Following his graduation *cum laude* in 1923, he set out on a long career of academic vagabondage; he spent a year at the University of California at Berkeley, where he heard Harry Ward lecture on his reasons for being a radical and came away deeply impressed; another year at Harvard where the chief attraction was Alfred North Whitehead, then at the height of his philosophical powers; from there to Union Theological Seminary to work under Harry Ward and Reinhold Niebuhr. In 1936, he received a joint Ph.D. from Columbia and Union; his thesis, "The Early Days of Christian Socialism in America," was later published.

During these years, Dombrowski's convictions led him from Methodism to Christian Socialism. Ward and Niebuhr influenced him greatly; of the two, Ward seems to have had the more lasting effect. For Ward's course on social ethics, he visited Elizabethton, Tennessee, in 1929 to observe the bitter textile strikes then in progress. In 1932, he took part in the formation of the Highlander Folk School and remained its staff director until he went to work for the Southern Conference. From 1929 to the present, he has devoted his life to a gradual, peaceful change of Southern social conditions.

A tall, spare man, Dombrowski is quiet, diffident, at times wryly humorous. His defenders verge on proclaiming him a saint; his detractors, although acknowledging his devotion to Southern reform causes, accuse him of deceit, fellow traveling, and of lacking contact with the South's masses.

Where Foreman is assertive, decisive, and perhaps a little rash, Dombrowski is self-effacing, cautious, at times inefficient. Where

Foreman is impatient for the advent of a better world, Dombrowski, although also eager for the new day, is more inclined to stoicism and quiet, diligent labor. Both rely primarily on economic analyses to explain Southern backwardness; yet where Foreman prefers political action, Dombrowski prefers educational programs.

Both had common qualities and both faced common problems. They were ambitious to make the Southern Conference a success. They sought adequate scope for their talents and wished to belong to an organization that would take the lead in the reformation of their beloved South. The Southern Conference's bleak wartime fortunes required them to work together, to overlook whatever personal antagonisms were latent in their respective characters. They had to define a program of action within the limits of the Conference's financial resources, its plan to promote total mobilization, and its new status as an educational organization.[5]

IV

During 1942, Dombrowski's careful management and skillful importunities improved the Southern Conference's financial position. Its total income for the year came to $14,983.66; $10,000 of that came from foundations, $2,901.95 from private contributors, and $2,007.52

5. Sketches of Foreman are numerous: Mary Braggiotti, "Southern Progressive," New York *Post,* March 3, 1945, Weekly Picture Magazine, copy SCEF possession; *Current Biography, 1948,* pp. 218–220; *PM,* undated clipping SCEF possession; M. Hobbes in *Negro Digest,* July, 1946, pp. 83ff. Interview, Clark Foreman, New York City, April 7, 1964. See also Dykeman and Stokeley, *Seeds of Southern Change,* pp. 157ff. Foreman's doctoral dissertation was published by Columbia University Press in 1933. Lastly, House Committee on Un-American Activities, *Hearings—Communism in New York,* 83 cong., 1 sess. (Washington: Government Printing Office, 1953), Part 6, p. 2133 for the testimony of Benjamin Gitlow; House Select Committee to Investigate Tax-Exempt Foundations and Comparable Organizations, *Hearings . . . ,* 82 cong., 2 sess. (Washington: Government Printing Office, 1953), p. 722 for the words of Louis Budenz; for Foreman's denial see *ibid.* p. 784 and the New York *Times,* January 14, 1953, p. 30; Foreman to Dombrowski, June 30, 1944, SCHW Records, TI, box No. 5; Shannon, *Decline of American Communism,* p. 212. On Dombrowski: SCHW Records, TI, box No. 6 has a brief biographical outline; *South Today* (Spring 1942), 52–53; New Orleans *Times-Picayune,* October 5, 1963, p. 2; *Early Days of Christian Socialism in America* (New York: Columbia University Press, 1936), Preface and pp. 3ff., pp. 191ff. *The Southern Patriot,* XXI (November 1963). Interview, James Dombrowski, January 3, 1964. Considerable information on both is scattered through the SCHW Records, TI, and the Foreman Papers, AU.

from membership fees. The Conference was affluent. Considering the amounts received by both the Civil Rights Committee and the Southern Conference in previous years, the Conference's annual income had been roughly doubled. But the sum was barely enough to cover operating expenses, Dombrowski's wages, and what few actions the Conference could afford to engage in. In 1943, the situation worsened. Total income was less than $8,000; in May, Dombrowski, in a desperate plea for funds, remarked that, owing to a lack of postage money, some Conference literature could not be mailed. Of the funds received, the bulk was again supplied by foundations and private contributors.

This paltry income paid for some work in support of the general program developed at the Nashville convention. On Bastile Day, 1942, a date chosen to indicate the Conference's agreement with Henry Wallace's characterization of the conflict with fascism as a people's war, the Conference initiated a Win-the-War meeting in Raleigh, North Carolina, to inspire patriotic support for the war effort. Other Conference activity tried to stifle anti-patriotic outbursts conducive to disloyalty and disunity. On August 16, 1942, after manifestations of racism, the organization paid for a full-page advertisement in the Birmingham *News-Age Herald* denouncing white and black racists as Axis agents and pledging to Roosevelt "full and unqualified support for every war agency and measure" and the preservation of "Southern unity, free from race conflict, behind our war effort." It counseled Southerners not to be provoked into anti-Negro or anti-white demonstrations. That same year, after three lynchings in a single week in Mississippi, the Conference sponsored an open letter in the Jackson *Clarion-Ledger* signed by 75 prominent Mississippians asking the governor to punish the murderers. In April 1943, following an incident in Nashville, the Conference asked the Department of Justice to investigate anti-Negro actions of the military police which had incited disunity in the region.

In the fall of 1942, the Conference executive board decided to begin a newspaper. Dombrowski wrote Clark Foreman:

The paper is to be directed to the mass of unconverted Southerners who economically and patriotically have every reason to support a liberal war policy, but whose ideas have been distorted by sentiment and prejudice. The editorial policy of the paper will call for the full utilization of all the people and the resources of the South in the war effort. The Southern Conference will be listed on the masthead as the publisher but the main effort will be directed at convincing Southerners that the ideas which the Southern Conference supports are correct, rather than that they should support the Southern Conference.[6]

The paper was christened the *Southern Patriot*, a title reflecting the Conference's 100 percent Southernism and its 100 percent Americanism.

The first number of the paper appeared in December 1942. Its declared purpose was "the complete and utter mobilization of all the people, Negro as well as white, and resources for the winning of this war." Although the paper eventually included book reviews, items of interest to Southern liberals, and reports of Southern Conference activities, its main concern during its first year or two of existence was the stimulation of support for the war. Editorially and in feature articles, the paper beat the drums of war. The first issue demanded "new plants, new dams . . . new credit for our small farmers . . . training schools in and out of industry . . . a better distribution of our labor supply . . . diversif[ication of] our agriculture to increase the production of milk, eggs, and meat, and vegetables." [7] Subsequent issues of the paper included features on freight-rate differentials, on food rationing, on the potential of Negro manpower, on a possible anti-New Deal coalition under governors Jones of Louisiana and Dixon of Alabama which might disrupt the war effort, on Southern health problems, on ways to increase agricultural production, and on the poll tax. Here older voices spoke: "The South is ripe for a political turnover. It will happen whenever the new army of industrial workers realizes the vast power within its reach, and when the poll tax system has been broken." [8] No detail affecting

6. October 7, 1942, SCHW Records, TI, box No. 5.
7. *The Southern Patriot*, I (December 1943), 1.
8. *Ibid.*, (August 1943), 1.

maximum use of Southern resources was neglected. A plan to use neighborhood leaders to stimulate support for the war received *Patriot* commendation and additional recommendations; block leaders, the paper suggested, should explain to mothers ways to save kitchen grease, find out which working mothers' children needed nursery care, and inform their neighbors of methods for consumer enforcement of federal price controls.

By the middle of 1943, the paper had a circulation estimated at five thousand. Issues of the paper featuring special subjects were taken up in additional lots by interested organizations: labor unions, consumer groups, church organizations. For the remainder of the Southern Conference's ill-starred career, the *Patriot* was one of the organization's most unqualified successes, and it exists to the present day, under the sponsorship of the Southern Conference's successor, the Southern Conference Educational Fund.

The *Patriot*'s feature articles derived from the investigations of other voluntary organizations and academic and governmental institutions; it digested and presented for popular consumption information taken from the works of Odum and his students, from federal and state government reports such as the National Emergency Councils' *Report on the Economic Conditions of the South,* and from studies of such organizations as the Citizens Fact Finding Movement of Georgia. For articles on current affairs, the paper relied upon Conference members with journalistic training and on other contributors. The details and the generalizations the *Patriot* could include were of necessity fewer than those in the studies on which it drew; it hoped to popularize the results of these studies and to use them to propagate support for domestic reform as a means to victory. In this, the paper was usually accurate. Its weaknesses lay elsewhere.

It was addicted to a glib use of pejoratives; in the space of a few sentences, Governor "Sad Sam" Jones of Louisiana was changed from a Tory candidate for the gubernatorial post into a "stooge candidate of refined Fascism against hoodlum Fascism [the Long organization]." Irate protests from Edgar Stern, a New Orleans businessman whose benefactions had previously been bestowed on the Southern Conference, and from Will Alexander, then on the *Patriot* editorial board, drew a lame defense; in the exchange, Dombrowski limped to the irrelevancy that Jones opposed Roosevelt and thus hindered the war effort. With distressing frequency in the *Patriot,* tories became conservatives, conservatives became reactionaries, reactionaries became fascists. Occasional conservative protests against the New Deal and outbursts of anti-Negro violence turned into portents of an imminent fascist apocalypse. Here and there absurdities appeared: the abolition of unequal regional transportation charges, the paper argued, would have a greater effect on the South than *Uncle Tom's Cabin* and the *Bible.*

Since the *Patriot* merely executed Southern Conference policies and expressed sentiments and opinions common to many of its members, its deficiencies resulted from the deficiencies inherent in the organization and from the revised program that the Nashville convention had adopted. Certainly, tactical considerations justified emphasizing victory over reform, victory through reform, and reform through victory. A superpatriotic attitude placed the Conference's good faith and loyalty beyond question—although its opponents continued to question them—and permitted the Conference to continue to enjoy unofficial patronage from the New Deal. Unquestionably, domestic mobilization would have been more thorough if the Conference's prescriptions had been followed. Presumably, the Conference's influence and power would have increased as the reforms it championed were effected. Yet its descent into the witless rhetoric of American jingoism was both deplorable and unnecessary: its failure to denounce the disgraceful violations of the constitutional rights of the Nisei gave partial lie to its pretension of concern for violations of democratic principles wherever they occurred; and its frequent cry of "traitor" at Roosevelt's domestic opponents was of the same pitch as Martin Dies's cry of "Communist" at critics of the House Special Committee on Un-American Activities.

These strictures aside, this much has to be said: the policies of the Nashville convention came close to success. At the end of the war, the Southern Conference for Human Welfare almost became the leader of all Southern reform organizations.[9]

9. Financial Report, Southern Conference for Human Welfare, 1942; Financial Report, Southern Conference for Human Welfare, 1943: SCEF. *The Southern Patriot*, I, II, all issues. Edgar Stern to Will Alexander, May 25, 1944; Alexander to Clark Foreman, May 31, 1944; Dombrowski to Alexander, June 27, 1944: SCHW Records, TI, box No. 5.

6

PREPARATIONS FOR THE POSTWAR WORLD

BY late 1943, the Allied Powers had taken the worst the Nazi war machine could fling at them and had begun to destroy its products almost as fast as they came off the assembly line. On the western front, they had conquered Italy up to Monte Cassino. On the eastern front, the Russians had turned the Germans back at Stalingrad and their counter offensives had carried them to the Dnieper, where they held several bridgeheads. An invasion of France was in the offing for 1944. Barring some fantastic secret weapon, Hitler's thousand-year empire would crumble in one or two more years. In the Pacific, American forces had isolated the Japanese stronghold of Rabaul and secured Tarawa and Makin in the Gilbert Islands. An assault on the Philippines impended; so did an amphibious campaign to provide the United States with air bases within striking distance of the Japanese home islands. The extended members of the Greater East Asia Co-Prosperity Sphere and the Third German Empire had either been clipped or hacked off; the end, to paraphrase Churchill, had begun. American liberals could divert more attention to domestic reforms and they could begin to plan for the forthcoming peace.

Meanwhile domestic developments had threatened the New Deal. The elections of 1942 had gone against the Administration. Both the House and the Senate, as a result, were under control of Republicans and conservative Democrats. A majority of the state governments were in similar hands. Southern Democrats, angry over the edicts of the Fair Employment Practices Committee, verged on an open break with the President. American conservatives seemed ready to substitute an old deal for the New.

Between the elections of 1942 and 1944, however, liberals had at least one cause for optimism. In the spring of 1944, the United States Supreme Court, having three years before held that state primaries intimately bound up with federal elections were subject to federal regulation, declared the Texas Democratic party's white primaries unconstitutional within the meaning of the Fifteenth Amendment. Here was indirect judicial sanction for the Southern Conference's criticism of Southern voting restrictions. Although the Court had refused to reverse its opinion affirming the constitutionality of the poll tax, it had at least overruled the more obvious attempts to keep Negroes from the polls. The Southern Conference could take heart; it could diversify its attempts to reform the South's undemocratic electoral system. Negroes now had federal support for their efforts to participate in Southern politics. Southern liberals of both races could add Negro voter registration drives to their labors against the poll tax.

International and national developments required reconsideration of both strategy and tactics. Broad goals had to be redefined—perhaps merely repeated—for the coming peace. Specific programs were needed; the electoral defeats of 1942 had to be reversed; the Supreme Court's decisions had to be implemented.[1]

II

At the Nashville convention, Conference members voiced concern for the character of the peace to follow the defeat of international fascism. Hoping to avoid the mistakes of 1919, they had proposed a postwar association of nations built around the Big Three. Although primarily concerned with winning the war, they had demanded reforms to effect Franklin Roosevelt's four freedoms: freedom from want, freedom from fear, freedom of speech, and freedom of religion. The organization had dwelt mainly on the first two freedoms; its proposals, for the most part, dealt with economic problems and with the economic sources of personal and social insecurity. Only secondarily was the Conference concerned with freedom of speech and freedom of religion: and, here, it advocated limitations on the First Amendment freedoms of some of Roosevelt's most bitter critics.

With peace clearly in view, Conference leaders initiated a reconsideration of the organization's program. As early as 1942, Dombrowski and Foreman began to solicit suggestions from members of the executive board about the Conference's work after the war.

Lillian Smith, the Conference's most persistent gadfly, complained of the excessive number of Negroes and laborites in the Conference, for they were blindly partisan. She begged Dombrowski to remember that

> The South desperately needs men and women with enough vision, imagination, knowledge and selfless interest to see the whole picture, to strive to develop the whole region. Which explains my monotonous urging upon those who have most influence in the Conference to invite and encourage more and more social scientists . . . more and more intellectuals and more

1. Since the above information is readily available, citations would be superfluous. The Court cases are: *United States* v. *Classic*, 313 *U.S.* 299 (1941) and *Smith* v. *Allwright*, 321 *U.S.* 649 (1944).

and more representatives of professional groups and the "white collar worker"! [2]

Her complaints exhausted, she urged the organization to continue working for the abolition of the poll tax and to cease pussy-footing on the race question; she wished a forthright stand in favor of integration.

For Arthur Raper, the sociologist, the country's central problems were the peace settlement, full employment, and democratic control of economic and political concentrations of power. Raper merely outlined the problems; he was unable to say how the Southern Conference might help to solve them.

Tarleton Collier, briefly chairman of the Conference in 1943, was clearer. The Southern Conference's first task, he realistically noted, was to stay alive; alive, it could voice protests of Southern liberals where conditions and developments seemed to warrant them. Alive, it could work for the extension of democracy. The Conference should work against race discrimination, or, failing that, work to mitigate the evils of segregation. It should press the labor movement to admit Negro workers in every trade and occupation. The Conference should disseminate opinions favorable to a global entente of the democratic powers to keep the peace. Collier was equally clear about the means the Conference had to use. "I have become confirmed," he told Clark Foreman, "in the conviction that we are not going to do anything . . . in the South without organization of the little people"—a patronizing phrase common among Southern Conference leaders and among American liberals generally during the New Deal—"and that this is not going to be accomplished except through a widespread, democratic and UNIVERSAL labor movement that will . . . prevail against the red herring of race, communism, cio [sic], etc. etc. There flatly isn't any other way than through power." [3]

2. Smith to Dombrowski, June 1, 1942, SCHW Records, TI, box No. 5.

3. Collier to Helen Fuller, December 12, 1942, SCHW Records, TI, box No. 6; the quote is from Collier to Clark Foreman, undated [1943 (?)], Foreman Papers, AU. The capitalization of universal is his.

Several of the executive board's labor representatives disagreed. M. C. Plunk, General Chairman of the Gulf States Federation of the Brotherhood of Maintenance of Way Employees, acknowledged the nation had to win the war and secure the peace; but the Southern Conference, he argued, should concentrate on abolition of the poll tax and on promotion of better understanding between capital and labor. Hollis Reid, who had been a La Follette progressive in 1924 and subsequently chairman of the Legislative Board of the Brotherhood of Locomotive Firemen and Engineers, hoped the Southern Conference would help to stimulate a spiritual awakening; "a real observance of the philosophy of the man Christ as recorded in the New Testament would do more to bring the peoples of the earth to a better understanding than all the political moves backed by the popes [sic], Bishops and rabbis." Nor would political schemes mitigate the conflict between capital and labor; "Employer and employee must meet on the broad ground of friendship and understanding. . . ."[4] Aside from applied Christianity and amity between capital and labor, Reid urged the Conference to support labor's demands for a just and living wage; employers unable to pay such a wage should go out of business. Reid also favored the establishment of an organization for the prevention of war.

One labor representative offered a dissenting opinion. Lucy Randolph Mason, CIO public relations director in Atlanta, a devoted member of the Conference from 1938 to 1947, agreed with Collier; Conference demands could not be effected without the support of a strong labor movement. The Conference, in short, needed power to transform its fair words into fair accomplishments.

Although Negro members of the executive board differed among themselves on some details of the Conference's program, they were at one on the need for an attack on segregation. John P. Davis recommended a mass propaganda campaign to show that "the rank and file of the white South is fully prepared to see the Negro accorded a fair opportunity to participate in the war effort. This is

4. Reid to Dombrowski, January 4, 1944, SCHW Records, TI, box No. 5

what we mean by mobilizing the South for victory." [5] F. D. Patterson, President of Tuskegee Institute, suggested the Southern Conference work to end sectional discrimination against the South and "injustice and discrimination..., especially as it relates to the various minority groups such as Negroes, labor and women." [6] Additionally, he wished the Conference to work to create a climate of opinion favorable to progressive legislation. Charles S. Johnson wanted the Conference to face four main issues: postwar planning for the South, the poll tax, vote for the soldiers serving overseas, and racial segregation. He was especially concerned about segregation within the labor movement; "the restrictive and exclusive racial policies of a group of unions... are seriously qualifying the moral as well as social and economic underpinnings of organized labor." [7] Rufus Clement hoped the Conference would honestly assess the Southern race problem and declare itself in favor of the soldiers' vote bill. Clement, too, seems to have hoped the Conference would increase its work against the Jim Crow system.

All of these suggestions agreed on one point: the peace of the world had to be secured. Once it was, the Southern Conference could pursue its reform work without fear of international distractions. The differences over the details of the program required the Conference to adopt a program of action broad enough to satisfy as many of its supporters as possible.

On January 22 and 23, 1944, the Conference executive board met at Black Mountain College in North Carolina. Clark Foreman, Charlotte Hawkins Brown, who, in the style of Mary McLeod Bethune, had founded her own school, Gerald Harris, F. Clyde Helms, a Baptist minister from South Carolina, Tarleton Collier, Lillian Smith, and James Dombrowski were the only official members able to attend. Concentrating on domestic problems, the board proposed an excess war-profits' tax to be used to retire the war debt

5. Davis to Dombrowski, January 27, 1943, *ibid.*
6. Patterson to Dombrowski, May 8, 1943, *ibid.*
7. Johnson to Dombrowski, January 3, 1944, *ibid.*

and prevent inflation. It supported uniform freight rates, food subsidies, the Farm Security Administration's rural rehabilitation programs, and a federal anti-poll tax statute. In connection with the latter proposal, the board wired Senator Mead of New York in support of a bill then pending in the Senate to abolish the tax. The board regretted Congress' failure to provide federal aid to education. These were familiar demands, familiar oppositions, familiar regrets.

The necessities of total war gave vitality and increased importance to new demands. The board sent a telegram to Virginius Dabney of the Richmond *Times-Dispatch* commending his "valiant efforts to bring an end to the practice of segregation in transportation carriers as a move in behalf of the causes for which the nation fights today which is essentially a struggle for democracy and human dignity." The year before, the Conference had come to the support of the President's Fair Employment Practices Committee; at Black Mountain, the board reiterated the Southern Conference's support of the FEPC and condemned a group of Southern railroads that had defied FEPC orders. It asked Roosevelt to take "uncompromising action to uphold the original order, for the sake not only of free and equal opportunity in America, but as well, of the integrity and strength of all our institutions." The Conference's initial opposition to segregation of its meetings had expanded in the space of six years to an outspoken opposition to segregation in some aspects of Southern life—a transformation largely ascribable to the need for total war mobilization.

At Black Mountain, the executive board also decided to set up state committees. The idea dated back to 1939 when a few state study groups had been established. They discussed some and did little. Scarcity of funds had prevented the Conference from hiring full-time administrators to keep the groups in operation. Yet Conference leaders had continued to hope and to plan for the day when state committees would be practicable. By 1944 they were optimistic; revenues were increasing and the Conference's program for the postwar South demanded local organizations. The state committees would lobby for the Conference's legislative program and work to increase the Southern electorate—especially the Negro electorate. What was now needed was either a respectable name or a powerful ally.[8]

III

The search for a respectable name had begun before the war. In 1940, during the prolonged struggle between the Conference's interventionists and isolationists, Frank Graham and Clark Foreman had tried to persuade Will Alexander to assume the Conference chairmanship and Howard W. Odum to take on the executive secretaryship. Both had declined. Alexander retained an interest in the Southern Conference, agreeing to serve on the *Southern Patriot*'s editorial board. Odum, always suspicious of the Conference's sources of support and of some of its leaders, remained aloof; yet he counseled Conference members who sought him out and he at least considered plans for a merger of the Southern Conference and his Southern Regional Council. Had either the attempt to hire Alexander or the proposal to merge with the Regional Council succeeded, the Southern Conference would have had the active support of two of the most respected of Southern liberals—men whose Americanism, if not their Southernism, was beyond reproach.

Planning for the Regional Council had begun as early as 1938. Designed to replace the Commission on Interracial Co-operation, the Council rested on the assumption that the quiet, persuasive tactics of the CIC could now be supplanted by more forthright methods; Odum wanted sound, long-range planning to replace the CIC's piecemeal gradualism. The Council developed out of a series of wartime conferences. In October, 1942, leading Southern Negroes met at Durham, North Carolina to inform the South of the grievances of her black minority. The conferees declared their opposition to the poll tax, the white primary, and compulsory segregation;

8. Minutes Executive Board Meeting, January 22, 23, 1944, SCEF possession. The earlier resolution on the F.E.P.C. is in Minutes Executive Board Meeting, February 7, 1943, SCEF possession. Lucy Mason to Philip Murray, October 30, 1944, Mason Papers, Duke, Letters–1944 October—1947 February.

they demanded an end to all forms of discrimination and to police brutality. They asked that Negroes be admitted to jury duty. They asked for Negro sections in all public hospitals, for the employment of Negro doctors and nurses in such hospitals, and for slum-clearance and housing projects to help the Negro poor. Like the Southern Conference before them, the Durham conferees asked that the South live up to the promises of separate-but-equal educational facilities; they desired equal school facilities and equitable allocation of funds. Thus, although opposed to compulsory segregation, the Durham leaders were unprepared to demand—or unable to see the implications of their demands—a complete end to Southern segregation. They sounded a note of faith; "We . . . believe . . . that it is possible to evolve in the South a way of life, consistent with the principles for which we are fighting . . . , that will free us all, white and Negro alike, from want, and from throttling fears." [9]

The following spring, in Atlanta, Southern white liberals met to answer the Durham statement. Hailing it as frank and courageous, the Atlanta conferees pledged their co-operation. And in June 1943, at Richmond, Virginia, members of the Durham and Atlanta Conferences met to plan for a permanent organization. Eight months later, in February 1944, their plans matured in the Southern Regional Council. Its long-term goal was "the improvement of social, civic, economic, and racial conditions in the South." At the outset the Council's program was modest; it sought to co-ordinate the programs of numerous Southern reform agencies, it undertook studies of specific problems, it continued the CIC's newspaper, the *Southern Frontier*, it published educational materials, it offered advice to public and private agencies, and it initiated action "at every possible point on the social, economic, political, and racial problems of the South."

The Southern Regional Council thus had policies and programs in common—if not in competition—with the Southern Conference for

9. Quoted in Charles S. Johnson, *et al.*, *Into the Mainstream* (Chapel Hill: University of North Carolina Press, 1947), p. 8, and pp. 5–11 for the source of most of the rest of the information on the SRC. For Odum's earlier plans, see Chapter 2, section I above.

Human Welfare. The two organizations might either unite or co-operate.

From the beginning of the Council's preparatory conferences, Southern Conference officials interested themselves in the new organization. Home from a trip overseas, Clark Foreman, later a member of the Regional Council, called the Durham Conference the best thing he had heard since his return. "The statement of the Durham Conference," he added eagerly, "is so in line with the aims of the Southern Conference and so many of the membership are . . . members of the Southern Conference, that it seems obvious that we will have a broad basis for co-operation." [10] Others thought the two organizations should merge. When organization of the Council had been assured, Will Alexander asked members of the Southern Conference to confer with him and other members of the Regional Council to discuss unification of the two organizations. Charles S. Johnson, a member of both organizations, supported the proposal.

The proposed merger failed. The Southern Conference, Dombrowski later claimed, had agreed to unification only if membership were open to all who wished to join and membership conventions decided the organization's main policies. Council leaders, his account continues, rejected these stipulations; they wished to control both the membership and the organization's policies. On the other hand, early in 1944, Odum wrote to the Southern Conference advising against unification. And that ended the merger negotiations.

Although the two organizations failed to unite, they at least stayed out of each other's way and may have refrained from sniping at one another. In mid 1944, Lillian Smith asked to write a piece on segregation for the *Southern Patriot.* Miss Smith, who had refused to join the Regional Council because of its failure to declare itself in open opposition to segregation, was asked to refrain from voicing her criticisms of the new organization. "I don't want," Foreman told Dombrowski, "to attack the SRC in the *Patriot.* There is room enough for both organizations and if Lillian [Smith] wants to work only with us that's fine. But there are others who will work only with

10. Foreman to Charles S. Johnson, August 13, 1943, Foreman Papers, AU.

the SRC. So let's have both and no time wasted in attacking each other." [11] The Council, he had earlier told Dombrowski, was "developing into a pretty good organization." [12]

IV

The Southern Conference's attempt to unite with the Southern Regional Council may have resulted from its precarious financial situation. In addition to promising greater respectability for the causes the Southern Conference championed, merger may have seemed the only hope for a moribund organization.

Whatever the case, by early 1944 Conference hopes had revived. Victory over international fascism seemed assured. Pressing domestic concerns had to be dealt with. Roosevelt had to be re-elected to insure a lasting peace and the security of his domestic reforms. A large progressive vote had to be turned out in November; Negroes must register: the work against the poll tax had to go on. Fortunately, the Southern Conference found itself in agreement with the most progressive and politically active segment of the American labor movement.

The CIO had also taken alarm at the results of the 1942 elections. In the summer of 1943, the organization announced the formation of the CIO Political Action Committee under the direction of Sidney Hillman. Hillman toured the country's major industrial centers to plan a program and to discuss the possibility of a united labor league, including the CIO, the AFofL, and the Railroad Brotherhoods. In co-operation with other progressives, the projected league would support candidates for office and conduct voter registration drives.

11. Foreman to Dombrowski, June 22, 1944, SCHW Records, TI, box No. 5.

12. Same to same, May 2, 1944, *ibid.* On Alexander and Johnson: Dombrowski to Lillian Smith, June 16, 1944, SCHW Records, TI, box No. 6; Dombrowski to Foreman, October 16, 1943, SCHW Records, TI, box No. 5. Odum's letter was read to the executive board, January 22, 1944: Minutes Executive Board Meeting, January 22, 23, 1944, SCEF possession. Guy B. Johnson to author, May 11, 1965. Dr. Johnson was kind enough to read and criticize this section. In his letter, he indicates that Conference members did snipe at the SRC but gives few details.

At its 1943 convention, the CIO endorsed Roosevelt's re-election and the work of the CIO-PAC. "Our primary task . . . is to weld the unity of all workers, farmers, and other progressives behind candidates, regardless of party affiliation, who are committed to our policy of total victory and who fully support the measures necessary to achieve it and to lay the basis for a secure, peaceful, decent and abundant postwar world." [13] In January, 1944, in New York, the CIO-PAC sponsored a conference on full employment. Progressives of every occupation were invited: intellectuals, economists, businessmen, government experts, farm-bloc representatives, and social workers. They agreed that full employment should be one of the country's postwar goals; it would, they reasoned in the fashion of most American progressives, guarantee maximum domestic purchasing power. With maximum purchasing power, Americans could consume most, if not all, of the goods the country produced, thereby lessening its dependence on foreign markets. Every class, every occupational group, would benefit. To insure full employment, Franklin Roosevelt had to be re-elected.

Although the united labor league remained unborn, the CIO-PAC developed out of the conference on full employment a broader progressive coalition. During the summer of 1944, Sidney Hillman announced the formation of the National Citizens Political Action Committee, an organization of nonunion liberals, designed to get out the vote for Roosevelt and other progressives, to "bring out," in Clark Foreman's words, "the real issues of our time," and to publicize the records of candidates for public office. Frankly a development out of the CIO-PAC, the National Citizens Political Action Committee considered itself "the instrument at hand for concrete expression of progressive principles." [14]

Both Foreman and Dombrowski joined the NC-PAC; Foreman

13. Quoted in Delbert D. Arnold, "The C.I.O.'s Role in American Politics, 1936–48," unpublished Ph.D. thesis, University of Maryland, 1952, p. 97. Most of the information on the CIO-PAC comes from this thesis, pp. 92ff.

14. Clark Foreman, "Statement of the National Citizens Political Action Committee," *The Antioch Review*, IV (September 1944), 473–475. Interview, Paul Christopher, Knoxville, Tennessee, February 25, 1964.

was active in the organization from its inception to its merger with the Independent Citizens Committee for the Arts, Sciences, and Professions in 1947. Both took time off from the Southern Conference during 1944 to work with the CIO-PAC for Roosevelt's re-election. Together with Lucy Mason they solicited CIO help for the Southern Conference.

Immediately following Roosevelt's re-election, Foreman and Dombrowski submitted a memorandum to the CIO executive committee analyzing Southern political and economic developments, prescribing plans of action to further progressive causes, and requesting both formal endorsement and financial aid. The South, the memorandum argued in familiar terms, was at once the most reactionary area of the country and potentially its most progressive region. It was the source of poll-tax congressmen who dominated congressional committees, the origin of most of the nation's fascist and quasi-fascist movements, and the center of the country's most aggressive anti-labor organizations. No other region had so benefitted from the New Deal. The progressive South, the South of the workers, the small farmers, and the sharecroppers, would, if given the vote, return progressive candidates to office in overwhelming numbers. Two million Southerners belonged to unions; together with their families, they accounted for some ten millions of the South's total population. These seldom voted: in Alabama in 1944, the total vote for Dewey and Roosevelt had amounted to a mere quarter of the total number of industrial workers of voting age within the state; in Georgia, the total vote for Roosevelt and Dewey was a mere third of the total number of industrial workers of voting age; and in Virginia, the figure was one-half. In the seven poll-tax states, 2.6 million had voted; in these same states 6.6 million industrial workers of voting age lived and earned their bread. If these could be got to the polls, if they could be got to vote for their true interests, and if progressive candidates could be got to run for office, the South would be quickly transformed from the most reactionary to the most progressive region in the country.

Mass registration campaigns and active searches for progressive candidates, the tactics of the CIO-PAC and the NC-PAC, were needed. The South required, in short, the same cure which the CIO had prescribed for the rest of the country.

But the South, in its insistent peculiarity, would take such cures only from physicians with marked Southern drawls. The Southern Conference for Human Welfare was an organization of genuine, drawling Southerners; it had worked six years for goals compatible with the CIO's. Unlike the NC-PAC, it had nascent organizations in several Southern states; it would begin more, if it could acquire the necessary funds and personnel. It had a functioning regional organization; and it had a program and a plan of action.

It planned public relations work to "present the essential facts about the South in the fields of economics, politics, and race relationships . . . [and to bring] together for common action all of the persons in the South who have faith that a humane, decent, and rational world can be developed wherein intolerance and bitterness can be replaced by brotherly love. . . ." The Conference's regional office, through the *Southern Patriot* and special publications, would undertake the public relations work. Its state committees would lobby against the Christian American Association's right-to-work laws, promote progressive legislation, conduct voter registration drives, and work for the defeat of numerous Southern reactionaries up for re-election in 1946.

During the CIO's annual convention in November 1944, the organization's executive board endorsed the Southern Conference for Human Welfare. Since the Southern Conference sought to enfranchise the progressive Southern masses, the board resolved, it was "the natural and appropriate spearhead of the liberal forces of the South." The CIO should "give all positive and constructive support to the Southern Conference . . . in its efforts to abolish intolerance and discrimination, to expand to a maximum the voting population of the South, and to express the true liberalism of our great Southern states." Later the board asked its constituent unions to contribute money to the organization. Shortly thereafter, on November 25, 1944, the NC-PAC executive board adopted a similar resolution. In addition, the NC-PAC's executive board agreed not to establish branches of the NC-PAC in states where the Southern Conference had functioning committees.

The Conference's hopes had received marked stimulation. Now it had to make good on its promises and its programs.[15]

V

Between January 1944, and early 1946, the Southern Conference executive board developed in detail the organization's postwar program. Its primary aims were peace and international stability and industrialization of the South. The former aims had been implicit in the Conference's wartime campaign for victory. The latter had been the presupposition of the Conference's wartime demands for total economic mobilization; without industrialization the South could not have been expected to produce up to her capacity. Conference publications supported the Dumbarton Oaks, Bretton Woods, San Francisco, and Yalta agreements. (The Yalta agreements were supported because they promised free elections and were evidence of continuing co-operation among the Big Three, not because they involved capitulation to Russian demands.) The Conference was uncompromisingly internationalist; without international organization, the world would descend again into war, and war jeopardized the Southern Conference's domestic plans. "The South knows," the *Southern Patriot* proclaimed, "that industrialization is the answer to the problems of the South—not only its economic problems but its political and social difficulties as well. And industrialization of the South is possible only in a stable world of peaceful relations among nations."[16] Few means for bringing industry to the South were open to the Southern Conference: it could not offer tax credits; it could

15. Memorandum for the C.I.O. Executive Board, November 13, 1944, SCHW Records, TI, box No. 5. Foreman submitted drafts of the proposed resolutions to both the CIO's and the NC-PAC's executive board which were presumably adopted in substance; Foreman to Philip Murray, November 16, 1944, SCHW Records, TI, box No. 6. For a version of the resolution: SCHW Records, TI, box No. 3, "CIO Contributions File." On the relations between the NC-PAC and the Southern Conference: Dombrowski to Durward McDaniel, March 21, 1945 and Marge Frantz to McDaniel, October 19, 1944, SCHW Records, TI, box No. 4.

16. III (April 1945), 8.

not—and would not if it could—promise cheap and docile labor; it could not offer cheap power and ready access to transportation. It had to champion the one means available to it, namely, full employment. Since the Conference accepted prevalent economic notions that increased purchasing power automatically resulted in increased industrialization and production, and since only full employment could guarantee maximum purchasing power, it had additional, ideological reasons for favoring full employment. "In the South," the *Patriot* prophesied, "full employment would mean the development of more Southern industry, scattered in every state, ready to process farm products, ready to employ surplus farm labor and displaced workers." [17]

Without full employment and maximum purchasing power all other reforms would fail. The common people had to have sufficient money to pay for the things the Southern Conference demanded—and once they had sufficient money the South would no longer have to depend upon federal benefactions—including quality education, adequate medical and dental care, family-owned farms and farm equipment; they needed, in short, enough money to provide for their own wants. But this was a long-range possibility. In the meantime, the Conference would have to continue to ask for federal aid to the South and combine with kindred spirits against the region's conservatives, who, though similarly interested in industrialization, opposed a strong labor movement and an adequate system of public health and social security. But the Conference could not procure federal aid by demanding it; it lacked the popular support to make its demands effective. It would have to make a direct contribution to Southern progress in other ways. It could work for laws guarantying full and fair employment; it could agitate for the repeal of the poll tax. It could lobby at Southern state legislatures and in Washington. It could work for or against political candidates. It could, in a word, try to educate the South by spreading the gospel of the New Deal and try to reform the region by electing New Deal apostles to public office.

With its hopes and its fortunes on the rise, Conference activities

17. III (August 1945), 5.

picked up. During 1944 and 1945, it diversified its efforts to enlarge the Southern electorate. It secured 6,000 signatures to a petition in support of a Senate bill to abolish the poll tax in federal elections. It got several hundred Southerners to sign a public statement in favor of the Supreme Court's decision in the Texas white primary case. It publicized voter registration dates and registration procedures. In December 1944, in Atlanta, it initiated a meeting called the Committee of Writers and Editors of the South; the delegates unanimously favored the abolition of the poll tax and the white primary. (The meeting may have helped spur Governor Ellis Arnall to action; under his threats to abolish the poll tax by decree, the Georgia legislature repealed the impost early in 1945.) The Conference also secured the signatures of one hundred college professors to a petition protesting the dismissal of Homer P. Rainey from the presidency of the University of Texas. In 1944, it persuaded prominent Alabamans to protest against the injection of the race issue into the senatorial contest between Lister Hill and Jim Simpson. In 1945, after James O. Eastland had declared that the Negro soldier "was an utter and dismal failure" who "will not fight" and "will not work," the Conference conducted an informal poll of Southern newspapers; more than 80 percent of the 250 who replied declared that Eastland's remarks hindered the war effort and 75 percent claimed that the Senator's comments did not express true Southern opinion on the matter. The Conference also circulated petitions opposing Southern filibuster against a permanent FEPC.

Throughout the latter years of the war, the Conference's main regional enterprise remained the *Southern Patriot*. The paper's circulation continued to increase; by March 1945, its editions ran to seventeen thousand copies. It continued to editorialize in support of general Southern Conference goals, to provide items of interest to Southern liberals about international, national, and regional developments, and to run feature articles. It ran muckraking pieces on several Southern reactionary organizations: the Christian American Association, which under the leadership of Vance Muse and the financial support of John Henry Kirby, Texas oil and timber millionaire, had taken the lead in the campaign for Southern right-to-work laws; an antilabor, white supremacist paper called *Militant Truth.* It ran features on the South's special problems in health, education, agriculture, and industry. State government departments in North Carolina and Georgia used the health feature; and the United States Department of Agriculture Library ordered a thousand copies of the issue. A *Patriot* feature on freedom from want, advocating 65 cents an hour minimum wage, went to ten thousand Southern ministers. In addition to the *Patriot,* the Conference published other materials and made the publications of kindred organizations available to its readers. Its pamphlet "For Your Children Too," a favorable presentation of labor's case for unionism, collective bargaining, and high wages, received praise from *Labor,* the house organ of the railroad brotherhoods, which called it the best work ever done to interpret labor to a nonlabor audience. In Mississippi, Methodist church women distributed the tract to two hundred of their churches. Among the pamphlets the Conference disseminated were pieces denouncing antisemitism and white supremacy, and championing interracial toleration.

To supplement these educational activities, the Conference took direct political action in the states and municipalities. By the end of 1945, the organization had eleven state committees set up. Of these, the most active were in Alabama, Georgia, and North Carolina; the others were either inactive or ineffectual.

In the summer of 1944, the Committee for Alabama was established under the chairmanship of the Reverend Daniel Whitsett, a Methodist minister whose political preferences ran to Norman Thomas, and the executive secretaryship of Pauline Dobbs, whose husband had been active in the League of Young Southerners and the Southern Conference before the war. About one third of the original group came from organized labor; the Committee had the support of the Birmingham CIO chieftain, Carey Haigler, and of the local Mine Workers Head, William Mitch, even though John L. Lewis was still at odds with Roosevelt and his supporters. An additional third of the members came from religious organizations and the final third came from a hodgepodge of midde-class groups. Despite strong advice to the contrary from James Folsom, later governor of Alabama, and Luther Patrick, congressman from Birmingham, the Committee insisted on openly acknowledging its affiliation with the Southern Conference.

James Dombrowski instructed Mrs. Dobbs to get voters registered, to solicit letters in support of the army's desegregation policy, to lobby against right-to-work laws, to stimulate support for the extension of TVA power into Birmingham, and to work for bills to strengthen existing child labor and workmen's compensation laws. She was further told "to cement relations between [Lister] Hill and the group" through conferences "between Hill and a selected group of leaders from time to time when Hill is in the South," and to "see that labor and other leaders speak to [Luther] Patrick about his alleged opposition to federal poll tax repeal." [18]

She was explicitly directed to maintain cordial relations with organized labor. During the Birmingham municipal elections of 1945, the local CIO decided for some obscure reason to endorse Bull Connor for re-election as City Commissioner. Mrs. Dobbs planned to oppose Connor. Dombrowski warned her against an open break with the CIO over Connor;

> the qualifications of a given candidate are irrelevant so far as the policy of the SCHW is concerned. No candidate should be endorsed . . . whether for or against, until you have the unanimous agreement . . . of all of the labor groups co-operating with the Conference. . . . [Y]our disparaging reference to Connor . . . could be interpreted as endorsing his opposition. . . . [T]he fate of a local candidate is unimportant compared with the good will of one of the major labor groups.[19]

Mrs. Dobbs followed her orders.

She did so elsewhere as well. The Committee for Alabama got Arthur Shores and Crampton Harris to draft a model bill for the repeal of the state's poll tax and circulated petitions in favor of

18. Dombrowski to Mrs. Dobbs, September 6, 1944, SCHW Records, TI, box No. 4.

19. Same to same, May 2, 1945, *ibid.*

repeal among the American Association of University Women, the state's Business and Professional Women's Clubs, and other interested organizations. The Committee produced posters to advertise places and dates for voter registration, some of which were placed in store windows in downtown Birmingham. The Committee later developed more effective means of communication; it sponsored radio forums and sporadically published a newsletter, dealing with bills pending in the Alabama legislature. Mrs. Dobbs helped expose the right-wing priest, Arthur Terminiello, who was later a principal in a famous court case. The good woman even tried to interest more businessmen in the Committee; "Some effort, but by no means enough, has been made to include more business representation on the Alabama Committee." [20]

The Alabama Committee suffered from its connection with the Southern Conference. Too many in the state remembered the Birmingham convention's resolution on segregation. Too many thought the Conference advocated total integration of the two races. Some of the state's liberal politicians dealt with the Committee quietly, privately. Many interested liberals failed to join. The Committee's finances suffered. Few besides Mrs. Dobbs, her husband, after he returned from the war, and Aubrey Williams, who came home from Washington in 1945, were willing to devote much time to its affairs. Consequently, the Committee was largely ineffectual—although its efforts to register voters doubtless yielded some positive results.

The Georgia Committee fared better. Founded early in 1945, shortly after the meeting of the Committee of Writers and Editors, its initial membership numbered 105 persons. Harry Strozier, a Macon lawyer and part time contributor to the Macon *News*, chaired the group; Margaret Fisher, the organizer of the Committee of Writers and Editors of the South meeting, took the post of executive secretary; Benjamin Mays, President of Spellman College, became secretary treasurer; and Lucy Randolph Mason was the vice chairman.

20. *News of the Alabama Committee*, v. I, no. 1, *ibid.*

Miss Fisher, the guiding genius of the Committee, expressed its aims.

> If the efforts of business and professional people, ministers, teachers, labor, farmers, white collar workers, and all other forward-looking citizens in Georgia were united, it would create a climate throughout the state conducive to sound social and economic legislation. We need more and better schools, expanded public health services, increased employment opportunities, an unrestricted ballot, more representative government, more adequate housing and recreational facilities, increased aid to farmers, and many other advantages in order to have a healthy, prosperous, and democratic state.[21]

Having secured the active co-operation of the local CIO director, Charles Gillman, Miss Fisher first appealed to the voters of Georgia to deluge the state legislature with letters and post cards in favor of the repeal of the state's poll tax. Since both Eugene Talmadge and Governor Arnall had declared themselves in favor of repeal, this may have been unnecessary. In any event, the tax was repealed early in 1945. Subsequently, Miss Fisher organized opposition to a proposed right-to-work amendment, tried to drum up support for a permanent FEPC, and co-operated with the forces opposed to the state's white primary. She spoke to church, civic, and labor groups, encouraged letters to the newspapers, conferred with legislators, worked with other reform organizations, kept the voting records of Georgia legislators, and maintained friendly relations with journalists.

During its first year, the Committee for Georgia issued a newsletter, *Let the People Know,* as the occasion seemed to warrant, in which the Committee's views on major issues were publicized. Its first number summarized, discussed, and editorialized in favor of the full employment bill then pending in Congress, contending that the bill would foster and support free enterprise. The Committee later issued a pamphlet entitled *Your Part in Georgia's Politics* to interest more Georgians in public affairs. Appearing under the slogan that good government depended upon an informed citizenry,

21. Fisher to W. A. Swinson, January 6, 1945, *ibid.*

the pamphlet provided details about state registration procedures, voting regulations, primary dates, congressional districts, the county-unit system, the state's elections, the state's federal representatives and senators, and the state's executive, judicial, and legislative personnel. The Atlanta *Constitution* urged every citizen to get a copy of the pamphlet and commended the Committee: "The fine services of the Committee for Georgia, the League of Women Voters and similar groups will have their rewards in a government representative of all the people instead of a few favored cliques." [22]

The Committee's successes were reflected in its membership and its finances. By the end of 1945, the Committee had about 300 members. During its first eleven months the Committee's receipts totaled $5,755—a substantial sum by the Southern Conference's impoverished standards. During its short life, the Committee for Georgia remained one of the Conference's most effective state organizations.

The Committe for North Carolina began slowly. Conference leaders spent nearly six months looking for an executive secretary; in the summer of 1945, they were able to secure the services of Mary Price, a native North Carolinian who had worked for a time in 1940 and 1941 as Walter Lippman's secretary. She in turn spent another five months in search of a chairman; in November, she persuaded the Reverend Lee C. Sheppard, pastor of the Pullen Memorial Baptist Church in Raleigh, to take the post. She also had trouble interesting North Carolina liberals in the organization; many of them feared the Conference was a front for the CIO—a fear she, too, entertained and sought to allay in them and in herself. Once, she took Dombrowski to task for a speech in which he conveyed the impression that the Southern Conference was a tool of the Southern labor movement.

Having at last convinced a sufficient number of liberals of the Conference's independence of the labor movement, Miss Price was able to organize the Committee for North Carolina late in December 1945. With an initial membership of 105, its program included a denunciation of Truman's attempts to abridge the right to strike,

22. Editorial, April 14, 1946.

and declarations in support of a permanent FEPC, diversification of North Carolina's agriculture and industry, a 65-cent-an-hour minimum wage, adequate income for both farmers and workers, and equal educational facilities for whites and Negroes. It planned to secure the passage of a state Wagner Act and state minimum-wage-maximum-hour laws to cover workers not covered by the Fair Labor Standards Act. Its first accomplishment was a four-page leaflet, "Uncle Sam Needs Your Vote," urging North Carolinians to do their duty and vote.

These three were the only significant committees set up in Southern states toward the end of the war. Beginnings were made in South Carolina, Florida, Texas, Louisiana, and Tennessee. In the latter state, the Conference had had active members from its inception. These had worked in coalition organizations supported or initiated by the Southern Conference: the Conference on Democracy in Tennessee in 1939 and the Tennessee Commonwealth Federation of 1941, both mainly concerned with the repeal of the state's poll tax. Their efforts were rewarded after the war. Local groups existed in Nashville during the war and, after the war, in Chattanooga. The Nashville group labored to ease race tensions and to have Negro policemen employed. It also protested military and civilian police brutality to Negro soldiers and civilians. The Chattanooga group's doings cannot be traced.

Outside the Southern states, additional committees were formed in New York City and Washington, D. C. The New York Committee was organized early in 1945 to raise money for the Southern Conference. Including Mrs. Roosevelt, Channing Tobias, one of the few Negroes ever to achieve prominence in the YMCA, and other New York liberals, its members were barred from voting at Southern Conference conventions and none of them had significant influence over Conference policies.

The Washington Committee soon became one of the Conference's most vital local organizations. Because the District of Columbia was located in the South, the Washington Committee's members were granted voting rights in the Conference. The organization drew on the large number of liberal Southerners in the District for members and for funds. Organized in the summer of 1944, the Washington Committee stimulated interest in the Southern Conference's program, raised funds for the organization, and united D. C.'s Southern colony for action on specific issues affecting the South. The Committee included Mrs. Clifford J. Durr, chairman, Helen Fuller, vice-chairman, and such luminaries as Will Alexander, Frank Graham, Mary McLeod Bethune, Arthur Raper, and John P. Davis. At first it staged monthly lunches at which distinguished speakers discoursed on their special interests as these related to Southern problems. Both it and the New York Committee staged fund-raising dinners at which for the first time black and white members of the Southern Conference publicly ate together.

In 1945, The Washington Committee added a legislative office to keep accurate records on congressional voting, to prepare statements on bills pending in Congress, to get out mailings of Conference propaganda, and to co-operate with like-minded organizations. For the remainder of its existence, the Committee presented statements to Congress on nearly every important piece of domestic legislation dealing with economic and social welfare. Late in 1945, it adopted an ambitious program calling for adequate prices for farmers, expanded markets for their produce, application of science to industrial reconversion, public housing, slum clearance, rural housing projects, full employment, higher minimum wages, the Hill-Burton hospital construction bill, and other Southern Conference projects. If anything, its demands were more sweeping than the parent organization's. In one instance it went significantly beyond the Southern Conference; it demanded an end to discrimination in travel, recreation, and education. By the end of 1945, it had 288 members.

Thus six months after the war ended the Southern Conference had greatly expanded its sphere of activities. It had the endorsement of the CIO and its financial support. Although its local committees had made but modest starts, they were functioning in some places and in others growing. The Conference had grown rapidly, and found many new sources of support. Its good fortune and changed plans necessitated an internal reorganization.[23]

VI

The Conference's increased range of activities attracted attention. Not only did the CIO executive board endorse the organization's efforts to extend the franchise but the regional CIO convention in Atlanta in September 1945 also declared its support. In 1944, the N.A.A.C.P. executive board adopted a resolution endorsing the Conference's work; a year later Thurgood Marshall, in a speech to the Georgia N.A.A.C.P., praised the Southern Conference and requested financial aid for it. New York and Washington newspapers reported the fund-raising dinners of the local Conference Committees. The *Southern Patriot*'s features were taken up in bulk lots; its specials on Southern reactionary organizations were used by Northern liberal columnists and newspapers. Thomas L. Stokes mentioned the Conference favorably, as did Frank Kingdon, Walter Winchell's substitute, and J. Raymond Walsh, a New York newscaster. Both *PM*, Marshall Field's liberal tabloid, and the New York *Post* ran special articles on the Southern Conference. Conservative and white supremacist delegates to Congress from the South also took notice; late in 1945, Theodore A. Bilbo called the organization the South's number-one enemy.

23. Executive Secretary's Report for 1944; Minutes Executive Board Meeting, January 27, 28, 1945; Minutes Executive Board Meeting, April 4, 1945; Dombrowski to Members of the Executive Board, April 25, 1945; same to same, July 18, 1945; same to same, August 7, 1945; Executive Secretary's Report, September 12, 1945; Minutes Executive Board Meeting, September 12, 1945: SCEF possession. Southern Conference for Human Welfare, Activities 1945–1946, SCHW Records, TI, box No. 3. *The Southern Patriot*, II and III, *passim*. Committee of Writers and Editors of the South, *We the People* (n.p.: n.p., n.d.); Clark Foreman, "Georgia Kills the Poll Tax," *The New Republic*, February 26, 1945, pp. 291–292. On the Committee for Alabama: P. Dobbs to Marge Frantz, October 10, 1944; same to Dombrowski, April 30, 1945: SCHW Records, TI, box No. 4. On the Committee for North Carolina: Marge Frantz to Eleanor Hoaglund, June 8, 1945; Mary Price to Dombrowski, July 25, 1945; same to same, August 24, 1945; same to same, October 12, 1945; same to same, November 11, 1945; Lee C. Sheppard to Dombrowski, December 10, 1945; Carolyn Goldberg to Dombrowski, December 12, 1945: SCHW Records, TI, box No. 4. Foreman Papers, AU, contain a file on the Washington Committee and some information on the New York Committee.

As Conference fame and notoriety spread, its membership and its wealth increased. At the Birmingham Convention, the Conference had enrolled about 1,250 persons. During the years before the war, the total membership seems to have declined—to a low point in 1942 of some 500. But by mid 1945, the organization had 1,224 Southern members and 1,525, non-Southern or associate members. In addition nearly 10,000 persons subscribed to the *Southern Patriot.* The Conference's greatest increase in memberships came early in 1946; by the middle of that year the organization claimed more than 6,000 members—many recruited by Mary McLeod Bethune during a speaking tour for the Conference early in 1946.

In 1944, the Conference drummed up $17,166.70; $7,477.94 came from private individuals, the Conference's loyal, wealthy friends, and its rank-and-file members. Foundations contributed $5,500 and unions contributed $4,100. That amounted to 100 percent increase over its income in 1943. In 1945, the Conference's total income was $82,583: members and private contributors accounted for $34,475.27; unions gave $28,395; and foundations added $17,234.37. In one year, Conference income had quadrupled.

The Southern Conference's good fortune coincided with and stimulated its plans of action for the postwar South. By the end of 1945, these plans had produced several functioning state committees and several more embryonic ones. These, however, transformed the Conference from an educational into an educational and political organization. As such, it could no longer receive tax-exempt donations, nor claim tax exemption for itself. At a meeting of the executive board in May 1945, a committee was established to reorganize the Conference. Consisting of Frank Graham, Josephine Wilkins, Palmer Weber, Helen Fuller, Charles Webber, Paul Christopher of the CIO in Knoxville, Frank Prohl, the Teamster's representative on the executive board, the committee's labors were completed in the fall and the draft of a new constitution, largely Miss Wilkins's work, was sent out for the consideration of the members of the board. At a meeting of the executive board in Durham late in January, 1946, the Southern Conference reorganized itself. The original charter issued to the Southern Conference for Human Welfare by the state of Tennessee in 1942 had chartered it as an educational corporation. That charter was amended: the name of the educational organization was changed from the Southern Conference for Human Welfare to the Southern Conference Educational Fund. The Fund would direct the Conference's regional educational activities and be eligible to receive tax-exempt donations.

The Conference's political activities in Washington, D. C., and in the Southern states would be under the guidance of a newly formed Southern Conference for Human Welfare, which appropriated the name but not the functions of the organization that had been chartered in 1942. Contributions to the new Southern Conference for Human Welfare were expected to come from the state committees, from unions, and from Northern friends. These would not be exempt from taxation. The generic name of the organizations would remain the Southern Conference for Human Welfare and a single administrative system would control the affairs of both organizations. Clark Foreman would be president of both and James Dombrowski their administrator. The Southern Conference was now a single-headed, siamese organization, whose joined bodies were inadequately distinguished from one another. Their identities were confused—and confusing both to members and subsequent commentators. Confusion of function, ill-defined spheres of jurisdiction, and different interests eventually helped split the twins' personality.

Nevertheless, by the end of January 1946, the Conference had—for the first time—nearly enough money to carry on a broad program; it had a rapidly growing membership, and it had an organization ready to use political and educational action to meet whatever problems might arise in the immediate postwar years. Conference leaders had reason to be optimistic—for about four months.[24]

24. Dombrowski to Executive Board, August 7, 1945; Executive Secretary's Report, September 12, 1945: SCEF possession. Foreman Papers, AU, have materials on 1944 finances; the figures for 1945 come from SCHW Records, TI, box No. 3. The membership figures were compiled from both these sources. Minutes Meeting of the Executive Board, January 22, 23, 1946, SCEF possession.

7

THE YEAR OF CRISIS: 1946

AFTER the war, the CIO planned a drive to organize the South's large nonunion labor force. The CIO National Executive Board established a Southern Organizing Committee under Van A. Bittner and budgeted one million dollars for the campaign. The proposed drive quickly excited the interest of Northern liberals and radicals and it was quickly christened Operation Dixie—a name reminiscent of the code names given to Allied military operations during the war. In the spring of 1946, a group of New York progressives prepared a "Help Organize the South" rally in Harlem to raise money for the unionization campaign.

On April 18, 1946, Van Bittner publicly denounced the proposed Harlem rally. The CIO, Bittner exclaimed, wished no help from outsiders, whether Socialists, Communists, or members of other political faiths. "That," he added caustically, "goes for the Southern Conference for Human Welfare and any other organization living off the CIO." [1]

The immediate occasion for Bittner's reference to the Conference was a letter from one of its field representatives, Osceola McKaine, to CIO Vice-President Allan S. Haywood. McKaine, a Negro, had written Haywood on behalf of the South's black minority to hail the announced organization campaign and to complain about

> the attitudes of a certain number of white CIO organizers in this region ... [who] could be readily mistaken for AFL or Railway Brotherhood organizers if one judged them by their racial attitudes and approaches. They should be told that the CIO expects them ... whenever and wherever it is possible, to practice what the CIO professes. I can be more specific if you so desire.[2]

Haywood replied irately:

> There isn't a movement in America doing as much to overcome the unjust and discriminatory practices against not only the colored but other groups, than the CIO is [sic], and the men on our staff in the South in the main deal with the problems they have in a realistic way, having one objective in mind, that is, the elimination of these conditions referred to and establishing for all our people the things ... which must be established ... in order to maintain and perpetuate our democracy.[3]

The day Haywood replied, Bittner, having seen McKaine's letter, issued his public statement.

Bittner's remarks reflected more than annoyance at unwanted criticism of the CIO. They reflected a revision in the union's conception of its function in American society; they reflected a change in union tactics; and they may have reflected a decline in the CIO's militant opposition to segregation. During the war, labor's no-strike pledge had precluded organizational campaigns; the pledge limited labor to attempts to conserve its prewar gains and to political action. Although its political efforts had been repaid, the CIO still existed primarily to protect the interests of the American worker. Political

1. The New York *Times*, April 19, 1946, p. 4.
2. McKaine to Haywood, April 14, 1946, SCHW Records, TI, box No. 3.
3. Haywood to McKaine, April 18, 1948, *ibid.*

action had hitherto been a less effective defense of the unorganized worker than a strong, militant union. Progressive politicians could not bargain for higher wages; an effective union could. The end of the war freed labor from the no-strike pledge and the nation's unions planned drives to organize the unorganized; they could now devote as much, if not more, energy to unionization as they devoted to politics. The CIO thus had less need for political allies, including the Southern Conference, who could not organize workers. At most, they could provide favorable publicity, which they would do even if the CIO withdrew some of its financial support. Funds previously donated to the Southern Conference and kindred organizations were needed to finance the organization drive. Bittner's sarcastic reference to organizations living off the CIO reflected a desire to be rid of entangling alliances—or at least less dependent on them. The CIO would wage its own campaign, fight its own battles.

Then and since, others besides Osceola McKaine have accused the CIO of opportunism on the race question during Operation Dixie; wherever expediency seemed to require it, the charges run, the Southern Organizing Committee chartered segregated unions. The counterclaims of CIO leaders and labor intellectuals have usually failed to meet the issue. Haywood's reply to McKaine was irrelevant; McKaine had not criticized general CIO policies, but their violation by "a certain number of white CIO organizers in this region." Paul Christopher, CIO representative on the Southern Conference executive board, narrowed the issue, contending Jim Crow locals were never chartered within his jurisdiction in Tennessee. Lorne Nellis, an official of the Steel Workers in Atlanta, contended that the Southern Organizing Committee's main problems resulted from the unfortunate nickname, Operation Dixie, given to it by Northern radicals. Perhaps true—obviously an evasion. Bittner and the CIO, Kenneth Douty, one of the Conference's socialist members and critics, retorted, had done more for the Negro worker than the Southern Conference and Conference leaders should not have cast stones at the CIO. Certainly true—certainly an evasion. If then, the CIO had decided to abandon its demands for interracial unions where expediency required it, Bittner's remarks reflected an additional annoyance; he had been caught with his principles down.

After his denunciation of the Conference, Bittner and officials of both the CIO and the Southern Conference tried to reconcile the two organizations. McKaine apologized for his letter. Dombrowski and Allan Haywood agreed to have the leaders of the two groups conduct all future discussion between them. Bittner assured Clark Foreman he had "nothing but the friendliest feelings for the Southern Conference." [4] In May, the CIO chief agreed to attend a dinner sponsored by the Southern Conference's Washington Committee. By way of Paul Christopher, Bittner sent word that his remarks "were in no way intended as a reflection on the Southern Conference" and that he wanted "all the moral support . . . the members of the Southern Conference can . . . give to the drive, but he is very adamant . . . that the tenor of the campaign must be entirely organizational." [5] By early 1947, according to an official of the Textile Workers' Union, Bittner "regretted the blast he issued against the Conference. . . . [He] had been talked to by [Philip] Murray and a couple of others. . . . Van would like to co-operate with the Conference in the future and to make some amends for his earlier action." [6]

Amends could not be made. Bittner's assurances of friendly feelings for the Southern Conference and his denials of intent to criticize the organization could not gloss over his acidulous reference to it as a parasite on the CIO. Nor could they repair the Conference's damaged prestige.

Amends were not made. In 1945, organized labor gave more than $28,000 to the Conference; most of that came from CIO unions. In 1946, CIO unions contributed between $13,000 and $18,000 to the organization, a decline of at least $10,000. After Bittner's public statement, CIO National Office donations to the Conference ended. During the second half of 1946, the organization's revenues fell off 50 percent—a loss ascribable in large part to Bittner's remarks.

4. Foreman to Paul Christopher, April 22, 1946, Foreman Papers, AU.

5. Paul Christopher to Foreman, May 3, 1946, *ibid.*

6. Malcolm C. Dobbs to Clark Foreman, January 4, 1947, SCHW Records, TI, box No. 6.

Early in 1947, the CIO Executive Board published a list of organizations approved by CIO departments and commissions. The Southern Conference did not appear on the list. Clark Foreman wrote Philip Murray:

In view of the very strong endorsement we have received from the CIO Executive Board and the increased strength and importance of our organization since that endorsement, I can understand how there would be some confusion in people's minds as a result of the publication of this list. I think it would help considerably in our work in the South and in our relations with the CIO if there could be some clarification from you on this matter.[7]

But clarification did not come.

In eight months, one of the Conference's main supports had become shaky. A CIO leader had publicly denounced the organization; CIO contributions had markedly declined. In subsequent months, most CIO representatives quietly withdrew from the Southern Conference. As the CIO support weakened, most of the others began to follow.[8]

II

Yet the Conference was at its peak in 1946. It had its largest membership—some 10,000 counting Southern members and Northern associates—and its largest annual income; by one calculation,

7. Foreman to Murray, January 20, 1947, Foreman Papers, AU.

8. *CIO News*, March 18, 1946, p. 2; March 25, 1946, p. 9; April 15, 1946, p. 6; April 22, 1946, p. 10; April 29, 1946, p. 5: for information about Operation Dixie. Other sources for this section are McKaine to Haywood, April 24, 1946, SCHW Records, TI, box No. 3. William Mitch to Clark Foreman, April 25, 1946; Witherspoon Dodge to Van Bittner and to Clark Foreman, April 25, 1946: Foreman Papers, AU. Christopher interview previously cited. Telephone conversation with Lorne Nellis, Atlanta, Georgia, February 13, 1964. Kenneth Douty, "The Southern Conference for Human Welfare," pp. 144ff. For independent confirmation of McKaine's charges—and the general charge against the CIO—see Ray Marshall, *The Negro and Organized Labor* (New York, London, and Sydney: John Wiley and Sons, c.1965), pp. 42–45, especially the remark on p. 45: "A few CIO unions permitted segregation where it was considered a prerequisite to unionization." Financial information comes from: Foreman to Edmonia Grant, May 26, 1947, SCHW Records, TI, box No. 6 and from Dombrowski to Board Members, December 24, 1946, Foreman Papers, AU. The CIO's list of approved organizations is in *CIO News*, January 13, 1947, p. 7. Neither the Foreman Papers nor the Philip Murray Papers, Catholic University, Washington, D.C. contains a reply to Foreman's letter to Murray cited in note No. 7 above.

its revenues for the year totaled $116,844.97. By mid-April it had enough money to continue effective work despite Bittner's remarks. It went on in its accustomed ways, propagating support for the New Deal, meeting local issues in the South, and moving closer to a thoroughgoing opposition to Southern and national segregation.

The *Southern Patriot* featured articles on Southern education, requesting federal aid, on Claude Pepper, using him as an example of an enlightened Southern politician, on the region's farm problem, demanding federal purchase and redistribution of large plantations on easy terms to small farmers (perhaps the most radical demand it ever made), and on the Klan, exposing that noisome organization's plans. The *Patriot* editorialized for higher minimum wages, for continuation of the OPA, and for the Full Employment Act. It publicized Operation Dixie and opposed limiting amendments to the Wagner and Norris–La Guardia Acts. Clark Foreman appeared before congressional committees to testify for continuation of the OPA, for repeal of the poll tax, for a higher minimum wage, and for a permanent FEPC. In support of the last-named measure, the Conference secured a petition signed by 4,000 Southerners opposing the filibuster against the bill; about 100 of these came from Mississippi whose senior Senator, Theodore A. Bilbo, expressed the wish to filibuster both the FEPC and the Southern Conference out of existence. The organization sponsored pro-FEPC meetings in nine Southern cities and ran ads in its behalf in ten Southern newspapers. Most of these demands were denied. In 1946, effective price controls ended and the permanent FEPC died. A year later, in the Taft-Hartley Act, Congress added stringent amendments to the Wagner Act. Yet a few of the Conference's reform hopes were fulfilled; the Full Employment Bill became law and the minimum wage rate was eventually raised.

Late in 1945, the Conference hired two field representatives, Witherspoon Dodge, a Unitarian minister who had gone to work as a CIO organizer in the late thirties, and Osceola McKaine, former editor of a Negro newspaper in Charleston, South Carolina. They sought additional members for the Conference and worked on voter-registration campaigns in Atlanta, Augusta, and Savannah, Georgia, and in Birmingham, Alabama. Together with other organizations, they added numerous voters to the registration lists; in Savannah, voter-registration workers claimed an increase in total registrants from 15,000 to 60,000 and in Negro registrants from 900 to 19,000.

In Alabama, the state committee worked against the Boswell Amendment, Alabama's attempt to thwart Negro voter registration drives by lodging registration authority exclusively in local boards of registration. The Committee for Alabama sponsored a conference on the amendment at which organized labor came out against it; it mailed an analysis of the measure to 8,000 prominent Alabamans; it urged candidates for public office to declare against it; it persuaded the Catholic Bishop of Mobile to come out publicly for defeat of the amendment. But its efforts were in vain. In the general elections of 1946, the voters of Alabama, by a majority of 53 percent, adopted the Boswell measure, only to see it voided three years later in a federal district court. The Committee worked in the successful gubernatorial campaign of James B. Folsom, whom it claimed as a member and for whose campaign program it took some credit.

In Georgia, the Southern Conference state committee sponsored two test suits challenging the constitutionality of the state's county unity system, helped secure an equitable proportion of a school bond issue for Negro schools (increasing the Negro schools' share from $1,000,000 to $4,000,000), and worked quietly against Eugene Talmadge during the gubernatorial race of 1946. Both test suits failed. So did the quiet opposition to Talmadge. Before his inauguration, Talmadge died; the Georgia legislature elected his son, Herman, to succeed him. When the incumbent governor, Ellis Arnall, refused to relinquish his office to the younger Talmadge, Herman's forces stormed and took possession of the state house. Against such high-handed tactics, the Committee for Georgia's quiet methods were ineffectual.

The Committee for North Carolina, in co-operation with the state's

AFofL and CIO offices, sponsored hearings on an increased minimum wage law. It worked to register new voters, to lower the voting age to eighteen, to increase the number of supervisors in the state educational system, to win state Wagner and Norris–La Guardia acts, and to extend the coverage of the state's unemployment compensation system. It asked for state grants to aid consolidating school districts and to finance a state symphony orchestra. Of these, only the voter registration work achieved any significant success.

By the end of 1946, the Washington Committee had 850 members and an income of $22,000. The most powerful of the Conference's local committees, it opposed the reassignment of Theodore Bilbo to the Senate District of Columbia Committee, sponsored a civic meeting to endorse a report favoring an end to compulsory segregation within the District, co-operated with other organizations to oppose an increase in the local ceiling on rents, and supported a strike of government cafeteria workers. It lent $200 to the National Negro Congress to aid its campaign to have the Capitol Transit Company hire Negroes. The Committee tried to persuade officials of George Washington University to admit Negroes to performances at the school's Lisner Auditorium. Although most of these were in vain, some bore fruit in later years.

Local committees were begun in several other states: Louisiana, Virginia, and Texas. By December 1946, the Committee for Louisiana had 593 members and a program centering around voter registration, public housing, rent controls, industrialization, and diversification of the state's agriculture. Although one of the Conference's largest local organizations, the Committee for Louisiana's members came almost entirely from New Orleans and Baton Rouge and it remained nearly ineffective. In November, a Committee for Virginia was put together. Its first act was to elect delegates for the Southern Conference's postwar convention in New Orleans. In Texas, the Conference began several city groups. Its El Paso chapter sponsored forums, tried to facilitate communication between the city's Mexican-American and Anglo-American communities, and to disseminate the Conference's program. It successfully opposed the deportation of a Nicaraguan labor organizer for the International Union of Mine, Mill, and Smelter Workers, one Humberto Selix.

In Kentucky, where a similar but independent Committee for Kentucky had been active for five years, nothing of consequence resulted from the Conference's organizational efforts. Nor did anything of consequence result from Conference efforts in Mississippi, South Carolina, and Oklahoma, though in the latter state Conference members included the Reverend John B. Thompson and Roscoe Dunjee, editor of the *Black Dispatch* and head of the state N.A.A.C.P. In Tennessee, the work of Conference organizer, William Cornelius, attracted a few members and small sums of money. Tennessee Committtee members worked to prevent Kenneth McKellar's re-election to the Senate. For their efforts they were vilified in editorials and cartoons in the Nashville *Banner* as minions of the CIO and the Communist party; and McKellar won the primary and general elections. At the end of 1946, the Tennessee Committee's extreme poverty caused Cornelius to resign to seek another, more secure position.

The Conference's high hopes for the postwar South went unfulfilled. It received inadequate compensation for its labors. With but one exception, the future promised even smaller rewards.[9]

9. James A. Dombrowski, "The Southern Conference for Human Welfare," *Common Ground*, VI (Summer 1946), 14–25. *The Southern Patriot*, IV (January 1946), (April 1946), (June 1946), (November 1946). On the Alabama Committee: Malcolm Dobbs to Dombrowski, October 7, 1946; same to same, November 5, 1946; Dobbs to Aubrey Williams, November 5, 1946; SCHW Records, TI, box No. 3. Dobbs to Clark Foreman, June 8, 1946, Foreman Papers, AU. On the Committee for Georgia: Frank W. Spencer to John W. Melton, November 7, 1946, SCHW Records, TI, box No. 3; Josephine Wilkins to Clark Foreman, September 3, 1946, Foreman Papers, AU. The test suits against the county unit system are not identified in the Conference's extant records; they were probably *Turman et al.* v. *Duckworth*, 68 *Fed. Supp.* 745 and *Cook* v. *Fortson* 68 *Fed. Supp.* 624. On the Committee for North Carolina: the Dombrowski piece in *Common Ground* cited at the beginning of this note; the Committee for North Carolina, Legislative Program, SCHW Records, TI, box No. 3. On the Washington Committee: scattered materials in SCHW Records, TI, box No. 3 and in the Foreman Papers, AU. On the Committee for Louisiana: Executive Secretary's Report, January 1947, SCHW Records, TI, box No. 3. On the Committee for Virginia: Virginia Beecher to Dombrowski, November 24, 1946, SCHW Records, TI, box No. 3. On the Committee for Tennessee: William Cornelius to Dombrowski, November 12, 1946; same to same, December 17, 1946; Dombrow-

III

At its birth, the Southern Conference inherited the ambiguous racial attitudes common to most Southerners. It expressed sympathy for the Negroes' plight, demanded the right to hold integrated meetings, admitted Negroes to its executive councils, and worked for the abolition of the poll tax—an indirect demand for partial integration of Negroes into Southern political life. But here its integrationist tendencies ended. It supported separate and equal schools and playgrounds and, by its silence and its equivocations, accepted the prevailing social segregation in housing and public accommodations and the prevailing segregation in hiring practices. Before the war, the Conference would not attack segregation where it was strong—and it was strong nearly everywhere.

Conference militants, however, expected to change the Conference's attitudes and its programs. In 1938, they had pushed for a strong denunciation of Jim Crow practices; their insistence was largely responsible for the Conference's refusal to hold future meetings in cities requiring public segregation and for the Conference's admission of Negroes to its executive ranks. The fight against the poll tax, they reasoned, was but the first battle in a war against the measures taken between 1890 and 1910 to disenfranchise and disqualify Negro citizens.

The most prominent integrationists in the organization were—or came to be—Clark Foreman, whose work in race relations dated back to the 1920s, Joseph Gelders, whose conversion probably occurred in the early years of the depression, Mrs. Clifford J. Durr, whom Foreman and Gelders converted, James Dombrowski, who expressed integrationist sentiments in the pages of the *Southern Patriot* from its inception, Lillian Smith, who, during the war, badgered Conference leaders for a forthright denunciation of segregation, CIO representatives, all of whom were wedded to the principle of inter-

---

ski to Cornelius, December 26, 1946: SCHW Records, TI, box No. 3. Other materials on the state committees are scattered in the SCHW Records, TI, and in the Foreman Papers, AU. The Southern Conference Educational Fund has two scrap books of clippings dealing with the Conference's work during 1945 and 1946; the author is indebted to Dr. Dombrowski for permission to use them.

racial unionism, and the Conference's Negro members, whose demands for justice, no matter how timid, pointed ultimately to an end to segregation.

Circumstances worked for them. The controversial Birmingham antisegregation resolution drove politicians and timid liberals, who could least afford association with an integrationist organization, out of the Conference. They could not obstruct progressive developments in the Conference's racial program. The war, too, aided Conference integrationists; total mobilization required full economic and military privileges for Negroes. The Conference therefore came out for fair employment and an end to military segregation.

The Conference's postwar plans wrought further changes in its race program. Permanent peace required amity among men of all races; that, in turn, required equal but not separate treatment in the South as well as in other parts of the world. The war had been fought against fascist racism; segregation entailed capitulation to domestic racism. Negro soldiers, having fought well in the war, deserved equal treatment for their services. To help Negro soldiers readjust to civilian life, the Conference circulated "Look Him in the Eye," a pamphlet daring White Americans to scorn Negroes' contributions to Allied victory by forcing them to resume their former subordinate position in American society. To spread the word of interracial harmony among the semiliterate, the Conference disseminated a comic book, "There Are No Master Races," presenting in pictorial form the scientific arguments for racial equality. The tract marshalled arguments familiar to a generation of liberal biologists: the white and black races had the same anatomical structure and the same four basic blood types; differences in environment, not innate characteristics, produced differences in skin pigmentation; education, not nature, produced intelligence. When Europeans had been chasing women about with clubs, the book remarked, the darker races of North Africa had developed a highly sophisticated civilization. Toward the end of 1946, the Conference produced another pamphlet on the race problem, "Would You Smile?" to afford white readers a glimpse into the commonplace deprivations of a Negro's existence. Fewer Negro than white mothers survived childbirth. Negroes, on the average, could expect to die ten years sooner than whites. The careers of Marian Anderson, George Washington Carver, Mary McLeod Bethune, and General Benjamin O. Davis offered evidence against dogmas of inherent Negro inferiority. If the reader were black, the pamphlet resolved, he would love his country and fight for full citizenship.

Along with the Conference's propagation of interracial amity went increased participation in the nation's crusade against lynching. During 1945, according to Tuskegee Institute's Records, only one such brutal execution occurred; in 1946, six Negroes were so murdered. Conference officials lobbied for a federal antilynching law and, following an atrocity in Georgia involving the death of a Negro ex-GI, participated in a large memorial service for the victims in Washington. They also worked on the worst racial incident of the year in Columbia, Tennessee.

There, late in February, 1946, following the threatened lynching of a returned Negro serviceman who had fought with a white man, some 500 Tennessee state guardsmen and policemen, at the request of local police who claimed to fear a Negro uprising, cordoned off the town's Negro district and invaded it, wantonly destroying several Negro businesses and looting others. Although the Negroes did not fire a shot during the invasion, the invaders sprayed numerous residences and businesses with machine gun bullets. They arrested scores of Negroes without warrant and beat some of their captives with blackjacks. While under questioning, two of the prisoners were shot to death. Twenty-five Negroes were subsequently brought to trial for attempting to lure whites into the Negro district and for fomenting riot and murder. Twenty-three were acquitted; the other two were sentenced to twenty-one years in prison.

In collaboration with the N.A.A.C.P., the Southern Conference investigated the incident, publishing its findings in a short pamphlet. With the National Federation for Constitutional Liberties and the International Union of Mine, Mill and Smelter Workers, it formed the United Committee Against Police Terror in Columbia, Tennessee, to persuade Attorney General Tom Clark to investigate the incident for possible violations of federal civil rights statutes. Later, Conference leaders helped merge this organization with the N.A.A.C.P.-led National Committee for Justice in Columbia; Southern Conference members of the former group realized, in Clark Foreman's words, "the necessity of putting the issue above any ideological or organizational differences."[10] The Southern Conference stimulated twenty-thousand protest notes to Governor McCord of Tennessee. It helped raise money for the legal expenses of the twenty-five Negroes who went on trial. In gratitude, Walter White addressed the Conference's New Orleans convention in November.

At the end of the war, the Conference became an equal-opportunity employer; Osceola McKaine, one of its two field representatives, was a Negro. It sent Mary McLeod Bethune on a tour of cities in the Carolinas, Georgia, and Alabama to raise money and recruit new members. Her speech—so the mimeographed version of it runs—challenged her audience to have the courage to fight for the abolition of segregation and racial discrimination.

At the Conference's New Orleans convention in November 1946, the organization rose to meet her challenge. It condemned discrimination in employment and wages, in housing, transportation, and government services, in education, and in voluntary organizations. Yet it also supported the Hill-Burton Hospital Construction Act which contained provisions for the construction of segregated hospitals; and some of its state committees continued to work for equal and separate public school systems.

By the end of 1946 then, the Southern Conference had adopted a forthright denunciation of segregation, though hedging—perhaps for tactical reasons—that denunciation with specific proposals that would perpetuate Jim Crow practices.[11]

10. Foreman to Walter White, April 20, 1946, Foreman Papers, AU.

11. *Birmingham Proceedings*, pp. 13, 21; "Chattanooga Resolutions," p. 4; *Proceedings of the Nashville Convention*, pp. 4ff.; *The Southern Patriot*, I–IV, *passim*. The three pamphlets on the race problem are in SCEF possession; Clark Foreman, "Fascism Has Foot in Door," *PM*, August 23, 1946, pp. 8–9; Dombrowski in *Com-*

IV

War restrictions on travel and financial difficulties prevented the Conference from holding a full convention after the Nashville gathering of 1942. Postwar expansion and reorganization further delayed a meeting of the Conference membership. By mid-1946, plans could be made for a Conference convention to reacquaint members with each other and with the organization's purposes and to consider changes in the program. In September, the executive board decided to convene the Conference in New Orleans during Thanksgiving week to express its gratitude for the defeat of fascism, the establishment of the United Nations, and the region's economic progress.

On November 28, 1946, in Carpenters' Hall, the convention opened. Only 269 official delegates attended—a figure lower than the figure for the wartime meeting in Nashville. Some 40 to 60 percent of the delegates were Negroes. A few labor leaders, a small group of Socialists, several Communists, and a large number of liberals, whom one of the Socialists called "a lot of YMCA-ish people," made up the rest of the delegation. Significantly absent were representatives of the New Deal. Although President Truman had exchanged several letters with James Dombrowski, he did not accord the Conference his Administration's unofficial patronage. No prominent person connected with the Administration appeared in New Orleans. Even Mrs. Roosevelt stayed away; disillusioned with Communism, she opposed the Southern Conference's occasional connections with fellow travelers and known American Communists. Yet she telegraphed her good wishes—as did Henry Wallace, Philip Murray, A. F. Whitney, Walter Reuther, and James G. Patton.

---

mon Ground (Summer 1946), pp. 14ff. The Southern Conference for Human Welfare, *The Truth About Columbia, Tennessee, Cases,* (n.p.: n.p., n.d.); Robert Minor, *Lynching and Frame Up in Tennessee* (New York: New Century Publishers, 1946). The N.A.A.C.P. and the SRC also issued pamphlets on the outrage. Alva Taylor, "One Justice for All," *The Christian Century,* LXIII (December 11, 1946), 1501–1502; *A Monthly Summary of Events and Trends in Race Relations,* IV (October 1946), 76. Mrs. Bethune's speech is in SCHW Records, TI, box No. 3. During the war, Dombrowski tried without success to hire a Negro secretary. The source for the New Orleans resolutions is cited in note 12 below.

Only two prominent politicians, Claude Pepper and Ellis Arnall, attended the convention; the former's Senate term would not expire until 1950 and the latter's term as Governor of Georgia was close to an end. The Conference had lost support in nearly every quarter. It had lost its tenuous connection with the national administration; it was losing the support of organized labor; even its white middle-class support may have weakened. Only the Negroes had an increased interest in the organization; in time, they would become its major source of popular support.

The major addresses reiterated the Conference's primary articles of faith and re-emphasized its program of action. Clark Foreman's opening speech reminded the delegates to be thankful for victory, increased industrialization, and New Deal social and economic reforms. Styling the Southern Conference "a conservative organization, preserving and cultivating the finest traditions of our forefathers," [12] he invoked the shades of Thomas Jefferson, Andrew Jackson, Henry Grady, Charles Brantley Aycock, and George Washington Carver. The Conference hoped, he explained, to make the South "the land of freedom and opportunity envisioned for all men by great Southerners from Thomas Jefferson and Andrew Jackson to Hugo Black and Claude Pepper." Mary McLeod Bethune called the ends of the Southern Conference—peace, justice, freedom, and economic security—the needs of humanity; she urged Negroes to register and to vote, and to use their political power to achieve the rights of first-class citizens. Senator Pepper demanded an end to freight-rate differentials and all forms of monopoly; he asked for federal public works programs and for federal aid to Southern farmers and to Southern education. He challenged the South to become the nation's major trader with Latin America and to become the leader of American progressivism. Walter White demanded an end to segregation; "the alternative to one world and one nation is no world and no nation." Governor Arnall, recipient of the Thomas

12. This and other materials on the convention come from Southern Conference for Human Welfare, "Stenographic Report of the New Orleans Convention," SCEF possession.

Jefferson award, prescribed more democracy to cure the ills of democracy; he asked for educational reforms, extension of public health services, full employment, and an end to the South's colonial economic status. "Let us then—you and I, the little people—roll up our sleeves and make democracy live."

After sessions on social welfare in the South, propaganda techniques, and Southern political and economic problems, the convention delegates, the so-called little people, decided on a program to vitalize democracy in the South. The Conference declared for the rational use of the region's natural resources through regional and local planning modeled on the TVA. It asked that Southern housing, income, public-health facilities, and educational institutions be brought up to national standards. It recommended diversification in agriculture and rapid development of Southern-owned industry. Collective bargaining should be extended to all workers and citizens should have the right to vote without arbitrary restrictions; here the delegates resolved against racial discrimination. They also pledged to continue to work to increase the Southern electorate, to support progressive candidates, and to lobby for progressive federal, state, and municipal laws. Reaffirming their faith in the good sense of the people, the delegates promised to "conduct an intensive and broad educational campaign, utilizing conferences, publications, radio, films, records, posters, and other media of communications to give the facts, aid understanding and stimulate action on issues relevant to this program." They thought a "more prosperous and democratic Southland" would be their "best contribution to a peaceful and democratic world; yet not shirking our responsibility as citizens of a national and world-wide community."

This avoided taking sides in the developing cold war. It may have been an indication of the Conference's declining vitality. It may have resulted from serious differences within the organization over the proper attitude to take toward the split between Russia and the West. It may have been an attempt to avoid adding another problem to the Conference's growing list of problems.

Conference revenues had fallen off drastically; the wages of its state executive secretaries were months in arrears; payments from the regional Southern Conference to the local committees had come to an end; its debts mounted faster than the organization could pay them. To deal with this problem and others, Conference leaders scheduled a meeting of the executive board to follow the adjournment of the convention.[13]

V

The delegates to the convention had elected a 34-man executive board, 9 of whom were on hand. On December 1, these 9 and the organization's administrative officers met to deal with the Conference's financial crisis. Acting in accordance with Clark Foreman's argument that the administrative work of the Conference had become too complicated for one man, the executive board unanimously adopted Foreman's motion to remove James Dombrowski from the dual position of executive secretary (administrator) of both the Southern Conference for Human Welfare and the Southern Conference Educational Fund and to transfer him to the position of administrator of the latter half of the organization. The Board appointed Branson Price, executive secretary of the New York Committee, to the position of administrator of the Southern Conference for Human Welfare.

Dombrowski's inefficiency, Foreman and other members of the Board believed, had increased the Conference's operating expenses; his talents were better suited to educational work. Miss Price, on the other hand, was efficient and effective. With her as Southern Conference administrator, Clark Foreman would be free to devote his time exclusively to the Conference's central problem, fund-raising.

The Board's decision deeply hurt Dombrowski. From the time of his appointment in 1942, he had devoted most of his energies to

13. In addition to the stenographic report of the convention, this section relies upon the following: Agnes M. Douty to Bill [Becker (?)], December 11, 1946; Tom Leonard to Harry (?), December 5, 1946, Socialist Party Papers, Duke, Letters, 1946-November 15, 1947. The phrase "a lot of YMCA-ish people" is Mrs. Douty's. *Daily Worker*, December 2, 1946, p. 8; *Alabama*, XI (December 6, 1946), 3.

the organization; he had kept the Conference alive during the lean years of the war. No other member of the organization had worked as hard to keep it viable. Dombrowski interpreted his replacement as part of an attempt to make Foreman the organization's undisputed head. Since the reorganization of the Conference in January 1946, the political activities of the Conference had overshadowed its educational operations; the Educational Fund's budget was half that of the Southern Conference for Human Welfare. With Dombrowski confined to the organization's educational operations and Miss Price responsible for the Conference's Southern office, Foreman alone would be responsible for the program and activities of both organizations.

Although Dombrowski accepted his replacement as Conference administrator, he would not accept his new position. The executive board, he argued in letters to its members, had lacked a quorum; its creation of a new position, Southern Conference administrator, violated the organization's bylaws. Foreman had failed to give advance notice of the proposed changes, and his replacement and reassignment had been effected by a virtual coup. The Board had thus disregarded normal democratic procedures.

Dombrowski's serious pique moved nearly every member of the executive board to ask Foreman for a reconsideration. Outnumbered, Foreman assented, scheduling a Board meeting for Greensboro, North Carolina, in January 1947.

Before the meeting, Dombrowski prepared an analysis of the Conference's administrative problems. In it, he argued that the twin organization needed a Southern office under one administrator to co-ordinate the work of state committees and the Educational Fund. The administrator would direct all Conference programs, oversee the organization's internal administration, control its finances and raise money in the South, represent the Conference at liberal meetings in the region, and appoint executive secretaries to the state committees who would be directly responsible to him. Subordinate administrators would deal with finance, with the organization's publications, with memberships, and with the details of office management. The president of the Conference would represent it at national legislative hearings, raise money in the North, co-operate with Northern progressive groups, and consult with the administrator about important matters of policy. The administrator would control most of the Conference's activities and most of its internal affairs; the president would be a mouthpiece, a fund-raiser, and an adviser. Dombrowski intended to be the administrator; he presumably intended Foreman to retain the presidency. The rift between the two men had become, in part, a struggle for power.

January 5, 1947, at Greensboro, the Southern Conference executive board reinstated Dombrowski as administrator for the Southern Conference for Human Welfare. Holding to its conviction that administration of both parts of the twin organization was too much for one person, it resolved to appoint a second administrator to oversee the operations of the Educational Fund. It established a three-man administrative committee to co-ordinate the work of Dombrowski and the Educational fund administrator. Foreman remained president.

This was a compromise. Dombrowski's plan for reorganization was not adopted. Nor did he acquire full control over Conference activities and internal affairs. But his reinstallation as Southern Conference administrator gave him a large measure of control over its political program, its major postwar concern. Foreman's contention that one person could not administer both parts of the siamese organization was accepted, and so, by implication, was his contention that Dombrowski was inefficient.

Yet compromise failed to restore the trust and good will that had existed before the attempt to remove Dombrowski. Effective co-operation between Foreman and Dombrowski became difficult. In the summer of 1947, Dombrowski voluntarily moved over to the Education Fund; gradually he disassociated it from the Southern Conference. Several members of the Executive Board thought Foreman's attempted removal of Dombrowski devious and unscrupulous. Subsequent incidents hardened their suspicions.

The Conference had added a serious internal split to its list of woes. Its financial position continued to worsen. It was losing the support of organized labor. Its failure to take a stand on the cold war convinced many that it was a Communist front. In subsequent months, numerous persons left the organization.[14]

14. Dombrowski to Foreman, December 6, 1946; Myles Horton to Dombrowski, December 10, 1946; Dombrowski to Foreman, December 12, 1946; Dombrowski to Members of the Executive Board, December 6, 1946; Dombrowski to Aubrey Williams, December 28, 1946: SCHW Records, TI, box No. 3. Lucy Mason to Foreman, December 8, 1946; Foreman to Lucy Mason, December 11, 1946; Foreman to Mary McLeod Bethune, December 11, 1946; Foreman to Myles Horton, December 11, 1946; Foreman to John B. Thompson, December 11, 1946; Lewis Jones to Foreman, December 11, 1946; Frank Prohl to Foreman, December 18, 1946; Foreman to Dombrowski, December 21, 1946; Dombrowski to Foreman, December 26, 1946; Margaret Fisher to Foreman, December 29, 1946; James Dombrowski, Memorandum on Organizational, Administrative and Financial Problems Confronting the Southern Conference for Human Welfare; Foreman to Frank Graham, January 6, 1946 [1947]; Foreman to Mary McLeod Bethune, January 6, 1947; Mary McLeod Bethune to Foreman, January 13, 1947: Foreman Papers, AU. Kenneth Douty, "The Southern Conference for Human Welfare," p. 158.

8

DEATH AND TRANSFIGURATION

VAN BITTNER'S denunciation of the Southern Conference, the rift between Foreman and Dombrowski, and the Conference's refusal to take sides in the cold war gradually debilitated the organization. Throughout 1947, prominent members resigned. By the end of the year, nearly all of the labor leaders on the executive board had quit the Conference. Others, pleading lack of time for Conference business, followed suit; the toll of resignations included Mary McLeod Bethune; Roscoe Dunjee, head of the Oklahoma N.A.A.C.P.; Tarleton Collier, long a Conference stalwart; and Harry Schacter, head of the Committee for Kentucky. Within the Conference, sordid, petty squabbles broke out. Early in the year, the Committee for Georgia suspended operations; cautious whites in the Committee opposed Foreman's vociferous opposition to segregation and were driven to quiet fury when photographs of Foreman and the prizefighter, Joe Louis, taken at a Conference fund-raising dinner in New York, circulated in Georgia. For his part, Foreman sharply criticised the Committee for its failure to declare publicly its opposition to the Talmadge forces during the gubernatorial race in 1946. A serious difference in principle stood behind the disputants: Georgia Committee members wished the Conference to remain a decentralized, grass-roots organization, with a minimum of dictation from the regional leaders; Foreman, as the Conference's principal officer, claimed the executive prerogative to intervene in matters of local policy. Still, without the ill will which Margaret Fisher, Lucy Randolph Mason, and other members of the Georgia Committee bore Foreman—a result of his attempt to move Dombrowski to the Educational Fund—the disagreement might have been compromised. On April 19, 1947, the Georgia Committee suspended operations. Several Conference members resigned over the Conference's attempt to ignore the cold war. Henry Hamill Fowler, later Lyndon Johnson's Secretary of the Treasury, quit the Committee for Virginia after it failed to adopt his resolution barring Communists from membership. Three important members of the Committee for Louisiana resigned for similar reasons. George Mitchell, former head of the CIO-PAC in the Southeast, left the Conference during the summer of 1947 after the executive board agreed to sponsor Paul Robeson on a tour of the South. (The tour never materialized.) Although none of these contended that the Conference was under Communist control, they all thought its refusal to ban Communists, to take sides in the cold war, and to cease trafficking with known Communist sympathizers serious enough to warrant their resignations.

The Conference's financial position deteriorated. By the beginning of the year, the organization was $23,000 in debt. Its first-quarter revenues came to $12,240. At that rate the Conference would have taken in $49,000 for the year, half its budgeted figure of $100,000. As it was, the Conference raised about $30,000. Union contributions fell off; some of the CIO's radical unions sent small sums and the Amalgamated Clothing Workers gave $1,000. Fund-raising efforts yielded less, and what they yielded was often grudgingly given. An appeal to the Brotherhood of Railway Trainmen went unfulfilled; the Union's constitution required unanimous consent of the executive board for all donations; two members inflexibly opposed a grant to the Southern Conference. In the spring, Clark Foreman appealed to Nelson Rockefeller for a $5,000 grant for the Educational Fund. This, too, was in vain. An appeal to the Julius Rosenwald Fund met with a similar rejection. In April, Marshall Field sent the Conference $1,000 with a letter indicating that he would not contribute further to the organization. After the House Committee on Un-American Activities attacked the Conference, Aubrey Williams sent out a mail appeal for funds; the cost of the mailing exceeded the returns. In November, a Conference-sponsored tour of the South by Henry Wallace netted approximately $5,000. It was not enough.

The decline in revenues caused internal reorganization and killed most of the state committees. In the spring, Frank Bancroft, an assistant editor of the *Patriot*, was released. In the summer, James Dombrowski voluntarily moved from the Conference administrative leadership to the lower-paying position of Educational Fund executive secretary. And Clark Foreman went off salary. (He was later hired at half salary by the Washington Committee.) Dombrowski's replacement, Edmonia Grant, a graduate of Fisk and Columbia Teacher's College, agreed to work for less than Dombrowski had. In December 1946, the Southern Conference suspended payments to the state committees. Their executive secretaries' wages fell farther and farther in arrears. By the end of February 1947, Margaret Fisher had not been paid since the previous November. Mary Price went without pay after March 1947. By September 1947, only two local committees were active: the Washington and North Carolina Committees. The others were either defunct or moribund.

The decline in revenues produced—and was produced by—a decline in members; friends and members from the first had provided the bulk of the Conference's finances. At the beginning of 1947, the Conference claimed 10,000 members, many of them recruited a year earlier during Mrs. Bethune's speaking tour. As their renewals came due many failed to continue their memberships. By the end of 1947, the Conference total membership stood at 5,500, about half of what it had been at the outset of the year. Between 1,000 and 1,500 of these had joined after Henry Wallace's fall tour under Conference auspices. After Wallace's tour, Conference leaders failed to find ways to attract new members to the organization. The Wallace tour only temporarily arrested the rapid decline in Conference membership.[1]

II

Even under these limitations, the work of the Conference went on. The *Southern Patriot* continued national and local news of interest to Southern liberals and progressives. It noted Southern Conference activities and editorially supported the Conference's New Orleans program. The remaining state committees followed suit. With the passage of the Taft-Hartley Act imminent, the *Southern Patriot* put out a special issue opposing the bill; the law, the paper predicted, would break up national unions and usher in an era of injunctions and armed violence against the labor movement. It urged its readers to ask their senators and representatives to vote against the bill, to set up labor defense committees and propagandize against the law,

1. Minutes, Meeting of the Administrative Committee, January 19, 1947; Minutes, Meeting of the Administrative Committee, April 19, 1947; Minutes, Meeting of the Administrative Committee, June 21, 1947; Minutes, Meeting of the Executive Board, July 12, 1947; Minutes, Meeting of the Board of Representatives, October 16, 1947; Foreman to Dombrowski, January 25, 1947; Edmonia Grant to Foreman, April 12, 1947; same to same, August 7, 1947; Mary Price to Stella Landis, July 22, 1947; Lucy Mason to Edmonia Grant, March 18, 1947; Report of the Administrator for the Second Quarter of 1947; Report of the Administrator for the Third Quarter of 1947: SCHW Records, TI, box No. 6. Edmonia Grant to Foreman, April 25, 1947; Foreman to Dombrowski, February 10, 1947; Foreman to Louis Weiss, April 8, 1947; Foreman to Marshall Field, April 9, 1947; Foreman to Nelson Rockefeller, January 24, 1947; A. F. Whitney to Foreman, June 25, 1947; Dombrowski to J. Daniel Weitzman, May 29, 1947; Frank Bancroft to Clark Foreman, May 16, 1947; Tarleton Collier to Edmonia Grant, August 28, 1947; Roscoe Dunjee to Mrs. Grant, Charlotte Hawkins Brown to Mrs. Grant, September 23, 1947; Memorandum from Mrs. Grant, January 23, 1947 [1948]; Financial Report Last Half of 1947: Foreman Papers, AU.

and, if it passed, to demand a presidential veto. State committees dutifully followed the *Patriot*'s lead; the Alabama Committee sent three thousand post cards to Lister Hill and other expressions of opposition to John Sparkman; the North Carolina Committee secured 7,000 signatures to a petition opposing passage.

The regional and state organizations also continued to support rent controls, to oppose right-to-work laws, to aid voter registration drives, and to fight Southern attempts to evade the *Smith* v. *Allwright* decision. The Alabama Committee had supported James B. Folsom's successful gubernatorial campaign in 1946; after his election, the Committee initiated expressions of popular support for the governor's program and several of its members assumed minor positions in Folsom's administration. The Committee for Louisiana held fund-raising dinners and undertook to inform New Orleans tenants of their legal claims against rent-raising landlords. The Georgia Committee used its remaining resources to oppose a bill that would have enabled the Democratic party to exclude Negroes from its primaries. In Florida, the short-lived Fourth Congressional District Committee of the Southern Conference for Human Welfare initiated a meeting of state liberal organizations in Winter Park, March 22, to mobilize opposition to the Matthews bill, a proposal to turn primary elections over to the Democratic party and thus enable the party, as a private body, to exclude Negroes. The Fourth District Committee can claim partial credit for the measure's eventual defeat.

Aside from its successful work against white primary laws, Conference labors were futile. The Taft-Hartley Act became law over Truman's veto. Federal rent controls and price controls were never re-enacted. Numerous Southern states adopted right-to-work laws, among them North Carolina, Virginia, Georgia, Tennessee, and Texas.

Even the Conference's most vital local committees, the North Carolina and Washington Committees, labored partly in vain. Although the former's advocacy of increased teacher salaries, increased wages for state employees, and higher appropriations for public health had been successful, it failed to block the passage of a right-to-work law and its demands for a minimum-wage-maximum-hour law and enfranchisement of eighteen-year-olds were ignored. By their nature, its activities made results difficult to assess. Radio broadcasts, public forums, and pamphlets such as "Your Part in North Carolina's Politics," issued early in 1947, were attempts at public education—artificial seedings of the clouds of public thought to produce a climate of opinion favorable to progressive legislation. The North Carolinians, like their Conference colleagues elsewhere, failed to find ways to translate public education into positive legislation; the Committee's dwindling membership rolls gave the lie to its claims to speak for the mass of the people of the state. Its effectiveness as a lobby was thus severely limited. Its increasing financial difficulties crippled it; after the middle of 1947, its activities virtually came to an end.

Only the Washington Committee remained as active in 1947 as it had been in 1946. During the year, it raised about $33,000—more than the regional organization itself netted. It sponsored testimony in behalf of a proposed national health law, got up a petition to the Senate protesting Senator Bilbo's continuation on the District of Columbia Committee, and arranged a panel discussion in favor of a permanent Fair Employment Practices Committee. It sold a thousand recordings of Paul Robeson's "Freedom Train." It unsuccessfully worked for the appointment of Charles Hamilton Houston to the District of Columbia Commission, basing its support on Houston's promise to work for hospital improvements, low-cost housing, slum clearance, and taxation according to ability to pay. It, too, worked against the Taft-Hartley Act through public forums and radio announcements. Anticipating home rule for the District, it briefly tried to organize the voters of the city's southeastern quarter. The Committee took up practical, effective work against segregation in the city. It raised funds for an interracial nursery school, sent delegations to two local hospitals to protest their discriminatory hiring practices, and worked to have playgrounds in the District opened to children of both races. Several members of the Committee, in their private capacities, purchased the DuPont Theater which they opened to members of both races without discrimination in seating, thus shattering the pattern of theater segregation that had hitherto prevailed in Washington. These, too, briefly operated a radio station, WQQW, which practiced the Conference's demands for an end to employment discrimination; WQQW hired a Negro announcer, a Negro engineer, and Negro receptionists. To raise funds, the Committee solicited the aid of its members, of kindred organizations, and of wealthy liberals. Additionally, it sponsored speeches and dinner meetings for prominent persons; it held a party for the Hollywood Ten on the mistaken assumption that they were liberals.

On June 16, 1947, the Washington Committee sponsored a speech at Washington's Watergate Auditorium by former Vice-President Henry Wallace. There Wallace warned of an impending war between the United States and the Soviet Union. There Wallace advocated a meeting between President Truman and Premier Stalin to settle points in dispute between their countries and to negotiate a treaty to provide the basis for lasting world peace. With peace between Russia and the United States assured, Americans could devote their energies to their domestic problems: the prosperity-depression cycles that had interrupted American economic progress for 150 years might be broken; unemployment might be reduced to a minimum; Wall Street domination of American foreign policy could be ended; and the nation's wealth could be diverted from armaments to peaceful purposes. In the meantime, the United States and the Soviet Union, democratic capitalism and democratic socialism, could peacefully compete for the leadership of the world. The United States could find in the Soviet Union a large market for its surpluses and a source of raw materials. "Our first duty to ourselves," Wallace declared, "is to protect our international markets by reaching an agreement with Russia." Neither major political party, Wallace went on, recognized these needs of the hour; both had adopted policies leading to war and depression. If the country continued its conservative trend, the Republicans would capture

Congress in 1948. A Republican-dominated Congress would "kill the capitalistic democracy some of us are fighting so hard to save." Unless the Democrats reversed their policies, unless they returned to the policies of Franklin Roosevelt, American liberals and progressives would have to form a third party for the 1948 elections.

Neither the Committee for Washington nor the Southern Conference officially endorsed the contents of Wallace's speech. Conference leaders merely wished to afford the former Vice-President an opportunity to express his views; they wished the nation to hear a point of view at odds with the policy lines of the Republican and Democratic parties. Clark Foreman later claimed to have invited former Secretary of State James F. Byrnes to appear at the Watergate meeting to answer Wallace; Byrnes either declined or failed to reply to the invitation. The Southern Conference thus persisted in its refusal to take sides in the cold war. Like Henry Wallace it did not wish a plague on either the Russian or the American house; it merely wished a *pax* on them.[2]

2. Wallace's speech may be found in the New York *Times*, June 17, 1947, p. 4. For receipts see *ibid.*, June 19, 1947, p. 3. The rest of this section draws on: *The Southern Patriot*, V, *passim;* Some Highlights of the First Quarter of 1947; Edmonia Grant to Foreman and Dombrowski, undated [June (?), 1947]; Minutes, Meeting of the Executive Board, July 12, 1947; Malcolm C. Dobbs to Dombrowski, January 15, 1947; Committee for Alabama, "For Your Information," March, 1947; Malcolm C. Dobbs to Members of the Committee for Alabama, May 22, 1947; same to Dombrowski, July 7, 1947; Edmonia Grant to Dobbs, December 19, 1947: SCHW Records, TI, box No. 6. Aubrey Williams to Foreman, April 28, 1947; Minutes, Special Meeting of the Committee for Georgia, July 26, 1947; Minutes, Meeting of the Executive Board, April 19, 1947; Margaret Fisher to J. Daniel Weitzman, February 17, 1947; Fisher to Dombrowski, February 24, 1947; Mary Price to Dombrowski, February 27, 1947: SCHW Records, TI, box No. 3. North Carolina Committee, "Citizens in Action," May, 1947: SCHW Records, TI, box No. 2. *Your Part in North Carolina Politics*, SCEF possession. New York Committee, Fact Sheet, April 1947; Donald Rothenberg to Robert Ware Straus, September 16, 1947; North Carolina Committee, "Citizens in Action," October 8, 1947; Minutes, Meeting of the Executive Board of the Washington Committee, June 25, 1947; Minutes, Meeting of the Executive Board of the Washington Committee, October 8, 1947; Minutes, Meeting of the Washington Committee, October 22, 1947; Minutes, Meeting of the Executive Board of the Washington Committee, November 5, 1947; untitled typescript summarizing Washington Committee activities for 1947, misdated February 25, 1947 [1948]: Foreman Papers, AU. Interview, Clark Foreman, New York City, April 7, 1964; interview, Dr. Joseph L. Johnson, Washington, D.C., April 1, 1964.

III

Four days before Wallace's speech, on June 12, the House Committee on Un-American Activities issued a *Report on Southern Conference for Human Welfare.* Produced to discredit the Southern Conference and thereby—presumably—Wallace's speech, the *Report's* conclusions were: the Southern Conference was a "deviously camouflaged Communist-front organization"; it had shown "unswerving loyalty to the basic principles of Soviet foreign policy"; it had "consistently refused to take sharp issue with the activities and policies of either the Communist Party, USA, or the Soviet Union"; it had "maintained in decisive posts persons who have the confidence of the Communist press"; it had "displayed consistent anti-American bias and pro-Soviet bias, despite professions, in generalities, of love for America."

Two of the *Report*'s conclusions were absurd; the Southern Conference had not shown unswerving loyalty to the basic principles of Russian foreign policy and it had not displayed a consistent anti-American bias. The organization's initial declaration on foreign policy supported the policies of Franklin Roosevelt and Cordell Hull, not Russia's policy of collective security. At Chattanooga, the Conference denounced Russian as well as German aggression. During the war, its superpatriotism supported the Roosevelt administration. After the war, the organization refused to take a stand on foreign policy. Indeed, its declarations in favor of lasting peace were sufficiently vague—not to say mealy-mouthed—to appeal not only to the Communist party but also to the Republican and Democratic parties.

Two of the *Report*'s other conclusions had a measure of accuracy; the Southern Conference had seldom taken issue with the policies of the Communist party or those of the Soviet Union, and some of its officers received favorable mention in the Communist party press. The significance of these conclusions is another matter; by themselves, they do not sustain the charge that the organization was a Communist front. They ignore the lack of clear differentiation among liberals, radicals, and Communists between 1936 and 1946. They overlook the Communist party's bland evolutionary policies. They fail to consider the wartime *de facto* alliance between the Soviet Union and the Western powers; criticism of the Soviet Union between 1941 and 1945, in light of the Southern Conference's hyperpatriotism, would have seemed treasonable. And these two conclusions, along with the others, rest on a hodgepodge of inaccurate quotations, ridiculous inferences, and an occasional accuracy.

According to the *Report,* the Conference's official report of the Birmingham convention was "extraordinarily vague" about the group's origins, but "the Communists were not nearly so reticent in claiming responsibility for the Southern Conference. . . ." The first contention was roughly accurate; the second mistaken. The latter rested on quotations from Rob Hall's report on the convention. The Alabama Communist, according to the *Report*'s quotations, considered the Southern Conference "a brilliant confirmation of the line of the democratic front advanced by Comrade Browder at the tenth convention. . . ." But, on the basis of the *Report*'s quotations, Hall specifically denied Communist responsibility for the convention. Communists, he remarked, "naturally watched the conference preparations closely and helped wherever possible. . . ." Only "five southern Communist delegates" attended the convention. "Our party contributed in a modest but constructive manner to the success of the conference. . . ." An additional, highly doctored quote from Hall was used to support the claim that the Southern Conference "supplemented the activity of the American League for Peace and Democracy"—a claim Hall himself did not make.

Subsequent quotations were equally misleading. One which the *Report* ascribed to James W. Ford in the *Communist* was not on the page cited, nor had Ford authored the text on that page. Subsequent evidence was either inadequately explained or offered in ignorance of contrary or qualifying information. The *Report* noted Browder's reference to the Southern Conference as a transmission belt without indicating how he had defined the term. As evidence of Communist party control, the *Report* alleged that William Weiner, party treasurer, had sent funds to the South in 1938 when the Conference was founded without noting his denial of the assumed connection between the funds and the conference. Rob Hall, it contended, had discussed the Southern Conference with party leaders in New York; the party's Central Committee had considered the Conference, and Earl Browder had complained of the hardships the party endured to maintain the "growing southern movement." The first two contentions were irrelevant; so was the third which did not refer to the Southern Conference for Human Welfare.

As evidence of Communist manipulation in the Conference, the *Report* claimed that at Birmingham the Communists had worked in the panels which initially framed the convention's resolutions. In one panel, Paul Crouch, then a known member of the Communist party, introduced a resolution on education which the convention unanimously adopted. Members of the Resolutions Committee, the *Report* further alleges, failed to oppose the activities of "such outstanding Communists as Paul Crouch, Robert F. Hall, Ted Wellman, John P. Davis, and Edward E. Strong."

The ease with which Crouch's resolution passed indicated the widespread agreement among Southerners on the need for federal aid to Southern education to correct its manifest deficiencies, not Communist manipulation. The lack of opposition to the activities of Crouch and the other alleged Communists cannot be used to support the claims of Communist manipulation. More plausibly, this simply proves that Crouch and his friends were innocuous. Indeed, the *Report* only identified four "Communist Party line resolutions"; in addition to the resolution on education, these were the resolutions demanding the release of the Scottsboro boys, endorsing the Congress of Mexican and Spanish-American Peoples of the United States, and condemning the Dies Committee. Aside from the dubiety of these as evidence of Communist manipulation, the four resolutions amounted to a small fraction of the total number of sixty adopted. On the *Report*'s own showing then, the Communists controlled only one fifteenth of the first meeting of the Southern Conference for Human Welfare.

As additional proof of Communist control and manipulation, the *Report* considered numerous members and friends of the Southern Conference some of whom had been named as Communists in testimony before it, others of whom had had past associations with alleged Communist fronts, yet others of whom had spoken in defense of the Communist party or of Communists under federal or state indictment. The list included Joseph Gelders, John P. Davis, Yelverton Cowherd, Edward Strong, Howard Lee, H. C. Nixon, Don West, Langston Hughes, Paul Robeson, James Dombrowski, Frank Graham, Edmonia Grant, and Clark Foreman. The *Report* also listed in tabular form some sixty-two members, executives, and sponsors of the Southern Conference and then indicated whether each had ever made statements in defense of the Communist party, or in defense or support of individual Communists; whether each had ever held membership in organizations defending Communists, or in pro-Russian relief and propaganda organizations, or in organizations defending Russian foreign policy. Since the Communist party was not proscribed in American law, statements defending it were innocuous. Statements supporting or defending individual Communists were similarly innocuous, especially where these statements were concerned with elementary Constitutional rights. Memberships in alleged fronts might or might not prove anything. The *Report*'s tabulation failed to test the quality of the membership: had the accused member been active? Had he merely paid his membership fee and then neglected the organization? Did membership prove that the accused subscribed to all of the organization's policies? Were the policies of the accused organizations subversive? Nor could the tabulation answer the important questions about the accused persons' connections with the Southern Conference. What policies were they responsible for? Were these policies subversive? In short, the *Report* reduced each accused person to a disease-bearing automaton; once tainted with even the remotest connection with communism, the *Report* assumed, no person could join another organization without transmitting the taint to the latter organization.

Of those friends and members of the Conference whom the *Report* mentioned at greater length, Joseph Gelders, John P. Davis, H. C. Nixon, James Dombrowski, Frank Graham, and Clark Foreman have been given sufficient consideration. Yelverton Cowherd, ironically, was known as a red-baiter in Birmingham; the *Report*'s claim that he appeared before the La Follette Committee to defend Joseph Gelders was both irrelevant and untrue. Frank Bancroft, assistant editor of the *Southern Patriot*, may have defended Sam Darcy, signed a letter favoring closer co-operation with the Soviet Union, and once edited *Social Work Today*, "a publication which promulgated Communist propaganda among social workers." None of these was necessarily subversive; during his employment on the *Southern Patriot*, he was a loyal Conference member. He may have been responsible for the *Patriot*'s short book notices, some of which occasionally recommended publications of such organizations as the National Council for American-Soviet Friendship. Edmonia Grant may have defended the Communist party—although the *Report* fails to indicate why—and she was indeed a member of the National Negro Congress. She was also a member of the N.A.A.C.P. None of the documents in the Southern Conference records indicates that she ever tried to subvert the organization or use it to further Communist purposes.

The *Report*'s claim that the Conference's "unvarying conformance to the line of the Communist party in the field of foreign policy" clearly indicated that its purpose "was to serve as a convenient vehicle in support of the current Communist party line" rested on gross misinterpretation of the evidence. By its own showing, the Birmingham declaration of foreign policy was a clear endorsement of Roosevelt's foreign policy, not Stalin's. The Chattanooga resolution denouncing Communist and other forms of aggression was a clear defeat for the Communist bloc at the convention, not a "convenient sop" the "Communists could grant their opponents." The Nashville convention's support of total war was primarily a defense of the policies of the Roosevelt administration, only secondarily co-incident with the aims of Russian foreign policy. After late 1946, the Southern Conference as a corporate entity refused to take a position on foreign policy. Members of the Conference, as the *Report* indicates correctly, expressed fear of an impending third world war. But they did not at any time favor "Russian expansionism." The evidence the *Report* cites in support of this latter claim was taken from excerpts from a Senate speech by Senator Claude Pepper which the *Southern Patriot* reprinted. The *Report* incorrectly identified Pepper as "a leading conference spokesman." The quotes from Pepper's speech do not in fact indicate support for Russian expansion. The *Report* further inaccurately claimed that the leading speaker at the New Orleans convention had "devoted most of his talk to a defense of Russia"; actually, the leading speaker, Senator Pepper, had devoted his entire talk to American and Southern domestic problems. His remarks about the Soviet Union had been made to reporters outside the convention hall.

The *Report* attempted to demonstrate the Conference's connections with communism by listing its joint activities with Communist fronts. It noted several "groups following the lead of the Communist Party in supporting" the Southern Conference; one of its proofs was an article in the American Federation of Teachers'—"at that time under Communist control"—publication *American Teacher.* The article had been written by Stanton Smith, an anti-Communist Socialist. Other examples of the Conference's co-operation with front groups failed to indicate the purposes for which the co-operative enterprises were undertaken. The Conference had, indeed, co-operated with the National Federation for Constitutional Liberties in 1946, as well as the International Union of Mine, Mill, and Smelter Workers to aid the victims of the Columbia, Tennessee, outrage. Later the Conference helped merge the organization thus formed into a larger organization under control of the N.A.A.C.P. Other examples were trivial: *Daily Worker* endorsement of Conference policies; the *Patriot*'s recommendation of radical publications to its readers (it also recommended publications by moderate liberals such as Howard W. Odum and publications by the United States government); the *Patriot*'s publicizing the activities of "such other front organizations as the Southern Negro Youth Congress and the National Committee to Abolish the Poll Tax." Still other examples were misleading; in 1942, the Robert Marshall Foundation, "an organization which has donated heavily to the support of Communist-front groups," gave money to the Southern Conference after receiving assurances that the Conference was not Communist-dominated—a fact not mentioned in the *Report*.

The *Report* thus rested on dubious evidence which had been tortured by dubious methods to support even more dubious conclusions. At most, its array of evidence proved what everybody already knew and what few Conference leaders ever attempted to deny: the Southern Conference was a popular-front group, containing but not controlled by Communists.

In addition to being an intellectual failure, the *Report* was almost a complete tactical failure. The Governor of Arkansas used it to force several state employees to resign from a nascent Committee for Arkansas thereby destroying that organization; the *Report* ended tentative plans for a state committee in Mississippi. Otherwise it boomeranged. The Wallace meeting drew a large crowd and grossed about $20,000. Before the *Report* appeared, several prominent members of the Southern Conference had planned to quit the organization. The *Report* changed their minds and most of them postponed their resignations. Many newspapers in the South attacked the document. The Greensboro *Daily News* scored the *Report* for claiming that the Conference was a Communist front and that Frank Graham had joined numerous Communist fronts. It doubted the Conference had followed the Communist party line in foreign policy. The St. Petersburg, Florida, *Times* denounced the *Report* as a devious attempt to abridge Wallace's freedom of speech through an attack on his sponsors. Several papers protested the Committee's failure to grant the Conference a hearing—and Foreman had asked for one—including the Winston-Salem *Journal* and the Shelby, North Carolina, *Daily Star*. The Charlotte *News* condemned the Committee's methods. The Asheville *Times* criticized the *Report*'s manifest lack of solid evidence. Major Southern newspapers also criticized the *Report*, including the Birmingham *Age-Herald* and the Atlanta *Constitution*. The *Report* drew a full, excellent criticism from Walter Gellhorn, a law professor at Columbia University. Yet, the *Report* had its defenders; the New Orleans *Times-Picayune*, the Nashville *Banner*, the Memphis *Commercial-Appeal* and the Danville, Virginia, *Register* announced their agreements with its conclusions.

The bulk of these commentaries were concerned with the *Report*'s accuracy, not with the character of the Southern Conference for Human Welfare. Here perhaps was an indication of the Conference's diminishing prestige. And so perhaps were attacks on the Conference from other quarters.

In 1946, after the Conference moved its regional headquarters from Nashville to New Orleans, it ran into recurrent criticism from local newspapers and from the city's Young Men's Business Club. The papers spread stories of the Conference's left-wing connections and scored it for its failure to offer realistic solutions to Louisiana's problems. The young businessmen seldom passed up an opportunity to broadcast the conclusions of the House Committee on Un-American Activities. Criticism of the Conference came from the Socialist followers of Norman Thomas and from members of the newly organized Americans for Democratic Action. In 1946, Southern Socialists reported to the national headquarters of the Socialist party that the regional offices of the Southern Conference were in Communist control, but that the state committees remained in safe hands. Another Socialist, Barney B. Taylor, in a review of Conference member Stetson Kennedy's *Southern Exposure*, ridiculed the organization; Kennedy had called the Southern Conference the hope of the South and Taylor remarked that if Kennedy were correct then he would have to surrender to despair. This same Taylor later organized an ADA chapter in Memphis and tried at the same time to prevent the organization of a Southern Conference committee in the city. Privately, Conference leaders complained to ADA officials about rumors spread by the ADA. And the ADA did more than spread rumors. In North Carolina, ADA supporters drained funds from the Conference. CIO Textile Workers' Union officials, according to Mary Price, threatened to withdraw support from the Committee for North Carolina unless Negroes were given less prominent roles in the Committee and their reform demands were muffled. The Textile Workers, she further complained, switched their financial support from the Committee to the state ADA chapter. Shortly after the House Committee on Un-American Activities' *Report,* the nationally syndicated Marquis Childs, an ADA member, criticized Henry Wallace's Watergate speech for its left isolationism; in the course of his article, Childs accused the Southern Conference of left isolationism between 1939 and 1941, of collaboration with the American Peace Mobilization, and of helping "to keep the United States unprepared for the blows that fell at Pearl Harbor." Childs's criticisms received support from L. M. Birkhead, guiding light of the Friends of Democracy which had financed some of John Roy Carlson's exposés and technical adviser to Sinclair Lewis for *Elmer Gantry.* Birkhead told Mrs. Isaac Heller, wife of one of the Committee for Louisiana's most effective fund-raisers, that the Conference had followed the Communist party line from 1939 to 1941 and that several of its leaders were habitual fellow travelers. Birkhead persuaded Mrs. Heller and her husband who thereupon resigned from the Committee for Louisiana. Although both Childs and Birkhead had overemphasized the Conference's connections with the American Peace Mobilization and with other party-line organizations, Conference leaders' denials were in vain. In the fall of 1947, the Conference drew severe, sarcastic comments from a former sponsor, Ralph McGill; in one attack, McGill referred to the Conference as Communist-infiltrated, compared the "mental mechanisms" of the Conference leaders with those of the leaders of the Klan, and called the organization's leaders a "set of discredited professional phonies." Under threat of a libel suit, McGill eventually printed a partial retraction; but his remarks remained on the record—and undoubtedly lingered in his readers' memories longer than his retraction. Conference prestige was sinking as fast as its finances and its membership.

Most of the attacks on the Conference either missed the mark or exaggerated the influence of the alleged Communists within the organization. Owing to the possibilities for libel inherent in the charges, persons who criticized the Conference outside of Congress refrained from mentioning names. A careful synthesis of the charges against the Conference and a scrupulous search for evidence could have resulted in a plausible argument that the organization was indeed a Communist front. Kenneth Douty's unpublished study came close to meeting these requirements. Yet Douty carefully avoided concluding that the Conference had been Communist-dominated. And justly so. The available evidence fails to sustain the charge of Communist domination no matter how it is spelled out: whether the interpretation claims Communist origin and domination or liberal origin and subsequent Communist capture.

Most of the real and imagined Communists and fellow travelers holding positions of importance within the organization have been previously indicated. Several others deserve brief consideration: Mary Price, Frank Bancroft, Malcolm Dobbs, Sam Carothers, and Leo Sheiner. In 1948, Elizabeth Bentley, a former functionary in the Russian espionage apparatus, appeared before the House Committee on Un-American Activities. There she alleged that Mary Price, while Walter Lippmann's secretary in 1940 and 1941, had passed on information from his files to Russian intelligence. During the war, Miss Bentley also alleged, Miss Price had passed information from Duncan Lee of the Office of Strategic Services to Russian intelligence. Later, in her public confession, *Out of Bondage,* Miss Bentley repeated her charges in greater detail. Between 1940 and 1944, Mary Price was supposed to have been a witting tool of Russia's American espionage operations. Although she failed to sue for libel, Miss Price denied the charges on their first appearance. After the passage of the Federal Immunity Act, she gave secret testimony before a New York Grand Jury; her revelations, if there were any, have never been made public.

After Frank Bancroft lost his job with the *Southern Patriot,* he went to work for the United Nations as an editor in its Documents Central Division. In 1952, Trygvie Lie dismissed him for his refusal to tell either a grand jury or the Senate Internal Security Subcommittee about his affiliations with alleged Communist fronts. He did, however, deny to the latter committee that he had been in the pay of a foreign power while in the employ of the United Nations and that he had ever been a spy.

In the fall of 1947, Malcolm Dobbs and his wife, former executive secretary of the Committee for Alabama, were expelled from the Birmingham CIO Council for their alleged Communist affiliations in proceedings which William Mitch, an anti-Communist, considered unfair. Nine years later, in testimony before the House Committee on Un-American Activities, Dr. William Sorum, a former Communist party member, claimed that during his association with the party Malcolm Dobbs had been his immediate superior.

From 1945 to the fall of 1946, the chairman of the Committee for Alabama was Sam Hall. In 1947, a Sam Hall—presumably the same man—became Communist party chairman in North Carolina.

In 1954, one James B. Nimmo claimed before the House Committee on Un-American Activities that while a member of the Communist party he had met Sam Carothers in closed party meetings. Carothers worked briefly for the Southern Conference in Florida in 1946 and even more briefly for the organization in Louisiana in 1947.

In 1954, during Senate Internal Security Subcommittee hearings on the Southern Conference Educational Fund, ex-Communist Paul Crouch, a witness of doubtful reliability, claimed to have known Leo Sheiner, one-time executive secretary of the Southern Conference's Fourth Florida Congressional District Committee, as a member of the Communist party. Before that committee, Sheiner denied having been a party member or a Russian intelligence agent. After the hearings, a Florida judge disbarred him. Later, he was reinstated.

Final, definitive judgments on most—if not all—of these charges are impossible. Statements given before congressional committees are often vague where they ought to be precise. Without more detailed information about the accusers and the accused, the good faith and objectivity of neither side can be adequately assessed. Nor can the evidence be properly weighed. Miss Bentley, for example, failed to explain how Russian intelligence could have been so stupid as to involve known American Communists like Earl Browder in the intimate details of its operations. Her book is laced with quotations from conversations that took place years before its publication, and this consideration casts at least partial doubt on the authenticity of her narrative. On the other hand, Mary Price's denials of Miss Bentley's charges quickly shaded off into indelicate suggestions that Miss Bentley was a lesbian, into plaints about red smears of the Progressive party, and into conjurations of a coming American fascism. Paul Crouch was an interested, not disinterested, party; the most important events of the last years of his life, the ones from which he presumably drew the greatest personal satisfaction, were those involved in the hearings where he bore witness. By dramatizing, not to say exaggerating, the importance and power of the Communist party, he dramatized, not to say exaggerated, his own importance and power: this involved naming a large number of real and imaginary members of the Communist party. Crouch's interest in his charges may have been as great—if such things are comparable—as the interest of those whom he accused in denying them. Some of the accused persons were never given a chance to confront their accusers or to answer the charges against them. The accusations usually failed to provide information about the character of the accused's connections with the Communist party or with front groups: why had they joined? what functions did they undertake? what specific subversions were they responsible for? Nor did the accusations provide information about the character of the accused's association with the Southern Conference for Human Welfare. On Miss Bentley's showing, Mary Price left the Washington spy ring in 1944, a full year before she became executive secretary of the Committee for North Carolina. There, incidentally, she was not known as a member of the Communist party; in 1954, before the House Committee on Un-American Activities, one Ralph Vernon

Long, a former member of the Communist party in North Carolina, testified that Miss Price had never been at party meetings which he had attended.

The central weakness of all the accusations against the Conference's members is that they fail to test their charges against specific activities of the accused while members of the Southern Conference and against the activities of the Southern Conference. Assuming for the moment that every charge made against members of the Conference was true, the question still remains: what subversive activities—or identifiable Communist activities—did the organization engage in? Accusations that the Conference followed the party line in foreign affairs cannot be substantiated. The organization never so much as flirted with Communist programs for Black Belt self-determination before or after the war when these schemes had some currency in the party press. When the American Communist party began planning a third party, when its foreign policy line began to deviate from the line of the Truman administration, the Conference adopted a mild resolution in favor of peace and thereafter avoided taking a position on foreign affairs; the conference never denounced either the Truman Doctrine or the Marshall Plan, the twin bugbears of American Communists and fellow travelers during the first years after the war. Its domestic programs aimed at bringing a humanized capitalism—or mixed economy—to the South, supported the mild social-democratic reforms of the New Deal, and pointed toward full justice for America's much abused black minority. Indeed, nonsocialist members of the Conference, at least, regarded the New Deal and the Southern Conference as agencies to save American capitalism from its stupidities. They similarly regarded attempts to increase purchasing power as a way to insure full production in the private sector of the economy; like the sponsors of the Full Employment Act, they advocated government action only when the private sector proved incapable of providing full employment. No amount of congressional pettifoggery can turn peaceful propaganda in support of New Deal reforms and Negro voter registration drives into subversive activities.

All of this does not deny some credibility to the charges against the Conference. Known Communists participated in the organization; they attended its general meetings and several served in administrative positions. Yet they failed to dominate the organization or to determine its major policies. These the full membership decided; specific programs of action were undertaken only if they commanded wide support among Conference members. Known Communists expressed interest in the organization and approved parts of its program; but known Communists expressed interest in Winston Churchill and approved some of his policies. The implications of this interest are difficult to determine. Earl Browder has acknowledged that the party was interested in the Southern Conference and at the same time claimed that he never considered the organization worth mentioning in his reports to party conventions. William Z. Foster, Browder's main antagonist within the party, has claimed that Communists were active and influential in the work of the Conference. But neither he nor Browder considered the Conference a Communist front.

The Conference seldom took sharp issue with the American Communist party and never spoke out against the barbarous tyranny and dubious democracy of the Stalin regime. The failure to take issue with the Communist party stemmed in part from the party's efforts to identify itself with programs appealing to all shades of the American reform spectrum; since poverty, race prejudice, and Southern Bourbonism were the Conference's main enemies, the organization took sharp issue with them and not with the small, nearly impotent contingent of Communists in the South. The failure to denounce Stalinism stemmed in part from the intellectual dishonesty characteristic of many American progressives who participated in popular fronts, in part from the consideration that Russia was our wartime ally, and in part from the Conference's postwar decision to confine itself to domestic issues.

Nor is this all. Not only were Communists in the Conference but so were Democrats, Negroes, anti-Communist Socialists, Christian Socialists, and a few Republicans. No one element ever dominated.

Nor did any one group ever subvert the organization. On the basis of the available evidence the Communists were one of the least subversive elements in the Conference. The chief wire-puller—if such a category has any relevance—was Franklin D. Roosevelt, whose bidding the Conference willingly did all his life and who gave almost nothing in return. The chief subversives—if such a term can be used without implications of treason—were John L. Lewis, who in 1941 tried to take over the organization, and Van A. Bittner, whose bitter public criticism in 1946 started the Conference toward its inglorious end.

The Southern Conference was not a Communist front but a popular front, a conglomeration of individuals from organizations as diverse as the Baptist Church and the Communist party united about a minimum program on which all of the constituent factions could agree. That minimum program aimed at repairing the defects of American capitalism, bringing the South up to the economic and social standards of the rest of the country, and finally obtaining elementary justice for American Negroes.[3]

3. House Committee on Un-American Activities, *Report on Southern Conference for Human Welfare*, 80 cong., 1 sess. (Washington: Government Printing Office, 1947). Newspaper comments on the *Report* are in Foreman Papers, AU. Walter Gelhorn, "Report on a Report of the House Committee on Un-American Activities," *Harvard Law Review*, LX (October 1947), 1193–1234; the present critique of the *Report* derives in large measure from Gellhorn's excellent article. Material on the Young Men's Business Club's attacks is in SCHW Records, TI, box No. 1. William Becker to Agnes M. Douty, C. C. Cloud, and Alice Labouisse, November 15, 1946; Tom Leonard to Harry (?), December 5, 1946; Agnes Douty to Bill [Becker (?)], December 11, 1946; Minutes, Meeting of the National Executive Board of the Socialist Party, November 8, 1946, Socialist Party Papers, Duke University. Barney B. Taylor, review of Stetson Kennedy's *Southern Exposure*, in *The New Leader*, XXIX (December 28, 1946), 13. Clark Foreman to Leon Henderson, April 29, 1947; Mary Price to William Poteat, January 9, 1948: Foreman Papers, AU. Childs's column appeared among other places in the St. Louis *Post-Dispatch*, July 8, 1947, p. 3B. L. M. Birkhead to Mrs. Issac Heller, August 14, 1947, SCHW Records, TI, box No. 6. Ralph McGill's criticisms appeared in the Atlanta *Constitution*, September 2, 1947, September 15, 1947, November 15, 1947, and his retraction on January 30, 1948; materials on the libel suit are in Foreman Papers, AU. Kenneth Douty, "The Southern Conference for Human Welfare," *passim*. On Mary Price: House Committee on Un-American Activities, *Hearings Regarding Communist Espionage in the United States Government*, 80 cong., 2 sess. (Washington: Government Printing Office, 1948), pp. 529–530, 687–689, 726, 729–730, 741, 755; Elizabeth Bentley, *Out of Bondage* (New York: Devin Adair, 1951), *passim;* Herbert L. Packer, *Ex-*

IV

Between the spring of 1947 and the late winter of 1948, the Southern Conference flirted with Henry Wallace and the Progressive party. On April 19, 1947, the Conference executive board expressed dissatisfaction with both the Republican and Democratic parties. "[T]he Southern people," it resolved, "must find a constructive solution to their greatest political dilemma since the Civil War." Opposed by tradition to the Republican party, "they are equally opposed to the present Democratic Party policies and to Southern Tory Democrats causing hysteria about the danger of a Third World War." Franklin Roosevelt had led them "to expect Democratic Party leadership toward a vital democracy and an in-

---

Communist Witnesses (Stanford: Stanford University Press, 1962), pp. 58, 105–106, 117; Mary Price's denials are in the Greensboro, North Carolina *Daily News*, August 9, 1948, p. 1; the New York *Times*, August 11, 1948, p. 3; *Daily Worker*, August 3, 1948, p. 11; for Ralph Vernon Long's testimony: House Committee on Un-American Activities, *Hearings—Communist Activities in Florida*, 83 cong., 2 sess. (Washington: Government Printing Office, 1954), Pt. 1, pp. 7364–7365. On Frank Bancroft: *The Christian Century*, LII (April 3, 1935), 444–445; *Social Work Today*, VII (February 1940), 16–18; VIII (October 1940), 7–9, IX (November 1941), 4–5, VIII (February 1941), 3–4; United States Senate, Committee on the Judiciary, Internal Security Subcommittee, *Hearings—Activities of United States Citizens Employed by the United Nations*, 82 cong., 2 sess. (Washington: Government Printing Office, 1952), pp. 29–40, 105–106; the New York *Times*, October 14, 1952, p. 1, and October 23, 1952, pp. 1, 8. On Malcolm C. Dobbs: House Committee on Un-American Activities, *Communism in New Orleans*, 85 cong., 1 sess. (Washington: Government Printing Office, 1957), pp. 158–159, 164–166, 171. For Sam Hall: Sam Hall to Frank Graham, March 19, 1947, Graham Papers, UNC; *Daily Worker*, September 20, 1946, p. 12. On Carothers: clipping from the Miami *Herald*, June 2, 1946, SCEF possession; House Committee on Un-American Activities, *Hearings—Communist Activities in Florida*, 83 cong., 2 sess. (Washington: Government Printing Office, 1954), Pt. 2, pp. 7427, 7439. For Leo Sheiner: Senate Committee on the Judiciary, Internal Security Subcommittee, *Hearings—Subversive Influence in the Southern Conference Educational Fund*, 83 cong., 2 sess. (Washington: Government Printing Office, 1954), *passim*. The last attacks on the Conference worth mentioning are Paul Crouch in *Plain Talk* in 1949, an article conveniently reprinted in the *Congressional Record*, 81 cong., 1 sess., 1949, 2998–3000; Crouch also testified before the House Committee on Un-American Activities: *Testimony of Paul Crouch*, 81 cong., 1 sess. (Washington: Government Printing Office, 1949), pp. 189ff. Browder interview, Yonkers, New York, April 13, 1964. William Z. Foster, *History of the Communist Party of the United States* (New York: International Publishers, 1952), pp. 378, 421; see also his, *The Negro People in American History* (New York: International Publishers, c.1954), pp. 485ff. David Shannon, *The Decline of American Communism* (New York: Harcourt Brace, c.1959), *passim*.

creased prosperity for the people. The Economic Bill of Rights gave [them] hope and confidence for the future." Postwar reaction had nearly destroyed the Southern people's bright hopes; wartime gains "are being taken from them." In place of continued progress, the Southern people got "the mutiliation of the Wage and Hour Act, the threatened destruction of the entire American labor movement, the increasing encroachment of absentee monopoly control of Southern business . . . [and] the threatened unemployment of millions of farm workers due to mechanization." Federal agencies "whose services are most acutely needed in the South" had been crippled and "social legislation to meet the most severe housing, education, health, child welfare and social security needs" had been neglected. White primary bills and an increase in lynchings had answered demands for more democracy in the South. Instead of increased productivity and a concomitant rise in American standards of living, the Southern people got "the fear of atomic energy as a means of universal destruction and the threat of World War III." Thus

> confronted with this dilemma, the greatest political need of the Southern people is to give urgent consideration through their churches, unions and associations of every kind, to the best way of reversing the present tragic trend. Effective action in this historic moment will lay the basis for a political decision in 1948 which will make it possible for the South to realize her own magnificent possibilities and to make her indispensable contribution to the national and international good.

The board then threatened the two major political parties; "the human needs and the political aspirations of the Southern people will not be frustrated by reactionary programs of either traditional party." Here began the Southern Conference's dalliance with the Wallace movement.

Conference sponsorship of Wallace's Watergate speech promoted "a free discussion of [American] policies before the American people without intimidation, any smears, any attempt to frighten people away"[4] and it anticipated a possible need for a third party in 1948.

4. From a transcript of a radio debate between Clark Foreman and Alvin O'Konski, SCHW Records, TI, box No. 3.

Although the Conference failed to seek formal alliance with Wallace's organization, the Progressive Citizens of America, it continued to collaborate with him and persons of similar convictions. In October, members of the Southern Conference in their private capacities undertook some of the arrangements for a Southern tour of Wallace's future running mate, Glenn Taylor, during which the singing Senator warned his audiences of the dangers of a third world war. In November, Wallace toured the South under Conference auspices, speaking in eight cities in four states to approximately 25,000 persons. The meetings were to spread Wallace's views and to aid the Southern Conference; "we are not coming South," Lewis Frank, Wallace's manager, told Clark Foreman, "just to add a few dollars to the SCHW treasury. We want to help you build . . . but these meetings must be as broad as possible and we want them to have some relationship to political organization and to reflect the ferment in the South." [5]

Prior to the tour, Foreman and Wallace's managers unwisely agreed to refuse to hold segregated meetings; Wallace therefore passed up opportunities to speak in Memphis, Nashville, and Little Rock, where he could have denounced segregation to his segregated audiences. Where he appeared he spoke forthrightly against the Jim Crow system, denounced the arms race, the Truman Doctrine, and aid to military dictatorships, and pleaded for a peace treaty with the Soviet Union, peaceful competition between Russia and the United States, and national economic planning. If the Democratic party failed to abolish segregation, he threatened in his speech in New Orleans, it would die "and there will be a new party—a people's party—a party of workers and farmers—a truely democratic party." [6]

Late in December 1947, Wallace announced his intention to seek the presidency. The announcement should have forced the Southern Conference to cease its coy flirtations—either to become an honest woman through marriage or to return, still chaste, to its Southern

5. Frank to Foreman, September 17, 1947, SCHW Records, TI, box No. 6.
6. A copy of Wallace's speech is in SCHW Records, TI, box No. 3.

domestic concerns. Yet, the Southern Conference would neither wed nor quite return. Wallace's domestic views closely paralleled the Conference's program for the South; "the Wallace candidacy," Clark Foreman contended, "offers the South the greatest chance it has ever had to escape from the feudalism that has been such a curse to its people and to the rest of the country." [7] Although convinced that Wallace was the South's best hope and active in his campaign, Foreman proposed to allow the Southern Conference leaders and its remaining state organizations to decide for themselves whether to join the Wallace movement. At a meeting of the executive board of the Conference in Washington, D.C., January 31, 1948, Foreman's proposal became official Conference policy. The forthcoming election, the board resolved, "will possibly be the most fateful of our generation" and "the Southern Conference for Human Welfare urges all Southerners to take a more active part in politics than ever before. Because the specific political situation in the various states differs, the Southern Conference . . . urges all its State Committees and its State and National Officers to determine their political course in the 1948 elections as these specific conditions may dictate, keeping in mind always the objectives of peace, security, democracy and full citizenship for which the Southern Conference . . . stands."

The Conference's state and national officers did as they were bid; some set their course for Wallace, others for Truman, and still others—perhaps—for Dewey. So did the state committees. The Committee for North Carolina refrained from endorsing a candidate. In the fall of 1947, by a vote of 46 to 5, its members rejected a resolution requiring them to declare their political affiliations, dubiously claiming, among other things, that the resolution involved red-baiting. The Committee then adopted a resolution declaring its disagreement with communism and declaring its support of the Constitutional rights of the Communist party. But the damage had been done; internal distrust and hostility were added to

7. Foreman to Members of the Executive Board, May 17, 1948, Graham Papers, UNC.

the Committee's financial woes. Early in 1948 Mary Price quit the Committee to work full-time for Wallace; she ran for governor of North Carolina on the Progessive ticket. Shortly after her resignation, the Committee died in the midst of suspicions and ill will. After six meetings of the membership and the executive board, the Washington Committee decided to refrain from supporting a presidential candidate. Foreman, the Committee's lobbyist, wished the Committee to stay clear of the presidential campaign; most of its members, as residents of the District of Columbia, could not vote, and he thought their efforts should be directed against Capital segregation patterns. Joseph Johnson, committee president, also opposed endorsing any one of the presidential aspirants; the Committee included Republicans, Democrats, and Wallacites and could not endorse a candidate without doing injustice to some of the Committee members. Johnson and Foreman prevailed. In May 1948, the Committee for Washington ended its operations. Only the Committee for Virginia endorsed Wallace; in March, the few remaining members of the organization voted to support the former Vice President's candidacy. The anti-Wallace members thereupon resigned.

Wallace's decision to run for the presidency effectively brought the Southern Conference for Human Welfare's political career to an end. It further split the badly split organization. Many left to work for Wallace, including Clark Foreman, Mary Price, Virginia Foster Durr, who ran for governor in Virginia as a Progressive, Alva Taylor, Robert Ware Straus, one-time executive secretary of the Washington Committee, Joseph Johnson, Donald Rothenberg, who had tried to organize the southeastern quarter of the District, and Samuel Rodman, a prominent member of the Conference's finance committee after the war. The close association of some of these with Wallace—especially Clark Foreman—drove anti-Wallace liberals out of the Conference. Both Melvyn Douglas, the actor, who had raised money in California for the organization, and Frank Karleson, a prominent New York lawyer, quit the Conference over Foreman's intimate role in the Wallace campaign. With the Truman liberals quitting the organization and with the defection of many Conference leaders to the Wallace movement, the Southern Conference for Human Welfare was left without leaders and administrative personnel. Only the Educational Fund remained. Under its future president, Aubrey Williams, a staunch supporter of President Truman, and James Dombrowski, who avoided the presidential campaign, the Southern Conference Educational Fund hobbled on in a different direction.[8]

V

At the New Orleans convention, the Southern Conference executive board decided to have the Educational Fund begin a campaign against Southern racial segregation. During the first half of 1947, the Conference's financial crisis and its internal feuds delayed attempts to implement the board's decision. In the summer of that year, after Dombrowski moved to the Fund, the work began.

The task required a reformation of Southern public opinion, a re-education of most Southern white adults and children. An educational organization, the Fund had to limit itself to propaganda; lobbying and participation in elections would have cost it its privi-

8. Minutes Meeting of the Executive Board, April 19, 1947, SCHW Records, TI, box No. 6. The resolution was reprinted in *The Southern Patriot,* V (June 1947), 4. Materials on the Conference's relation to the Wallace movement are scattered through the SCHW Records, TI, especially in box No. 6, and the Foreman Papers, AU. Foreman to Mortimer May, January 31, 1948, SCHW Records, TI, box No. 6. Minutes Meeting of the Executive Board, January 31, 1948; Foreman to the Members of the Committee for Washington, February 10, 1948; Foreman to Thomas N. E. Greville, October 3, 1947; Melvyn Douglas to Members of the Southern Conference, February 4, 1948: Foreman Papers, AU. Frank Karleson to Aubrey Williams, October 5, 1948, Williams Papers, Roosevelt Library, Hyde Park, box No. 39; James Dombrowski to Aubrey Williams, September 6, 1955, *ibid.,* box No. 38. Robert W. Straus to Joseph L. Johnson, May 19, 1948, Foreman Papers, AU. Johnson interview previously cited. This account of the Conference's relation to the Wallace movement differs from the one presented by Kenneth Douty; in the mid 1950s, Clark Foreman told Douty that Aubrey Williams alone had prevented the organization from endorsing Wallace. The evidence in the Foreman Papers and in the SCHW Records indicates otherwise; contemporary documents are presumably more accurate than Foreman's memory. For a recent account of the Wallace campaign by a participant, see Curtis D. MacDougall, *Gideon's Army* (2 vols., New York: Marzani and Munsell, c.1965). For Aubrey Williams's later years, see his obituary in *The Southern Patriot,* XXIII (March 1965); also interview, Aubrey Williams, Washington, D.C., March 23, 1964.

leges of tax exemption and thereby cut off its paltry revenues. Persuasion and gentle guidance, the techniques of public education, suited James Dombrowski's temperament and his talents. The Educational Fund thus reverted to the function the Southern Conference had claimed for itself before January 1946: to promote public welfare through public education. Public welfare gradually became synonymous with integration and New Deal reforms received less and less publicity.

In the fall of 1947, the *Southern Patriot* devoted a full issue to segregation in education. The paper pointed out the disparities between the wages of white and Negro teachers, between property valuations of white and Negro schools, and between per-pupil expenditures for white and Negro children. It deplored the lack of facilities for professional training for Southern Negroes, who had access to four law schools, two schools of medicine, and one university offering an advanced degree in library science. In consequence, the South had proportionately four times more white than Negro doctors, four times more white dentists, thirteen times more white pharmacists, thirty-five times more white lawyers, and two hundred times more white engineers. The journal argued that educational segregation, being inherently unequal, violated the equal-protection clause of the Fourteenth Amendment, that it was un-Christian, that it failed to train citizens for the postwar period, and that it impaired American relations with the colored nations of the world.

In a subsequent issue the paper attacked segregation in health. Negroes could expect to die sooner than whites, have more of their children die at birth, have more of their children's mothers die in childbirth, and have more stillbirths per thousand than whites. Deaths from pellagra, syphillis, and pneumonia were proportionately higher for Negroes than for whites. Only one percent of the hospital beds in the South were available to Negroes. Sixty-five percent of the region's Negro babies were born without the aid of a competent physician. Seventy percent of the Negro homes in the South lacked running water; 75 percent of the Negro families in the region existed on annual incomes of less than $1,000. The journal demanded an immediate end to segregated hospitals and a national health program. It also demanded an immediate end to all forms of segregation.

In addition to its feature articles, the *Patriot* reported civil rights battles and, in some cases, made news itself. Signs of hope appeared; at the University of Oklahoma, a thousand students, to protest University segregation, cremated the Fourteenth Amendment and sent the ashes to President Truman; a poll revealed that 60 percent of the graduate students at Alabama Polytechnic favored the admission of Negroes; at the University of Texas, at Tulane, and at Louisiana State University, applause greeted Henry Wallace's criticism of segregation; Federal Judge J. Waites Waring overruled two attempts of the South Carolina legislature to circumvent the Supreme Court's ruling on the white primary system; the admission of Negroes to professional baseball and other sports drew *Patriot* encomiums. Yet signs of despair persisted: for a time, the journal kept a tally of the number of Negroes killed by Birmingham police. James Dombrowski conducted several opinion polls; in one a majority of Southern social scientists who responded to Dombrowski's questionaire declared that segregation violated American political and ethical traditions and was contrary to the country's self interest. This same majority favored admission of Negroes to Southern graduate schools. A subsequent poll of the faculties of Southern state universities indicated that a majority of those who replied favored the admission of Negro students to white graduate and professional schools.

As the Educational Fund transformed itself into an antisegregation organization, it broke away from the Southern Conference for Human Welfare. After the summer of 1947, the *Southern Patriot* no longer appeared as the organ of the Southern Conference for Human Welfare but as the journal of the Educational Fund. After May, 1948, the paper refrained from commenting on the presidential race; it even failed to mention Henry Wallace, whose earlier tour of the South it had reported in great detail. Clark Foreman's work for Wallace effectively removed him from the affairs of the Fund and the termination of the remaining state committees early in 1948 left it the sole viable heir of the Southern Conference. In fifteen months, Aubrey Williams and James Dombrowski disengaged the Educational Fund from the Southern Conference. "We have," Williams told the Southern AFofL leader, George Googe, "completely severed all connections with the Southern Conference for Human Welfare." [9]

Shortly after the election of 1948, the Southern Conference Educational Fund reaffirmed its new role. On November 20, 1948, at Thomas Jefferson's home, Monticello, Virginia, the Fund sponsored a meeting of fifty persons—most of them middle-class white and Negro liberals—who adopted a declaration of independence for America's Negroes. Negro rights, the declaration stipulated, included "equality before the law, and freedom from any discrimination bolstered by law; a right to vote; freedom of expression; an unrestricted access to all institutions supported by taxes for the public welfare, schools and hospitals not excepted; equal pay for equal work, and equal opportunity to receive training and to gain employment; and the right of unsegregated transportation, housing and assembly." The delegates recommended individual, group, state, and federal action to end racial discrimination: individuals could speak out against discrimination and guard against personal prejudice; groups could end their own discriminatory practices; states could abrogate laws enforcing discrimination; and all government units could enact laws protecting the civil rights of their citizens.

From the adoption of the Monticello declaration to the present day, the Southern Conference Educational Fund has single-mindedly worked to end Southern segregation. It continues to feature articles on specific aspects of the Jim Crow system, report the signs of hope appearing in the South, lay bare the strategy and tactics of the region's white supremacists, and to stimulate new attacks on the system. The re-education of Southern whites has been a long and tedious task.[10]

9. Williams to George Googe, November 12, 1948, Williams Papers, Roosevelt Library, Hyde Park, box No. 39.

10. This section rests mainly on the files of the *Southern Patriot* after August 1947; specific issues of interest are October 1947, February 1948, March 1948, May 1948, August 1948, and September 1948. The Monticello declarations is in the *Southern Patriot,* VI (December 1948). Two hundred other persons signed the declaration. For other attempts to deny any vital connection between the Southern Conference for Human Welfare and the Southern Conference Educational Fund see the New Orleans *Times-Picayune*, October 5, 1963, p. 2.

VI

The day after the Monticello meeting, a rump group of former Southern Conference activists—including Clark Foreman, James Dombrowski, Aubrey Williams, Myles Horton, and Mrs. C. J. Durr —met in Richmond, Virginia, to bring the Southern Conference for Human Welfare to a quiet end. In debt and without income, the Conference paid off its obligations at 25 percent, its back wages at 15 percent. "[N]ew political alignments," the rump group's resolution of termination remarked, "have largely absorbed the political energies of the members of the SCHW and make its continuation unnecessary and a duplication of effort;" in short, the attempt to transform the Southern Conference into a political organization had utterly failed. Having failed politically, the Southern Conference in the corporate person of the Southern Conference Educational Fund would return to "educational work." Outside of the Conference, the death of the Southern Conference for Human Welfare went unnoticed; so did the Educational Fund's transfiguration from an unofficial propagator of the New Deal into a declared enemy of Southern segregation.[11]

11. The *Southern Patriot,* VII (January 1949), 4, has a copy of the resolution adopted at Richmond. Clark Foreman to Samuel Rodman, November 23, 1948; Clark Foreman to J. Daniel Weitzman, November 23, 1948; James Dombrowski to Clark Foreman, December 28, 1948; Clark Foreman to Robert Bialek, February 23, 1949; Clark Foreman to Frank Graham, June 15, 1949: Graham Papers, UNC.

9

POST MORTEM

THE Southern Conference for Human Welfare, whose birth had drawn regional, national, and international attention, thus died in obscurity, poor and neglected, forgotten both by its friends and its enemies. By the pragmatic test, its troubled life had been almost without importance. Its answers to the National Emergency Council's *Report on the Economic Conditions of the South* went unheeded in Congress. Its attempt to help liberalize the Democratic party through the abolition of the poll tax was a failure; and it could not take credit for the few successes of the 1938 purge. Its subsequent demands for reform were ignored—cries for aid that state and national politicians heard but failed, in the main, to act upon. Where Conference demands became law, its voice was only one of many, usually weaker and hoarser than the others in the clamant chorus of reform. Its recommendations for wartime mobilization were at best duplications of the efforts of official and unofficial patriots; only the Conference's insistence on continued reform and its concern for the Negro saved it from callous chauvinism. For all its huffing and puffing, the Southern Conference could not blow down the mansion of Southern conservatism—a failure ascribable either to the Conference's feeble breath or to the strength of the Southern conservative's edifice.

Even the Conference's postwar flurry of activity brought few tangible results. The *Southern Patriot* and the Conference's occasional pamphlets provided valuable information to the South's liberal minority. Yet the connection between these pamphlets and subsequent actions cannot be determined. Conference pamphlets favorable to organized labor and its outspoken support of organizing drives may have provided aid and comfort to the labor movement and to the unorganized worker; but no specific union successes can be traced to the Conference's labor propaganda. Its pamphlet on the Columbia, Tennessee, outrage drew attention to the plight of the Negroes there under indictment and money for their defense, but the heavy legal and financial burdens were carried by the N.A.A.C.P. Other Conference publications on the race problem may have converted moderate whites to integration, but they failed to stave off an increase in recorded lynchings after the war; and the Conference failed to win either federal or state antilynching laws. Conference lobbies in several Southern states and the District of Columbia were necessary aids to the forces of reform and no doubt helped produce some liberal legislation. Yet the balance sheet shows the Conference an over-all failure; most of its local demands were ignored and conservative forces came before the legislatures better financed and better organized—witness the large number of right-to-work laws passed in the South during and after the war. Conference efforts to register Negro voters were a vital part of progressive efforts to extend the franchise and increases in Negro registrants following the *Smith* v. *Allwright* decision were partly a result of its labors.

Here perhaps lay the Conference's most enduring successes.

It pioneered to break the chains of a half century of Southern racial customs. It may have been the first Southern interracial voluntary organization to speak out for an end to all forms of segregation. Its work in voter registration, its public demands for an end to all forms of segregation, and its local work against discrimination in Washington, D.C., anticipated—and may have prepared the way—for subsequent assaults on the Jim Crow system. Arguments used in the *Southern Patriot* after the war are now common among the activists in the freedom rides, the sitins, and the voter-education projects. The Southern Conference Educational Fund now works with militant Southern civil rights groups, including the Student Non-Violent Coordinating Committee and the Southern Christian Leadership Conference; its current president, the Reverend Fred L. Shuttlesworth, has long been active in the civil rights movement in Birmingham. The Southern Conference Educational Fund provides a direct link between the idealism and programs of the New Deal Era and the idealism and programs of the current civil rights movement.

Yet the Educational Fund is not a membership organization; persons who join receive the *Patriot,* nothing more. Its organized demonstrations are few and peripheral to the main tasks of the civil rights forces. It helps where it can; it has a few special projects; it provides favorable publicity; it tries to keep the frequently antagonistic organizations aware of one another's programs. All of this is a tacit admission of an earlier failure.

The Southern Conference for Human Welfare had aspired to become a mass organization. It had hoped to become the leader of the South's rural and urban dispossessed. It never remotely approached its goal. The South's rural masses, whether black or white, were without effective organization. The Southern Tenant Farmers' Union was small, and relations between its leaders, most of them Socialists, and the Southern Conference were seldom cordial; the former cried "Stalinist" at the latter too often and the leaders of the Conference ridiculed the Union's pose as a representative of all the South's rural masses. The Southern part of the National Farmers' Union was, if anything, even smaller than the Tenant Farmers' Union; a brief attempt by Conference member Gerald Harris to organize for the National Farmers' Union in Alabama in 1941 was inconsequential. The Conference never again attempted to organize in the rural South. If it had, it would probably have failed. The opposition was too strong and willing to use violence to defend itself—as it had readily shown in Alabama and Arkansas during the sharecropper organizing drives of the 1930s. If rural Negroes and whites could ill afford to pay their poll taxes, even less could they afford to subscribe to the *Patriot,* the Conference's sole means of reaching them. Some in both races would have been unable to read it. Whites would have been offended by a small paper advertising books by Negro authors and taking issue with the dogmas of white supremacy—dogmas so vital to the emotional well-being of the region's poor white farmers. With an occasional Theodore Bilbo to offer them hatred of both Negroes and Black Belt planters, why should they have been persuaded by the tame rhetoric of the Southern Conference's educated middle-class leaders?

Nor did the Conference acquire a sizable following among the region's workers. Union leaders spurned suggestions that they enroll their members *en masse* in the Southern Conference. The large labor delegations at the Conference's early conventions seem to have come at their leaders' behest; owing to confusions about membership requirements, they may not have formally belonged to the organization. The Southern Conference dealt with labor leaders, not with workers. When these labor leaders withdrew their support after the war, the Southern Conference began to collapse.

The Conference thus drew most heavily from the South's middle class. Its executive secretaries, its administrators, its office clerks, were usually educated Southerners of bourgeois origins. They kept the Conference in operation between conventions; they turned out its newspaper and its pamphlets; they did its lobbying. They and wealthy friends of the organization provided it with the bulk of its revenues. They stayed with the organization longer than any other group. Some of them—including middle-class Negroes—stayed with the organization after the death of the Southern Conference for

Human Welfare. Whether from timidity or wisdom, they kept the transformed organization small; they made no attempts to solicit mass support for it.

The failure to become a mass organization was fatal. Without an independent base of power, the Southern Conference could not carry on in the face of domestic and international political changes. Sired by national necessity out of regional circumstance, nurtured by a sustained international crisis, the Southern Conference by the end of the war had got a spurious growth. It was not, despite appearances, master of itself. Labor's first loyalty was to labor; the Socialists' to the Socialist party; the New Deal Democrats' to the Democratic party; the radical isolationists' to a party that would avoid the cold war for the sake of domestic reform. When the CIO split with the Conference, labor's financial support fell off and labor leaders began to withdraw from the organization. When international fascism went up in flames, the popular front went with it. When the cold war began, it forced Americans to take sides for or against the Soviet Union; critical discussions of Russian Communism could not be avoided. When the New Deal was threatened, the task of the Democrats was to preserve it through what became the Fair Deal. These were the country's pressing problems. The Southern Conference's growing weakness, its inability to find a formula for the problems of the world satisfactory to all its constituent elements finally destroyed it. Its members, acting on their primary interests, returned to their parties and to the tasks the era seemed to require. The Southern Conference Educational Fund stumbled on, supported by a small number of Negro activists and white integrationists. It too has not yet succeeded.

But human conduct may be judged not only by its results but also by its aims. Results presuppose motives. These involve, apart from animal urges and psychological impulses, principles and ideas. The Southern Conference's desire to democratize the South, to equalize the opportunities of her depressed masses, was as worthy as previous American reforms in the name of democracy. At least parts of the old Southern mansion needed replacement and at least some of the customs of its inhabitants needed changing: the Jim Crow shanties out in back, the rickety shutters used to close off the occupants when alien fashions and ideas appeared on the streets below, the basement sweat shops where the master's kinsmen worked long hours for low wages, the reliance on primitive health services to take care of the sick, the closets with the white sheets and the long ropes. The Conference failed to refurbish the mansion or change markedly the habits of its occupants because its means were disproportionate to its ends. Public education—the creation of a climate of opinion favorable to progressive legislation—and small-scale political action were inadequate for the large rebuilding job it had set for itself. But if it had not tried it could not have failed. The effort was enough; it stands in worthy contrast to the continued evasion of the region's most serious problems by the bulk of its political leaders.

BIBLIOGRAPHIC ESSAY

THE following list of manuscripts, interviews, and printed materials includes the sources basic to the preparation of this study. To save space, items which may be relevant but which were not of use have been generally omitted. Some of the printed materials listed in the footnotes have not been relisted here. Readers who wish a fuller bibliography are invited to read this essay together with the footnotes.

MANUSCRIPT MATERIALS

The Records of the Southern Conference for Human Welfare at Tuskegee Institute, Tuskegee, Alabama, consist of seven large boxes of poorly organized materials. The Institute lacks the funds and the staff to process manuscript materials and nothing had been done to the SCHW Records before the writer got to them. Large numbers of letters from leading participants in the Conference are in this collection, as well as information on the state committees, files of background materials for *Patriot* stories, financial information, minutes of the meetings of various executive boards, and some information on peripheral organizations: the Southern Regional Council, the Southern Tenant Farmers' Union, the American Peace Mobilization, the CIO, and the National Citizen's Political Action Committee. All of the materials in this collection were examined, about half of them in careful detail. Hastily skimmed materials included newspaper clippings and background materials for *Patriot* stories.

Materials at the Trevor Arnette Library, Atlanta University, were sent there by Clark Foreman and reflect some of his interests. Consisting of a four-drawer filing cabinet, a loose file drawer, and three loose boxes of materials on the fight against the poll tax, they contain information on the reorganization of 1946, on the background of the NEC *Report,* on

Henry Wallace, and on other politicians; there is an especially valuable file of letters organized chronologically which contains details on Conference operations for every year of its existence.

The Southern Conference Educational Fund, Inc., whose offices are now at 3210 West Broadway, Louisville, Kentucky, has a back file of the *Southern Patriot,* newspaper clippings covering much of the Southern Conference's lifetime but fullest for the last years of the war and the first years of the peace, and many official records, including minutes of meetings, a transcript of the New Orleans convention, and copies of the Conference's various Constitutions and by-laws. These records and the records at Atlanta University and Tuskegee Institute are the main sources for the history of the Southern Conference.

The University of North Carolina has the papers of Frank P. Graham, Howard W. Odum, and the Southern Tenant Farmers' Union. Of these, the Graham Papers were the most rewarding; they have been partially processed and a separate chronological file on the Southern Conference has been organized. Other sections of the collection include files on such organizations as the American Civil Liberties Union, the Friends of Democracy, and the Committee to Defend America by Aiding the Allies. The Odum Papers and the Tenant Farmers' Union Papers are chronologically organized and easily used. Neither collection offers much of value as commentary on the Southern Conference, but both are worth something as examples of attitudes toward the organization.

The Manuscript Division of Duke University Library has Lucy Randolph Mason's papers, the papers of the Socialist party, and the Southern Labor Archives. All are intelligently organized. Miss Mason's files yielded little that had not already turned up in the collections at Tuskegee and Atlanta; she seems to have asked the recipients of her most important letters to burn them. The Socialist materials contain interesting, unfriendly comments on the Conference by Socialist party leaders. The Southern Labor Archives consist in the main of materials bearing on organization campaigns, strikes, and union members; they afforded little that had not been found elsewhere.

The Library of Congress Manuscript Division has the files of the National Policy Committee and of its Southern affiliates; the files of the Alabama Policy Committee are indispensable for the origins of the Southern Conference.

A quick search of the Philip Murray Papers at Catholic University yielded nothing. This may indicate that SCHW and CIO leaders communicated verbally on most important matters.

Franklin Roosevelt's papers at the Franklin D. Roosevelt Memorial Library, Hyde Park, New York, contain several items of interest on the Conference's formation and early history. So do Aubrey Williams's papers. Mrs. Roosevelt's files had not yet been opened, but many of her letters turned up in collections at Tuskegee Institute and Atlanta University.

INTERVIEWS

Many Conference participants were still living when this study was undertaken. Wherever possible, they were reached by mail and interviews were obtained. More than 200 letters were sent; most of them netted answers, but a few did not. John B. Thompson, William Mitch, and Lillian Smith failed to reply. Many of those who responded remembered little of their association with the Conference. They were especially vague on matters of detail. The same was true of persons interviewed. But they did remember what it felt like to belong; they had a sense of the organization that could not be obtained from the documents. They helped the writer understand the temper of the period, some of its problems, and provided insights. Interview, Mike Baker, Minneapolis, Minnesota, November 1963, provided information about the functions of the Council of Young Southerners and the Southern Conference in Virginia before the war. Interview, Frank McCallister, Chicago, Illinois, December 17, 1963, provided helpful leads and a Socialist party view of the Conference. Interview, James A. Dombrowski, New Orleans, Louisiana, January 3, 1964, provided details about Dombrowski and his social and political attitudes. Interview, Mrs. Emily Blanchard, New Orleans, January 4, 1964, dealt with the Committee for Louisiana. Interviews, Mr. and Mrs. C. J. Durr, Montgomery, Alabama, January 11–12, and 18–19, 1964, provided information about Conference participants and about New Dealers, and insights about the Conference's relationship to the Roosevelt administration. Interviews, Claude Williams, Helena, Alabama, January 13–14, 1964, dealt with some of the Conference's radicals and with Williams's interpretation of the Conference, that of a radical Southern populist. Interview, Rufus Clement, Atlanta University, February 19, 1964, dealt with the Conference's relation to the race question. Interview, Paul R. Christopher, Knoxville, Tennessee, February 25, 1964, helped on the connection between the CIO and the Conference. Interview, Howard Kester, Black Mountain, North Carolina, February 26, 1964, turned on the question of the extent of Communist control of the organization and Kester's relations with its leaders. A phone conversation with William Poteat of Chapel Hill, North Carolina, March 21, 1964, yielded information about the last days of the North Carolina Committee from one of its anti-Communist liberals. Interview, Aubrey Williams, Washington, D.C., March 23, 1964, provided information about the rift between Clark Foreman and James Dombrowski in 1964, about the transformation of the Southern Conference Educational Fund, and about the connection between the Southern Conference and the Wallace movement. Interview with Dr. Joseph L. Johnson, Washington, D.C., April 1, 1964, supplied information about the Committee for Washington, about its work against segregation in the District, and about the relationship between the Committee and the Progressive party. Interview, Clark Foreman, New York City, April 7, 1964, supplied details about the last years of the Conference and supplied points of difference about the significance of the Conference. Interview, Roger Baldwin, New York City, April 9, 1964, gave Baldwin an opportunity to restate his views on the Conference. Interview, James Marshall, New York City, April 9, 1964, provided information about the Robert Marshall Civil Liberties Trust Fund and its relations with the Southern Conference. Interview, Earl Browder, Yonkers, New York, April 13, 1964, supplied some information on relations between the Communist party and the Southern Conference. Interview, Frank Graham, New York City, April 20, 1964, gave Graham a change to restate the views of the Conference which he held during his tenure as chairman.

PRINTED MATERIALS

Bibliographic aids: In addition to the general bibliographic aids familiar to students of American history, the following special aids were useful: For convenient entry into the maze of government documents United States, Superintendent of Documents, *Index to Monthly Catalog United States Public Documents* (Washington: Government Printing Office, 1930—) for the years after 1938. The title of the *Catalog* varies, but the basic words *Monthly Catalog* always appear. The House Committee on Un-American Activities, *Cumulative Index to Publications of the Committee on Un-American Activities, 1938–1954* (Washington:

Government Printing Office, 1962) has separate indices for persons, publications, and organizations. It is a handy guide to the Committee's enormous output. There is a *Supplement,* covering 1955 through 1960 (Washington: Government Printing Office, 1961). Some leads were found in American Theological Library Association, *Index to Religious Periodical Literature, 1949–1962,* 5v. (Chicago, 1953–1963). *Biography Index,* for the years after 1946, provided leads to the writings of Southern Conference officials and to writings about them. Fund for the Republic, *Bibliography on the Communist Problem in the United States* (New York: Fund for the Republic, 1955) is intelligently organized. Less helpful was Robert Finley Delaney, *The Literature of Communism in America: A Selected Reference Guide* (Washington: Catholic University Press, 1962). Donald Drew Egbert, *et al., Socialism and American Life:* II, *Bibliography: Descriptive and Critical* (Princeton: Princeton University Press, 1952). For the connection between religion, especially the Social Gospel, and the Southern Conference: Nelson R. Burr, *A Critical Bibliography of Religion in America,* IV, Parts 1 and 2, of *Religion in American Life* ed. James Ward Smith and A. Leland Jamison (Princeton: Princeton University Press, 1961) was helpful.

The Southern Conference for Human Welfare: the basic published works are: Clark Foreman, "The Decade of Hope," *Phylon,* XII (Second Quarter, 1951), 137–150, a short excellent article which relates the Conference to the period in which it lived, to the New Deal, to the CIO, to the Negro rights movement, and does not overemphasize its accomplishments. Foreman does, however, skirt the Communist problem and fails to mention some matters that might embarrass the organization's former members, including the rift between him and James Dombrowski in 1946; for an earlier interpretation, see James A. Dombrowski, "The Southern Conference for Human Welfare," *Common Ground,* VI (Summer, 1946), 14–25. Kenneth Douty's "The Southern Conference for Human Welfare," typescript Mr. Douty's possession, is an excellent piece of detective work that suffers from an inadequate perspective; Douty's central concern was the extent of Communist infiltration and this led him to minimize or neglect other aspects of the Conference's history—aspects more important than the Conference's connections with the Communist party. More severe on the Conference are House Committee on Un-American Activities, *Report on the Southern Conference for Human Welfare* (Washington: Government Printing Office, 1947); Senate, Internal Security Subcommittee,

Hearings Regarding Subversive Influence in the Southern Conference Educational Fund, Inc. (Washington: Government Printing Office, 1954) which appeared shortly before the Supreme Court's decision in *Brown et al.* v. *Board of Education of Topeka;* Paul Crouch's article in *Plain Talk* reprinted in *Congressional Record,* 81 cong., 1 sess., 2998–3000. With the exception of the arguments in Wilson Record's *The Negro and the Communist Party* (Chapel Hill: University of North Carolina Press, 1951) and his *Race and Radicalism* (Ithaca: Cornell University Press, 1964) most of the criticisms of the Conference in the last 15 years stem from Paul Crouch and the House Committee. The answer to the 1947 HUAC *Report* is Walter Gelhorn, "Report on a Report of the House Committee on Un-American Activities," *Harvard Law Review,* LX (October 1947), 1193–1234. On Paul Crouch, see Willard Shelton, "Paul Crouch, Informer," *The New Republic,* CXXXI (July 9, 1954), 7–9; Frank J. Donner, "The Informer," *The Nation,* CLXXVIII (April 10, 1954), 298–309. Crouch answered his critics in *The New Republic,* CXXXI (August 23, 1954).

Members of the Conference wrote a considerable amount and had considerable amounts written about them. Emma Gelders Sterne, *Mary McLeod Bethune* (New York: Knopf, 1957); W. T. Couch, ed., *Culture in the South* (Chapel Hill: North Carolina Press, 1934), the introduction by Couch. James A. Dombrowski, *Early Days of Christian Socialism in America* (New York: Columbia University Press, 1936) and his "Attitudes of Southern University Professors Toward the Elimination of Segregation in Graduate and Professional Schools in the South," *The Journal of Negro Education,* XIX (Winter, 1950), 118–123. John P. Davis, "A Survey of the Problems of the Negro Under the New Deal," *The Journal of Negro Education,* V (January 1936), 3–12. Clark Foreman, *Environmental Factors in Negro Elementary Education* (New York: W. W. Norton, 1932); *The New Internationalism* (New York: W. W. Norton, 1934) with Joan Rausenbush, *Total Defense* (New York: Doubleday Doran, 1940). Foreman also wrote numerous newspaper and magazine articles. Frank P. Graham, "The Meaning of the Civil War," *The Virginia Quarterly Review* XXXVIII (Winter, 1962), 36–70, provides an introduction to Graham's basic attitudes. Charles Granville Hamilton, "South Faces Its Own Race Issue," *The Christian Century,* LV (December 7, 1938), 1520–1521; and the same author's "He Sacrificed Himself Not His Principles," *The Christian Century,* LXXV (March 26, 1958), 375–376, on

Alva Taylor, another Conference Activist. Hamilton was a liberal Mississippi clergyman. Stetson Kennedy, *Southern Exposure* (Garden City, N.Y.: Doubleday, c.1946) and *I Rode With the Ku Klux Klan* (London: Arco Publishers, 1954). Paul B. Kern, "Hope Sees a Star," *The Christian Century,* LVI (March 29, 1939), 412–414; the author, a Methodist Bishop, was a Conference member. Lucy Randolph Mason, *To Win These Rights* (New York: Harper, 1952), an uncritical account of her work for the CIO in the South. Benjamin E. Mays, "Negroes and the Will to Justice," *The Christian Century,* LIX (October 28, 1942), 1316–1318, and Roscoe Dunjee, "Tis the Set of the Soul . . . ," *The Crisis,* LXIII (January 1956), 23–26, 60, and "Are Dixie Race Relations Improving?" *Negro Digest,* VI (April 1948), 52–57 indicate two Southern Negroes' attitudes toward the region's racial practices. H. C. Nixon's academic works are numerous: *Forty Acres and Steel Mules* (Chapel Hill: University of North Carolina Press, 1938), *Possum Trot* (Norman: University of Oklahoma Press, 1941); "The New Deal and the South," *The Virginia Quarterly Review,* XIX (Summer 1943), 321–333; see also his contribution to Twelve Southerners, *I'll Take My Stand* (New York: Harper, 1930). Jennings Perry, *Democracy Begins at Home* (New York and Philadelphia: J. B. Lippincott, 1944), and "Hillbilly Justice in Tennessee," *The New Republic,* CIX (July 19, 1943), 68–70, both of which deal with the fight against the Tennessee poll tax. Lillian Smith, *Strange Fruit* (New York: Reynal and Hitchcock, 1944) and *Killers of the Dream* (New York: W. W. Norton, 1949), are two of her best works. Her magazine under various titles, *The North Georgia Review* and *South Today,* contains many of her ideas in their original form. Alva Taylor, *Christianity and Industry in America* (New York: Friendship Press, 1933), "The Forgotten States," *The Protestant,* IV (February-March 1943), 31–34, and "Obstacles to Progress" in William P. King, ed., *Social Progress and Christian Ideals* (Nashville: Cokesburg Press, 1931), pp. 121–192, by a one-time professor of religion at Vanderbilt who was fired because of his radicalism. Helena Huntington Smith, "Mrs. Tilly's Crusade," *Colier's,* CXXVI (December 30, 1950), 28–29, 66–67, deals with a woman active in numerous good causes who was also a member of the Southern Conference. Charles C. Webber, "Sweet Land of Liberty," *The Christian Century,* LV (May 18, 1938), 624–625 and "A Worker's Education, Program for First Rate Citizenship," *Religious Education,* XLIII (September-October, 1948), 292–296; Webber was director of the CIO-PAC in

Virginia after the war and active in the Committee for Virginia. Josephine Wilkins, "Facts versus Folklore," *Proceedings of the National Conference of Social Work . . . 1939,* pp. 461–472, deals with the Citizen's Fact-Finding Movement of Georgia. The basic source for the opinions of the members of the Southern Conference is of course the *Southern Patriot,* I— (December 1942—).

New Deal: the background up to 1936 is most amply and intelligently treated in Arthur Schlesinger, Jr., *The Age of Roosevelt* 3v. (Boston: Houghton Mifflin, 1957–1960). A recent one-volume account is William E. Leuchtenburg, *Franklin D. Roosevelt and the New Deal, 1932–1940* (New York: Harper, 1963); Rexford G. Tugwell, *The Democratic Roosevelt* (Garden City: Doubleday, 1957); James M. Burns, *Roosevelt: The Lion and the Fox* (New York: Harcourt, Brace and World, c.1956); neither of these three treats the purge of 1938 in the same way that this study does. Richard B. Morris, ed., the *Encyclopedia of American History,* Vol. I (New York: Harper, 1953), provides a useful chronological survey of the period. Samuel I. Rosenman, ed., *The Public Papers and Addresses of Franklin D. Roosevelt,* 13v. (New York: Random House, Macmillan, and Harper, 1938–1950). George P. Rawick, "The New Deal and Youth," unpublished Ph.D. thesis, University of Wisconsin, 1957, provided understanding of the youth groups of the 1930s. The New York *Times* for the period is indispensable.

The South: C. Vann Woodward, *Origins of the New South* (Baton Rouge: The Louisiana State University Press, 1951); *The Burden of Southern History* (New York: Vintage Books, 1961); *The Strange Career of Jim Crow* (New York: Oxford Press, 1955) were all useful. Francis Butler Simkins, *A History of the South* (New York: Alfred Knopf, 1959), is a comprehensive survey. The outstanding work on Southern politics for the New Deal and Fair Deal periods is the severely scientific study of the late V. O. Key, *Southern Politics in State and Nation* (New York: Vintage ed., c.1949). Some of Howard W. Odum's best known works are: *Southern Regions of the United States* (Chapel Hill: University of North Carolina Press, 1936); *Race and Rumors of Race* (Chapel Hill: University of North Carolina Press, 1943); *The Way of the South* (New York: Macmillan, 1947). Wilma Dykeman and James Stokeley, *Seeds of Southern Change* (Chicago: University of Chicago Press, 1962), contains valuable information about Southern liberals and Southern liberalism for the period from 1910 to 1950. Files of *The Virginia Quarterly Review, The*

Journal of Southern History, and *The Journal of Politics* contain materials of importance on the period. W. J. Cash, *The Mind of the South* (New York: Vintage ed., 1960), though now 25 years old, still repays reading.

Negro: the basic work is Gunnar Myrdal, with the assistance of Richard Sterner and Arnold Rose, *An American Dilemma* (New York and London: Harper, c.1944). Charles S. Johnson, *et al., Into the Main Stream* (Chapel Hill: University of North Carolina Press, 1947); Robert Penn Warren, *Segregation* (New York: Vintage ed., 1956); Richard Bardolph, *The Negro Vanguard* (New York: Vintage ed., c.1959), provided leads and information. So did *The Negro Handbook, 1946–47* and the *Negro Year Book . . . 1941–1946;* both contain statistical information and list of organizations interested in race relations. The back files of *The Journal of Negro History, The Journal of Negro Education, The Crisis, Opportunity,* and *Negro Digest* afforded some information. Wilson Record's previously cited volumes were useful; William A. Nolan's *Communism Versus the Negro* (Chicago: Henry Regnery, 1951) was not. The works of Record and Nolan are treated critically in Vaughn D. Bornet, "Historical Scholarship, Communism, and the Negro," *The Journal of Negro History,* XXXVII (July 1952), 304–324. Will Alexander, "Our Conflicting Racial Policies," *Harper's Magazine,* CXC (January 1945), 172–179, points up the folly and the cruelty of educating Negroes without providing them with employment suitable to their education. The article indicated that part of the moderate white South had come to favor an end to discrimination in employment. W. E. B. Dubois, "The Negro Since 1900: A Progress Report," New York *Times Magazine,* November 21, 1948, is an interesting survey. Edwin Hoffman, "The Genesis of the Modern Movement for Equal Rights in South Carolina, 1930–1939," *The Journal of Negro History,* XLVI (October 1959), 346–369, places the origins of the current civil rights movement back in the New Deal period, as does this study. Louis C. Kesselman, *The Socal Politics of FEPC* (Chapel Hill: University of North Carolina Press, 1948), includes materials critical of the Southern Conference.

Labor: writings on the CIO are few; writings of substance on Southern labor even fewer. The following helped: United States Department of Labor, *Labor in the South* (Washington: Government Printing Office, 1947); Matthew Josephson, *Sidney Hillman* (Garden City: Doubleday, 1954); Milton Derber and Edwin Young, eds., *Labor and the New Deal* (Madison: University of Wisconsin Press, 1957); Saul Alinsky, *John L.*

Lewis (New York: G. P. Putnam, 1949); Max Kampelman, *The Communist Party* vs. *the C.I.O.* (New York: Praeger, 1957), provided several good leads; Horace Cayton and George Mitchell, *Black Workers and the New Unions* (Chapel Hill: University of North Carolina Press, 1939), was indispensable for the early years of the Conference; Cedric Belfrage, *A Faith to Free the People* (New York: Dryden Press, 1944), tells of Claude Williams, radical preacher and sharecropper organizer. Delbert D. Arnold, "The C.I.O.'s Role in American Politics, 1936–48," unpublished Ph.D. Thesis, University of Maryland, 1952, helped with the CIO-PAC and the NC-PAC.

Religion: Burr's *Critical Bibliography of Religion in America* and the *Index to Religious Periodical Literature* helped make some of the connections between radical Protestantism and the Southern Conference. Robert Moats Miller, *American Protestantism and Social Issues, 1919–1939* (Chapel Hill: University of North Carolina Press, c.1958), and Ralph Lord Roy, *Communism and the Churches* (New York: Harcourt, Brace and World c.1960), performed similar services. Back files of *The Christian Century* contain articles and reviews by Southern Conference members.

Communism: the only survey covering the party through the entire period is Irving Howe and Lewis Coser, *The American Communist Party* (New York: Prager, c.1957). David A. Shannon, *The Decline of American Communism* (New York: Harcourt, Brace and World, c.1959), deals with the party after the Second World War. The New York Public Library has a broken file of the party's first Southern publication, *Southern Worker*, and a file of its successor, *New South*, begun in 1937 and ended in the 1940's. Other information about the party comes from the *Daily Worker*, *The Communist* (changed to *Political Affairs* in January 1945), *Party Organizer*, and *The New Masses*. See also the works of Record, Roy, and Kampelman previously cited.

The Progressive party: Karl Schmidt, *Henry A. Wallace; Quixotic Crusade, 1948* (Syracuse: Syracuse University Press, 1960), is uncritical. For a critical view: Eric Goldman, *Rendezvous with Destiny* (New York: Vintage ed., c.1956); Arthur Schlesinger, Jr., *The Vital Center* (Boston: Houghton Mifflin, 1949); and the works of Shannon, and Howe and Coser previously cited.

Socialism: David Shannon, *The Socialist Party of America* (New York: Macmillan, 1955) and the files of *The New Leader* and the *Socialist Call.*

INDEX